GURUS AND THEIR FOLLOWERS

Gurus and Their Followers

New Religious Reform Movements in Colonial India

Edited by
Antony Copley

OXFORD
UNIVERSITY PRESS

OXFORD
UNIVERSITY PRESS

YMCA Library Building, Jai Singh Road, New Delhi 110001

Oxford University Press is a department of the University of Oxford. It furthers the
University's objective of excellence in research, scholarship, and education
by publishing worldwide in

Oxford   New York

Athens   Auckland   Bangkok   Bogota   Buenos Aires   Calcutta
Cape Town   Chennai   Dar es Salaam   Delhi   Florence   Hong Kong   Istanbul
Karachi   Kuala Lumpur   Madrid   Melbourne   Mexico City   Mumbai
Nairobi   Paris   Sao Paolo   Singapore   Taipei   Tokyo   Toronto   Warsaw
with associated companies in   Berlin   Ibadan

Oxford is a registered trade mark of Oxford University Press
in the UK and in certain other countries

Published in India
By Oxford University Press, New Delhi

ISBN 019 564 9583

Typeset by Wordsmiths, Delhi 110 034
nted by Rashtriya Printers, Delhi 110 032
ied by Manzar Khan, Oxford University Press
ary Building, Jai Singh Road, New Delhi 110 001

To
St Antony's College
and
two of its most distinguished historians
Sarvepalli Gopal
Tapan Raychaudhuri

Contents

Contributors   ix
Editorial Preface
    Antony Copley   xi

A SYNOPTIC APPROACH

A Study in Religious Leadership and Cultism
    Antony Copley   3

THE BRAHMO SAMAJ

Educating Women, Educating a Daughter: Babu
Navincandra Rai, *Lakṣmī-Sarasvatī Samvād* (1869),
and Hemantkumari Chaudhurani
    Ulrike Stark   33

THE RAMAKRISHNA MISSION

Swami Akhandananda's *Sevavrata* (Vow of Service) and
the Earliest Expressions of Service to Humanity in
the Ramakrishna Math and Mission
    Gwilym Beckerlegge   59
The Ramakrishna Mission: Its Female Aspect
    Hiltrud Rüstau   83

THE ARYA SAMAJ AND THE AHMADIYYA MOVEMENT

'Kindly Elders of the Hindu Biradri': The Ārya Samāj's
Struggle for Influence and its Effect on Hindu-Muslim
Relations, 1880–1925
    Harald Fischer-Tiné   107

'Duties of Ahmadi Women': Educative Processes in the Early
Stages of the Ahmadiyya Movement
    Avril A. Powell   128

THE THEOSOPHICAL MOVEMENT

Theosophy as a Political Movement
   Mark Bevir
                                                                159
Thinking Culture through Counter-culture: The Case of
   Theosophists in India and Ceylon and their Ideas on
   Race and Hierarchy (1875–1947)
   Carla Risseuw
                                                                180

SRI AUROBINDO

'The Error of All "Churches" ': Religion and Spirituality in
   Communities Founded or 'Inspired' by Sri Aurobindo
   Peter Heehs
                                                                209

Index
                                                                225

Contributors

ANTONY COPLEY is Reader in Modern History at the University of Kent at Canterbury. His most recent publication is *Religions in Conflict: Ideology, Cultural Contact and Conversion in Late Colonial India.* He is currently working on attitudes of Indian and British intellectuals towards Indian spirituality.

ULRIKE STARK studied French, Spanish and Indology at Bonn University and received a PhD in Modern Indology from Bamberg University in 1994. She currently teaches Hindi literature at the South Asia Institute of Heidelberg University and is engaged in a post-doctoral research project on 'The Diffusion of the Printed Word: The Newal Kishore Press in Lucknow and its role in the promotion of vernacular literature in Urdu and Hindi (1858–1895)'.

GWILYM BECKERLEGGE is a member of the Religious Studies Department of the Open University, UK. A recent article was on 'Iconographic Representations of Sri Ramakrishna and Swami Vivekananda' in the *Journal of Contemporary Religion,* 1996. He is currently completing a monograph on service to humanity in the Ramakrishna Math and Mission.

HILTRUD RÜSTAU is Reader in the History of Philosophy in South Asia in the Institute for Asian and African Studies, Humboldt University, Berlin. She is currently working on modern Advaita Vedanta and new religious movements in India, with special reference to the role of women.

HARALD FISCHER-TINÉ has published on the Arya Samaj in C. Weiss (ed.), *Religion-Macht-Gewalt.* He is completing his doctorate on educational institutions of the Arya Samaj at the South Asia Institute, Heidelberg.

AVRIL POWELL is Senior Lecturer in the History of South Asia at the School of Oriental and African Studies, University of London. Recent publications include *Muslims and Missionaries in Pre-Mutiny India* and 'Contested Gods and Prophets: Discourse among Minorities in late 19th Century Punjab' in *Renaissance and Modern Studies*, December 1995. She is currently working on the brothers, Sir William Muir and Dr John Muir, and the theme of Scottish Evangelicalism and the roots of Indian religions.

MARK BEVIR is Sir James Knott Fellow, Department of Politics, University of Newcastle, UK. He has published articles on Theosophy in *International Journal of Hindu Studies* and *Journal of the American Academy of Religion*. He is currently writing a biography of Annie Besant.

CARLA RISSEUW is Professor of Intercultural Gender Studies, Department of Anthropology, University of Leiden. She has published on gender and kinship in South Asia and Sub-Saharan Africa. She is working on a larger study of the activities and ideas of Theosophists in colonial India and Sri Lanka.

PETER HEEHS is Archivist in the Aurobindo Ashram. Recent publications include *Nationalism, Terrorism, Communalism* and *The Essential Writings of Sri Aurobindo*. He is currently working on a biography of Sri Aurobindo.

Editorial Preface

THIS COLLECTION OF ESSAYS brings together original research on a broad spectrum of new religious reform movements in late colonial India. The first, my own, is deliberately synoptic and frames the succeeding more specialized essays. These include: an essay on a Brahmo educationist reformer, two on the Ramakrishna Mission, one each on the Arya Samaj and the Ahmadiyya movement, two essays on the Theosophical movement, and one on Sri Aurobindo. Most were first given to a panel entitled New Religious Movements in South Asia, organized by Rüstau and myself, at the Fourteenth European Conference of Modern South Asian Studies, Copenhagen, August 1996. They have been revised in the light of our common purpose, and several completely rewritten. This collection is, in consequence, a new venture.

My own essay comes out of reading and teaching while a Professeur Invité at the University of Paris 8. I should like here to thank those postgraduate students who patiently sat through the seminar I conducted during the Winter semester, 1997–8.

IN SEARCH OF NEW PARADIGMS

Looking at the movements as a whole, a number of questions are posed. Are they best understood in common, as a collective response to the stress of modernization and the challenge of foreign ideologies? Alternatively, should they rather be seen as distinct and discrete responses, often regional rather than all-India in scope, within different faiths? Should we, additionally, try to place them in a longer chronology looking at causes and consequences rather than emphasizing their uniqueness in time? In other words, are there any agreed parameters and paradigms?

Clearly there is no agreement over the categorization of 'new religious movements'. Several contributors reject this categorization, in particular those addressing the story of Sri Aurobindo. I can remember myself being severely rebuked when I visited the Aurobindo Ashram in

Pondicherry, for referring to Sri Aurobindo's movement as 'religious'. It is seen as essentially an exploration of spirituality.

Several members within the movements under review, however, readily described themselves as members of a new religion. Guru Datta, a militant of the Arya Samaj, saw Dayananda as a *rishi* and his *Satyarth Prakash* as a sacred text. Moderates, on the other hand, revered him only as a great reformer.[1] If divided in its interpretations, the Arya Samaj became, to quote the most authoritative interpreter of these movements, Kenneth Jones, 'a creedal religion, repeatedly defined and explained through a system of proselytism and conversion'.[2] (Even so, during my visit to India in 1995 and after meeting officials of the Arya Samaj, I kept reminding myself that it was not so much a fundamentalist faith as a progressive social reform movement). Mirza Ghulam Ahmad, inspirer of the Ahmadiyya movement, claimed messiah status.[3]

It is not difficult to demonstrate how all the movements under review do revere their founders and ritualize certain texts and how they take on the character of sects. In colonial India, there were, anyway, as Jones has pointed out, good psychological reasons why members of India's elite, 'caught between their heritage and British colonial society'[4] should seek sanctuary in a quasi-religious movement. Even so, the categorization 'religious movements' is less restrictive than 'new religions'. Interestingly, Jones makes no mention of Sri Aurobindo in his textbook on socio-religious reform movements. A more acceptable concept should emerge with continuing debate.

Currently the most familiar paradigm for such movements is one that Jones discerned, the contrast between the 'transitional' and the 'acculturative'. This does not exhaust his list. There were also strictly conservative movements, in Jones's words, 'defensively orthodox'. It is far from easy, however, to see quite how binding the distinction between transitional and acculturative can be. Jones saw it in terms of timing. The threshold came with the emergence of 'a colonial milieu'. The 'transitional' drew on an Indian heritage and were not a response to a colonial presence. The 'acculturative', on the other hand, were keenly conscious of this presence and might well borrow some of its aspects.

As it happens, all the movements in this volume would come within Jones's paradigm of the acculturative. Yet both transitional and acculturative are seen as drawing on the same traditions of protest and both are movements of return. Jones hedges his bets. 'There was no clear point of beginning or end', he accepts, 'of the transitional movements of pre-British India.' In many ways the acculturative 'were in no way new or "modern", nor were they the creation of interaction with Christianity and western civilization.' They emerged within the colonial milieu as 'both a continuation of socio-religious dissent, and a modification of this tradition.'[5] The paradigms begin to look merely suggestive and unconvincingly defining. Jones speculates that quite often the leaders were transitional and the followers acculturative. Of course this whole analysis intersects with a more wide-ranging debate on to what extent, as revisionist historians now argue, India had begun to renew itself and embark on a process of modernization in the pre-colonial period, or alternatively, was colonialism itself the necessary catalyst for change?

It might help to look more closely at a movement that Jones defines as transitional, the Swaminarayan religion. It is one now brought strikingly to the attention of Londoners by its remarkable temple in Neasden. Williams in his study makes much of two crucial meetings between Sahajanand Swami and two leading Europeans—with Bishop Heber, 26 March 1825, at Nariad, a small town south of Baroda, and with the Governor of Bombay, Sir John Malcolm, 26 February 1830, at Kathiawar. It seems reasonable to assume that the division of the Swaminarayan movement into dioceses, exceptional in religious movements of this kind, was a result of the influence of Heber. Aspects of its ideology suggest a borrowing of Christian concepts. The relationship, for example, between Ramananda Swami and Sahajanand Swami could be seen as analogous to that between John the Baptist and Christ. Both the Swaminarayan movement and Company Raj contributed to the pacification of Gujarat. It is a moot point whether *Pax Swaminarayana* or *Pax Britannica* made the greater contribution, but they worked in harmony. Clearly, the Swaminarayan movement borrowed from both Church and State in the colonial presence, which suggests that 'transitional' should be redefined as 'tangential' or 'approximating' to the emerging colonial milieu. Raymond Williams identifies Sahajanand as 'the last of the medieval Hindu saints and the first of the neo-Hindu reformers'. His was a new religious movement 'which met the needs of the Gujaratis during the period of modernization and independence.'[6]

In the light of such ambiguities, without wishing to jettison Jones's paradigms, it seems wise to place the religious reform movements within a larger, more incorporating paradigm of modernization and change. Clearly, these movements met the emotional and spiritual needs of those caught up in the necessarily destructive impact of colonialism and modernization on a familiar world.

A comparative approach is also helpful. In the late nineteenth century in Europe and America there was a profound questioning of values, likewise to do with the shock of industrialization and the Darwinian challenge to faith. This was to take many forms—sexology, socialism, vegetarianism, aestheticism, psychoanalysis, spiritualism. It was, above all, an exploration of the personal. In time, such concerns were to be buried by the pressure of collective movements, such as socialism. There are parallels here to the way in which the reform movements in India were likewise examining a more personal approach both to religion and social questions, only for this to be overtaken by the larger demands of the collective nationalist movement. In a Nietzschean sense, the 'return of the oppressed' occurred in Europe in the 1960s: The revolutions of 1968 coined the slogan, 'the personal is the political'. Such a reassertion has yet to happen in India, though there are signs of it in contemporary Indian feminism.

But all the movements discussed in this text were in some of their aspects progressive movements which encouraged or, at least, sought accommodation to change. We have to ask of all of these movements: where did they stand on the great contemporary questions of political, social and religious or ideological change?

Professor Samiran Chakrabarty, from the Rabindra Bharati University, has argued that there was nothing new about movements of renewal within Hinduism, Islam and Sikhism. Whenever the religion fell into decadence such leaders would emerge. The distinctiveness of the late-nineteenth-century reform movements was just this concern with political nationalism and social justice: Theirs certainly was a major contribution to cultural revivalism.

More disturbingly, we have also to ask: to what degree did their religious fundamentalism contribute to the rise of communalism? It is difficult not to see in the mutual hostility of the Arya Samaj and the Ahmadiyyas in the Punjab, for example, a contribution to the rise of communalism in that troubled province, even though in time the heterodox Ahmadiyyas were to be equally embattled with orthodox Islam. As Jones tellingly puts it, 'each had the Punjabi tendency to see their ideas as the absolute, unbending truth.'[7]

If political nationalism was new and arguably an ideology alien to India, such was certainly not the case with movements for social reform. Jones writes of acculturative socio-religious movements as 'contemporary expressions of centuries-old dissent' though, he adds, they were 'a modification of this tradition'. They were a means by which 'progress' could be achieved 'by turning back to the righteous past'.[8] Jones is also right in saying of the Ramakrishna Mission that 'theirs was a doctrine of religious piety and social service that is the most dramatic expression of a Hindu social gospel.'[9]

I might here interject a personal experience. On returning from a visit to Bede Griffith's ashram, Santinavam, near Trichinopoly, my attention was caught by statues of Ramakrishna and Vivekananda outside a building. On entering I discovered it to be a hostelry of a boys' school. I was quickly taken by one of the swamis to the meditation room. To quote from my diary:

Here the community of monks meet twice a day. I have to say the presence of four to five monks in this bare room gave off a more intense religiosity than anything at Santinavam, or, indeed the Aurobindo ashram. The sight of the Abbot, or so I assumed he was, tugging the cloth around his waist to ensure greater concentration was charged with a spine-chilling sense of asceticism. Here was the medieval mendicant order recreated, a lifetime devoted to social service.[10]

One question that underlies this social dimension of the reform movements is the extent to which their awareness of the constraints of orthodoxy checked their more radical ideas on social change. Many would see, however, the greatest significance of these movements in their endeavour to fashion a new religious or spiritual outlook. Here were profoundly inward attempts to re-examine the tradition of Indian spirituality. There is an inevitable tension in hermeneutics between the historian, who seeks to contextualize or historicize these spiritual insights in their economic, social and cultural background, and those who argue instead for the autonomy of such systems of thought. Theologians and philosophers may adopt a quite different approach. It might be possible to try and make sense of the differing reinterpretations of Indian spirituality in such autonomous terms. There are those intriguing differences over the nature of religion and meditation between the Ramakrishna Mission and Sri Aurobindo, between an approach which emphasizes the uniqueness and equality of different religions and a belief in some transcendent spirituality, between a spiritual discipline which stresses the need to master all four of *jnana, bhakti, karma* and meditation, and Aurobindo's integral yoga. Beckerlegge believes that Vivekananda adopted a more evolutionary approach than Sri Aurobindo. Swami Bhajananda, in a fascinating conversation at Belur,[11] speculated that Vivekananda pioneered an entirely new form of spiritual enquiry. Whereas formerly this had always been constrained by reference to the sacred texts—a biblical spirituality—Vivekananda laid stress on personal experience. Chakraborty was not impressed by this argument, claiming that this element of a personal quest had always been there and that it sat well, anyway, with a biblical approach.

But the problematic arises: how to explain this spiritual quest by India's intellectuals at this particular point in time? Surely we are unlikely to find an answer solely by a contextualization within the tradition of spirituality itself. Here was a crisis of identity which laid bare an almost crippling sense of doubt as to the role intellectuals should play when challenged by new cultural and political values. Indian intellectuals share much of that self-doubt and introspection of European, particularly German and Russian intellectuals, confronted by the social and political backwardness of their societies at a time of radical change elsewhere.[12] Indian intellectuals likewise faced an entrenched traditional society and an authoritarian colonial state.

We also need to answer questions about how to interpret the intellectual outlook of the leadership of these movements. Many of them, including both Dayananda and Ramakrishna, started out in an exclusively Indian environment and only late in life came into contact with western thought. Are their intellectual enquiries understood best by reference to Indian culture from within or were they, equally, an Indian attempt to grapple with the implications of western thought and, by way of a challenge and maybe synthesis, to fashion a new religious outlook for a post-Darwinian age? Both theosophy and Sri Aurobindo were seeking a spiritual answer to the challenge of the Darwinian theory of evolution. Could one locate their exploration of the theory of the evolution of consciousness in narrowly Indian terms?

If we can point to common objectives in these religious reform movements, by no means was theirs a collective endeavour. Notoriously, Madame Blavatsky and Colonel Olcott fell out with Dayanand Saraswati in the early 1880s. Vivekananda and Colonel Olcott quarrelled and Vivekananda took a stand against the role of the occult in theosophy. A communal element crept into the interaction of the Arya Samaj and the Ahmadiyya movement in the Punjab. The Maha Bodhi Society, a neo-Buddhist reform movement not covered in this volume, came to blows with the Ramakrishna Mission.[13]

INTRODUCING THE TEXT

The essays in this collection are organized under the headings of the reform movements themselves. Each essayist has pursued, with a differing emphasis, the political, social or spiritual content of these movements. Here their main lines of interpretation will be briefly explored.

A Synoptic Approach

In my own essay, I pursue further some of the paradigms briefly sketched here. I am particularly concerned with exploring the nature of religious leadership, the status of the guru in these movements. This inevitably entails some discussion of discipleship. A comparativist approach with the psychoanalytical movement is adopted. The chapter is restricted to religious reform movements which come out of Hinduism. Each movement is considered in turn, looking more fully at its social, political and intellectual aspects. The dialogue with western science is considered. The chapter forms an introductory background to the chapters that follow, specializing on the various movements.

The Brahmo Samaj

Ulrike Stark's essay takes up the story of Navincandra Rai and his daughter Hemantkumari Chaudhurani, and their attempt to promote female education, mainly in the Punjab. It was just this concern that later split the movement, prompting Navincandra to abandon Keshab Chandra Sen for the Sadharan Brahmos. His was, partly, a utilitarian approach, that education led to prosperity. His was also a reverence for science, reflected in his campaign for the cause of female emancipation. At the same time, the preference for Hindi in the Nagari script reflected communal overtones.

The Ramakrishna Mission

Whether Vivekananda's emphasizing social service was a fulfilment or reorientation of Ramakrishna's wishes has always been a matter of controversy. There is, additionally, a dispute whether even setting up a *math*, let alone concentrating on social service, was true to the traditions of Hinduism. Did this emphasis on *seva*, service to humanity, in fact derive essentially from western influence? Gwilym Beckerlegge approaches these questions from a new angle, the influence of Swami Akhandananda on Vivekananda's commitment to social work. Both spent time in Gujarat and both were influenced by the social reform programme of the Swaminarayan movement, which points to a Vaishnavite, rather than a western inspiration for this approach. This may not, however, have been a direct one-to-one influence. Beckerlegge suggests that Akhandananda's correspondence with Vivekananda, who was then in the United States, was the crucial factor in winning him over to this programme. Even so, whilst recognizing Vivekananda's contribution as a strategist for the Mission, Beckerlegge squares the circle by seeing his humanitarianism in terms of a revitalization of Hinduism.

Hiltrud Rüstau discusses the role of women in the Ramakrishna Mission. Intriguingly, despite their rhetoric against 'women and gold', both Ramakrishna and Vivekananda enjoyed a warm relationship with women. Rüstau speculates on the impact of the suicide of his favourite sister on Vivekananda's attitude towards the role of women. Did the Mission's concern for women reflect some distinctive social development in Bengal? It certainly featured as a significant aspect of its social reform programme.

Rüstau begins with portraying an intriguing assemblage of non-Indian women attracted to the movement. Many were unmarried teachers from the lower middle class. Nevertheless, it was one of Vivekananda's wealthier disciples, Josephine Mcleod, who got Romain Rolland interested in the movement. With Margaret Noble, Sister Nivedita to be and Vivekananda's best known foreign follower, it was to be a process of reverse acculturation. Vivekananda saw in this daughter of an Irish clergyman and from a family caught up in Irish nationalism, someone who could advance the cause of female education in India, provided she underwent complete indigenization. Ultimately, however, Sister Nivedita's commitment to nationalist politics required her making a vow of formal separation from the Mission, her meeting with Sri Aurobindo in 1902 having led to her joining the executive committee of the Revolutionary Society in Calcutta.

Sarada Devi, wife and disciple of Ramakrishna, shared Sister Nivedita's commitment to female education. Rüstau considers her as Ramakrishna's first disciple. He worshipped her as Kali, the mother. She represented *sakti.* Both saw themselves as a manifestation of divine energy.

The Arya Samaj and the Ahmadiyya Movement

The Arya Samaj and the Ahmadiyya movement share a common characteristic of having been mutually antagonistic in the Punjab, and in exemplifying the paradox that reform movements often waged greater battle with their own orthodox majority than with other faiths. Harald Fischer-Tiné describes how the Arya Samaj, through its adoption and use of a technique of reconversion, the *suddhi* movement, which went a long way towards alienating Indian Muslims, was, in fact, ingratiating itself with orthodox Hinduism. In the 1880s the Arya Samaj did indeed drift into outright confrontation with Islam: not with Islamic orthodoxy but with the reformist sect of the Ahmadiyyas.

With power increasingly defined by census statistics the Arya Samaj sought a ritual of conversion, and found it in suddhi, traditionally the ritual cleansing ceremony for Brahmins who had transgressed caste norms. Suddhi was little used in Dayanand's lifetime, and not all *biradaris* welcomed suddhi converts. From 1896, the suddhi movement reached beyond individual to group reconversion, an obvious rejoinder to Christian so-called mass conversion of untouchables. But when extended to Muslims on this scale, it turned political.

Orthodox Hinduism, however, still looked askance at such contact with untouchables. The political alliance of Congress, Khilafat and Muslim League also proved equally distancing. It was the forced conversion of Hindus in Malabar in 1922 that altered attitudes and orthodoxy now welcomed the aid of the Arya Samaj to emerge out of its supposed inferiority complex. Even so, the convergence was temporary. Swami Sraddhananda was for pressing on with the Arya Samaj as a reform movement. The orthodox accepted suddhi as a tactic against Muslims, but still drew back from its use with untouchables.

The Ahmadiyya movement was one of several Muslim return movements, which contrived to make itself anathema to all other religious movements in the Punjab, and still survived. Straddling the urban–rural divide, the Ahmadiyya movement would not neatly fit into the categories of transitional or acculturative. Ghulam Ahmad's movement began in a village, Qadiyan, maintained its village origins, and continued to appeal to a rural and poorer, if upwardly mobile, community. Avril Powell in her contribution focuses on the social reformism of the movement, in particular its cautious but courageous approach to female education. Here is an interesting link with Ulrike Stark's paper.

Powell's point of departure is the startlingly high female literacy rate in the community. A number of texts inform her account: Mufti Fazl al-Rahman's biography of his wife, Hafsah, daughter of the first khalifah, Nur-ud-din; a sermon given by Mahmud Ahmad, the second khalifah at Sialkot in 1920; the biography by Zafrullah Khan, Pakistan's first Foreign Secretary, *My Mother*, the life of Husain Bibi. Powell's account emphasizes how patriarchal the Ahmadiyya movement remained in many ways. Ghulam Ahmad defended both polygamy and divorce. But we learn how wives could get round their husbands. The prejudice against education was being broken down. Those traditional meeting-places for village gossip, the *majlis*es, had, by the 1930s, become centres of serious educational and charitable activity. Not only were women called upon to educate their children in Islam, there were, by the 1920s, the beginnings of formal education for both girls and boys in the movement and girls were allowed to attend public schools. Given the constraints in orthodox Islam on female education, this was progress indeed.

The Theosophical Movement

The essays on theosophy explore its political ideology and its contribution to Indian nationalism, but also suggest how a movement inspired from outside India proved to be politically ambiguous and could not entirely escape the values of imperialism. Mark Bevir finds in neo-Hinduism a link between theosophy, the Ramakrishna Mission, Sri Aurobindo and, if more awkwardly, the Arya Samaj. Neo-Hinduism could both look back to a golden age and constitute a hiatus in Hinduism. As Bevir sees it, the crucial political question was, 'how best to return India to its true self'. Blavatsky was a reformer. She offset a contemporary exoteric Hinduism with its social blemishes of child marriage and sati, with an esoteric brahmanism; India 'needed to return to the pure ways of the Veda'. The Raj had corrupted caste into status rather than service. Admittedly, the romanticization of the Indian village by Theosophy raises anti-orientalist anxieties that it might likewise be depressing India into a decentralized, economically backward society. But one cannot quarrel with Bevir's mapping out of the way theosophists contributed to all-India nationalist organizations, from Allan Octavian Hume's contribution to the Indian National Congress to Annie Besant's Home Rule League.

Carla Risseuw addresses the disturbing paradox that theosophy could both challenge colonialism and stand for a theory of race. In an exploration of western intellectual history, she shows how from the fifth century BC there had been a repression of occultism, which had looked for inspiration from the East. In the nineteenth century there was to be a 'return of the oppressed' and a projection once again on to the East of this occult tradition. This 'old and diversified trend of European counter-thinking' was now, through the Theosophical Society, to be set up in India itself. As a counter-culture it was strongly opposed to the merely rational traditions of the West and to imperialism. It attracted to its cause outsiders and the oppressed, India's own intelligentsia, women, Irish nationalists and homosexuals. Yet how, she asks, can theosophy square its belief in Universal Brotherhood with its theory of race?

Risseuw's is a brave attempt to clarify Blavatsky's Secret Doctrine and to set out the main lines of its phantasmagoric evolutionary history. Here Darwinism and the occult join hands. (Not that theosophy was unique in such accounts in the nineteenth century; the utopian socialist, Charles Fourier, had an equally extravagant account of the history of civilizations.) Here, admittedly, was a theory of race which emphasized factors of mind and intelligence, rather than merely physical characteristics and this differentiates it from the crude materialist racism of much twentieth-century eugenics, to be shown, at its worst, in Nazi Germany.

We seem, in Blavatsky's strange mythological history, to hit familiar territory with her account of the Aryans, fifth of the Atlantean races, led by Manu, with their civilization in Central Asia. North Indian Aryans were deemed superior to the south Indian peoples. There was to be an evolution from 'old' to 'new' souls, a linkage of evolution and reincarnation. As Risseeuw tartly observes: 'in religious, scientific and (left-wing) political circles this approach is rejected as ridiculous.' Through such theory, theosophy shared in some of the basic assumptions of imperialism, with its hierarchical views on education, culture and race. Even so, aspects of theosophy, above all its high evaluation of eastern religions, have gained legitimacy in India. Risseeuw's interpretation carries seeds of controversy.

Sri Aurobindo

In his reflective essay, Peter Heehs moves beyond the territory I have myself explored on Aurobindo and nationalism, to an examination of the nature of his theory of yoga and to an exploration of its practice in the ashram at Pondicherry. It is very helpful, in assessing Aurobindo, to learn that he outgrew any account of himself as a Hindu and as a mere apologist of *sanatana dharma*. He drew a crucial distinction between religion and spirituality. His was to be a forty-one-year-long experiment in testing out this mystical approach to yoga. By 1911 his life's objectives were perceived: to reinterpret Vedantism; to reinvent yoga; to revitalize India's former greatness; to see the way towards a utopian society. The ashram at Pondicherry was to be the laboratory for these projects. It was not, he insisted, to deteriorate into a religious movement or church. In significant ways the practice of the ashram was to vary from the Brahmo Samaj, the Theosophical Society and the Arya Samaj. Peter Heehs then tries to place the Aurobindo project in a longer chronological framework.

Paradoxically, it can be argued that it was just this attempt to differentiate the Aurobindo movement from other religious movements, to mark it out as a special case, that encourages the view that, despite his denial, Aurobindo did take on the role of guru and that the Aurobindo movement did acquire some characteristics of a cult.

These are essays of reinterpretation and it would be premature to attempt conclusions. There is to be a second panel on this theme of Religious Reform Movements at the fifteenth European Conference on Modern South Asian Studies at Prague in September 1998. We hope we have encouraged a reconsideration of an attempt by Indian as well as European intellectuals in the late nineteenth century to articulate a more personal response to the challenge of social and religious change in India, an inward attempt, both by way of a reappraisal of India's own traditions as well as a response to a challenge from outside. This personalized endeavour gave way in the twentieth century to the more collectivized and impersonal movements of nationalism and communalism.

A similar fate befell attempts in Europe to fashion new personal moralities in the 1880s with the rise of totalitarian movements in the twentieth century. Maybe in a society of still disturbing inequality such as India, such inwardness is a form of self-indulgence. But with the rise of India's new ascendant middle class it will be interesting to see how the pursuit of the personal will unfold: will a western-style emphasis on the libertarian and sexual prevail, or a re-articulation of the concern for the religious, as expressed by the new religious movements studied in this text?

Canterbury
June 1998 ANTONY COPLEY

NOTES

1. See Kenneth Jones, *Socio-Religious Reform Movements in British India*, Cambridge, 1989, pp. 97–8.
2. Ibid., p. 103.
3. Ibid., p. 117.
4. Ibid., p. 214.
5. Ibid., pp. 210–11.
6. Raymond B. Williams, *A New Face of Hinduism: The Swaminarayan Religion*, Cambridge, 1989, p. 24.
7. Kenneth Jones, *Socio-Religious Reform Movements . . .*, p. 120.
8. Ibid., pp. 210–13.
9. Ibid.
10. *Exploring Indian Religion and Politics: Antony Copley's Indian Diary 1995–96*, Chennai, 1997, p. 24.
11. A personal conversation at Belur, 22 December 1997. I describe this in ibid., p. 67.
12. Somewhat improbably this came home to me in reading Aileen Kelly's *Mikhail Bakunin: A Study in the Psychology and Politics of Utopianism*, Oxford, 1982.
13. One interesting source for this is Sangharakshita's *In the Sign of the Golden Wheel: Indian Memoirs of an English Buddhist*, Birmingham, 1996.

A Synoptic Approach

A Study in Religious Leadership and Cultism

ANTONY COPLEY

IN THIS LONG JOURNEY through the Hindu or Indian Renaissance of the nineteenth century and into the twentieth, the focus will be on religious reform movements which spring from Hinduism, but analogous questions can be put to those that derive from Indian Islam and other Indian religions. A semantic question confronts us at the outset of such enquiry. In what senses are they religious? Farquhar in his classic text on this theme, published in 1915, categorized them. as modern religious movements.[1] Kenneth Jones, in a text which must rank as the contemporary equivalent to Farquhar's, published in 1989, preferred to categorize them as socio-religious reform movements.[2] In another contemporary text, edited by Robert Baird and published in 1981, they come under the heading of religion.[3] An obvious problematic is that several such movements reject any characterization of themselves as a religion at all, preferring an emphasis on their pursuit of spirituality. Undeniably, all have in common an engagement with the Indian tradition of spirituality. The approach here will be to establish to what degree their leaders became self-conscious gurus and their movements took on the character of cults.

This is a study of individuals and their disciples. It will incorporate Ram Mohun Roy and Keshab Chandra Sen and the Brahmo Samaj; Ramakrishna, Vivekananda and the Ramakrishna Mission; Dayananda Saraswati and the Arya Samaj; Madame Blavatsky and Annie Besant and the theosophical movement; Aurobindo Ghose and his ashram at Pondicherry. To answer the question whether these persons are self-conscious religious leaders or gurus necessitates a biographical approach. This being a cross-cultural study, some other questions also arise about these leaders: how far did they adopt western organizational models for their movements and to what extent did they borrow ideas from the West or draw on their own religious traditions? This opens up a significant debate on their relationship with western science, in particular the theory of evolution. The degree to which they depart from a scientific approach becomes one criterion for assessing whether they abandon an open-ended religious movement in favour of a more exclusive religion or cult.

A novel aspect of the Hindu renaissance was its reaching out beyond religious and theological questions into matters social and political. Given that the identity of a Hindu has always been defined more by social practice than by religious belief, this social dimension is not in itself surprising. Nevertheless, the readiness to reach out to visions of social change does represent a considerable extension of Hindu religious aware-ness. On a wider canvas this again is not surprising, for with the impact of modernity and the profound questioning of traditional forms of belief, religion did begin to attach itself to ideals of social transformation, most evidently so in nineteenth-century social utopianism.[4] More novel was the political breakthrough. Admittedly again, in a larger context, new expressions of belief had taken on a political character through the upheavals of the French Revolution, which can be classified as secular religions, the strongest among them being a kind of messianic nationalism. Already in the revolutionary years the cults of reason that emerged in consequence of radical de-christianization were turning into cults of *la patrie*. With the rise of romantic nationalism and in the writings of Michelet, Mazzini, Kossuth and others, nations took on the role of the divine, the means whereby, in a Hegelian sense, the Absolute realizes itself in time and history.

So another key indicator of these new religious movements in India is what attitude they adopt towards social and political issues. There are certainly quasi-religious visions of a caste-free society. In some cases Indian nationalism itself becomes a religion, with the Nation seen as the incarnation of the Mother, quite literally worshipped as a God.

GURUS AND THEIR FOLLOWERS

The guru is as much a western phenomenon as eastern. Kenneth Jones interprets theosophy as 'a religious movement of reverse acculturation, foreigners who adjusted to the realities of South Asia'.[5] But Madame Blavatsky and Annie Besant must nevertheless be seen as western gurus. Maybe non-Indians simply projected their own spiritual needs onto the Indian spiritual tradition. There is nothing uniquely Indian about spiritual pursuits, nor is India's culture uniquely spiritual. Gavin Flood, in a recent reinterpretation of Hinduism, writes of 'the reality being more complex as both cultures contain strong "spiritual" and "material" factors.'⁶ There is an equally rich, if less dominant, religious and mystical tradition in western culture. India's has a strongly materialist drive. Vivekananda was surely wrong to polarize a materialist West and a spiritual East. In India, as Anthony Storr observes, gurus are 'much more acceptable than they are to western Protestants or agnostics. Gurus are more embedded in the culture and their existence more taken for granted.'⁷ An exploration of the problematic of western gurus provides critical and novel insights into the role of their eastern equivalents.

The term guru can be pejorative. Storr certainly views them dimly, highlighting their narcissism, their claim to be above the law, and their ways of seeking attention. A guru 'demands that all his relationships are *de haut en bas* and this is why gurus have feet of clay.'⁸ They are an even bigger menace when authoritarian and paranoid. Such evidently deluded figures as Jim Jones and David Koresh have, predictably, given gurus a bad name. It is not surprising, therefore, that several of the spiritual leaders under review denied the status of guru and disclaimed any attempt to fashion a religious movement. Aurobindo is an obvious example. Yet it is not difficult to see how in an Indian context such transformation comes about. Raymond Williams, historian of the Swaminarayan movement, observes: 'the individual Hindu operates within a theological scheme in which the doctrine of the manifestation of god as experienced within a particular sect or regional form is accepted as the most adequate.'⁹ It is easy enough to see how this would predispose followers to convert their teacher into a quasi-godlike leader, to ritualize selected texts and to become a sect, even a new religion. Can we at the outset portray the characteristic features of gurus and their disciples?

The Sanskrit definition is 'one who brings light out of darkness.' Storr settles for 'spiritual teacher' as 'sufficiently accurate to indicate what is popularly meant by the term today. Anyone can become a guru if he or she has the hubris to claim special spiritual gifts.'¹⁰ Self-evidently, this is open to abuse: some gurus 'have been entirely unworthy of veneration: false prophets, madmen, confidence tricksters or unscrupulous psychopaths who exploit their disciples emotionally, financially and sexually'.¹¹ Storr tries to classify a range of figures, both Indian and non-Indian. Future gurus may well be isolated and narcissistic as children. Jung, for example, was an only child till he was nine: 'throughout his life Jung remained a solitary person who only felt fully himself when he was alone.'¹² There may be an early bereavement. Rajneesh, for example, lost a younger sister when only five and a much loved grandfather at the age of seven. Gurus are often indifferent to family ties. They may undertake particular kinds of journeys—and here Storr has Paul Brunton in mind—in search of the spiritual. Storr makes much of a 'creative illness', possibly a mid-life crisis, preceding a spiritual revelation. These may be manic-depressive, even schizophrenic. He believes that Freud underwent such an illness between 1894 and 1899, accentuated by his father's death in 1896, from which he was to emerge with his *Interpretation of Dreams*.[13] Rajneesh is seen as enduring a prolonged manic depressive illness from which he surfaced at the age of twenty-one, March 1951, with a new enlightenment. Exceptionally, gurus do not succumb to this cycle again; they are permanently changed. (Rajneesh did once again become depressed, but it was not manic-depression.) One explanation for the charisma of gurus—and such charisma is central to their success—is an immense self-confidence in their new revelation. It was Gurdjieff's 'own conviction that he had discovered the *answer* which made him charismatic and persuasive.' His followers 'believed that he *knew*.'[14] Rudolf Steiner, that 'mild gentle good kindly man' had also, at some level of personality an unshakeable conviction that he "knew".'[15] Such conviction comes from within: 'one of the characteristics of gurus is that they generalize from their own experience.'[16] Freud is an example. Jung likewise 'believed that he had privileged access to realms beyond consciousness.'[17] Simplicity can be the secret of their attraction, as in the case of Paul Brunton. Gurus are seen as offering 'holistic' and 'all-embracing' answers to problems. But Storr's account of the psychoanalytic movement and of the status of both Freud and Jung brings us to the heart of the controversy. Are we to look on a movement which originally laid claim to being a secular science as, instead, a religious cult?

But does the very claim to guru status camouflage, as Storr asserts, an inner doubt? We come here to the question of their relationship with their followers. Gurus tend to be elitist and authoritarian. They are intolerant of criticism: 'anything less than total agreement is equivalent to hostility.'[18] Freud's conviction that he was right 'was a matter of faith rather than of reason.'[19] Dominance rather than friendship defines the relationship of guru to disciple. But if they are 'unable to relate to anyone on equal terms at an ordinary human level',[20] it is just this dependence on disciples that begs the question of their credibility. Here we begin to touch on the attitude of disciples towards the guru, a large question and one that cannot be given sufficient attention here. Clearly, obedience to authority is attractive: 'for some people, complete submission to a higher power is seductive, in that it involves abrogating responsibility, doubt and anxiety.'[21] And, of course, such loyalty can be carried to excess. Some of Freud's followers, Storr asserts, 'became deluded fanatics.'[22]

These are risks in all esoteric groups: 'mutual reassurance systems, confirming each disciple's convictions', the belief that they have access to special insights as to how life should be lived which are denied to ordinary persons.'[23] Storr sees the dependence of the disciple on a guru as the equivalent of falling in love or transference. But the point to emphasize is that this is a two-way process and the guru needs such devotion to bolster his own self-belief.

In Richard Noll's recent study of Jung[24] we have a strongly defined case-study of a guru and his movement, which could serve as a paradigm for them all. This should, however, be prefaced by Storr's demurral, for despite his own critical commentary on Jung, he denies that he ever set out to create a sect: 'the idea of a universal Jungian church cannot really be sustained.'[25] To present this paradigm it is not necessary to recapitulate Jung's intellectual antecedents and his convergence with those *volkisch* beliefs that underlay Nazism. Jung's indebtedness to Nietzsche, to that quest for a new elite, has, however, to be acknowledged.

In Noll's account, Jung emerges as the epitome of a charismatic leader, who underwent an extraordinary reinvention, from his background in the Swiss Protestant pastorate and his own role as a nineteenth-century bourgeois Christian physician to becoming 'the leader of a movement of modernity that promoted the development of individuality.'[26] In common, though, was the role of the elites, the Swiss *pfarrenstand* or pastorate and the Nietzschean. Jung came out of a cultural background of like-minded movements. There was theosophy, Haeckel's *Monistenbund* (the Monistic alliance), Wagnerism. As early as 1907 Weber had detected in the Freudian movement the appearance of a quasi-mystical group. Jung's quest was part of a widespread European endeavour to fend off decadence and degeneracy, as well as coping with his own fears of hereditary mental illness on his mother's side of the family. It was Otto Gross (1877–1920) who introduced him to the counter-culture of the Schwabing-Ascona nexus,[27] vital for his own personal and sexual emancipation. By 1910 Jung began 'openly to acknowledge his desire to form a religious sect of psychoanalysis.'[28] In 1912 he established the Society for Psychoanalytical Endeavour. In a key essay, written late 1911 or early 1912, *New Paths in Psychology* and compared by Noll for its revolutionary significance to Lenin's 1902 pamphlet, *What is to be done,* Jung appealed for 'a revolution in the internalized European traditions that enslave the individual personality.'[29] In setting up the Zurich school for analytical psychology in 1913 he announced his break from Freud and in 1914 he resigned his post as President of the International Psychological Association. With the setting up of his Psychological Club in 1916, psychoanalysis had 'truly become a cultural movement with its own Weltanschauung'.[30] Jung's speech to the Club in 1916 can be read 'as a manifesto of a religious movement whose goal is not only the salvation of the individual but also of the world.'[31] In Noll's analysis, a religion replaced a religion. Here was Jung's version of a secret doctrine. But had Jung in the process laid claim to being a God?

Both Ernest Jones in his 1913 essay, *The God Complex* and Freud in his 1914 *Narcissism*, had in so many words said so. Through recognizing the impact of his powers of intuition and extra-sensory ability, Jung had certainly become increasingly aware of his charisma. In his essay written in 1916 in French, *La structure de l'inconscient*, Jung's riposte was to declare his own 'godlikeness' and to describe his own religious movement as one 'based on ideas of redemption, regeneration and rebirth through contact with a transcendental realm.'[32] Jung was offering 'something that could heal the festering *fin-de-siècle* neurosis produced by modernity: rebirth.'[33] In 1925, in his seminars on analytical psychology, significantly in English so as to attract a larger audience, Jung is seen by Noll as initiating a personality cult. Down to 1948, only those who had sat at Jung's feet were deemed capable of mastering 'individuation'. Becoming a Jungian analyst was like joining a secret church: you had to 'undergo a subterranean initiation into the mystery grotto of the collective unconscious in Switzerland.'[34] In Weberian terms Jung emerges as an exemplary prophet rather than an ethical, one initiating an elitist and hierarchical cult rather than a more egalitarian church. In time Jung's residence at Kushnacht-Zurich became a Jungian Bayreuth. Interestingly, the movement proved peculiarly attractive to women: 'like the Dionysian cults of antiquity the Jung cult seems to have started (and then prospered) as primarily a cult of women.'[35] But once this personality cult became entrenched, routinization could follow. In setting up the C.G. Jung Institute in Zurich in 1948 the need was recognized for a more permanent authority or, as Weber might have put it, 'charismatic exuberance became bureaucratized and Dionysian spontaneity is replaced by Apollonian regimentation.'[36]

So, had Jung fashioned a religion? Storr would disagree: 'Noll has constituted a conspiracy theory which does not bear examination.'[37] But whoever is right,[38] here is a benchmark for measuring the new religious movements in India.

A less extreme model and one maybe closer to the Indian situation, is provided in Raymond L.B. Williams' account of an Indian concept of *sampradaya:* 'a tradition which has been handed down from a founder through successive religious teachers and which shapes the followers into a distinct fellowship with institutional forms.'[39] But this is an account premised on there being a kind of apostolic succession of leaders, which was by no means the case.

In the Proustian concept of love there may be a further intriguing way of explaining the relationship between gurus and their followers. It is an insight that came from a visit to Sai Baba's ashram at Putta Parthi. In Proust's pessimistic account of love, on the impossibility of mutual love, the very force of the love of the lover is reflected back from the beloved, creating an illusion that the love is returned.[40] Might this not be the way Sai Baba engaged with his followers? As I reported it at the time, 'his achievement is somehow successfully to let others invest their hopes in him. He simply gives back to people what they give to him'.[41]

The way religious reform movements in India were organized owed much to the impact of European missionary movements. There was a running battle between Mission and Indian religions in the nineteenth century[42] and, to meet this challenge, exponents of Indian religions appropriated much of the style of their militant ideology and their embattled missionary organizations. But in a more positive way they also began to imitate the corporate life of Christianity, its communal prayer, its monasticism, also some of its religiosity, its concepts of sin, guilt, the need for repentance and grace. It can, of course, be argued that such mimesis was a sign of insecurity and that out of this defensiveness sprang modern Hindu fundamentalism.

THE BRAHMO SAMAJ, RAM MOHUN ROY AND KESHAB CHANDRA SEN

In many ways the Brahmo Samaj was to be the model for India's religious reform movements. Its contribution to 'the new age of the nineteenth century, was', Baird asserts, 'without parallel'.[43] To see its leaders in context and to sense its differing expressions we need a brief chronology. The Brahmo Samaj literally grew out of a friendship between Ram Mohun Roy and a Baptist missionary, William Adam, whom Roy, in one of those strange religious encounters of the century, had converted to unitarianism. For Roy religious debate had always been an intellectual exchange between friends and he had been perfectly happy for his own commitment to a new monotheistic Hinduism to be represented through his association with Adam's Unitarian church. Only in 1828 did another earlier informal discussion group of friends which he had set up on his arrival in Calcutta in 1815, but which had since lapsed, crystallize as the Brahmo Sabha. With his premature death in Bristol in 1833 the movement foundered, to be revived by Devendranath Tagore, both through his setting up in 1839 a parallel society, the Tattvabodhini or truth-seeking Society, and his joining the Brahmo Sabha in 1843. In 1859 the two organizations merged as the Brahmo Samaj.

In that year Keshab Chandra Sen joined, and he was to have a devastating effect on the movement. His social radicalism on matters of caste led to a split, formalized in November 1866, between the conservative Adi Brahmo Samaj, still under Devendranath's leadership, though in practice Rajnarain Bose became its leading protagonist, and Keshab's Brahmo Samaj of India. But Keshab's increasing retreat into a kind of neo-Vaishnavism put intolerable strains on more radically minded colleagues and in 1878 the Brahmo Samaj divided yet again, into the more socially radical Sadharan (or general, that is catholic and democratic) Brahmo Samaj and Keshab's minority grouping, to be named by 1881 the Church of the New Dispensation. It is the Sadharan which has remained the leading organization.

In one of his articles in *Bande Mataram* Aurobindo Ghose summarized Ram Mohun Roy's role in far too ambitious a way: 'the Brahmo Samaj was set on foot by Ram Mohun Roy with the belief that this would be the one religion which would replace and unite the innumerable sects now dividing our spiritual consciousness.'[44] Roy did not possess the charisma to undertake such leadership nor did he aspire to such a role. Certainly he was the *acharya* or teacher, but no guru. Throughout his life Roy displayed a measured intelligence, a reliance on reason, a humanitarianism which makes him an altogether attractive personality, one that anticipates the gravitas of Devendranath but has none of the histrionics of Keshab. He was instrumental in the revival of Vedantism but of the late Vedas, the Upanishads: he did not have access to the *Rig Veda*.

Ram Mohun's monotheism owed much to his early reading of Islam: on breaking from his parents through his reformist views he had taken himself off to Patna, where he studied the Qur'an in Arabic. He went on to Tibet to study Buddhism. In a four-year stay at Varanasi he mastered Sanskrit and was well qualified to be a critic of the Hinduism of his day. Through his exposure to western thought, to utilitarianism and to liberalism, and his polemical encounter with the Baptist Serampore missionaries, Roy sought a reform of Hinduism along rationalist lines. But this had universalist implications and this is one reason for denying that Roy had any intention of setting up a new religion or sect. Even though he was unable to see Christ as an incarnate God, he was quite happy to affirm the value of Christian moral teaching. Farquhar went so far as to argue that Roy, through his rejecting both reincarnation and the key Hindu concept of karma had ceased to be a Hindu, but that he fell short of any new theology and that Roy's, at best, was a variant of deism. But this is to underplay Roy's contribution to a new monotheistic Vedantic Hinduism. If Roy did not become a cult leader, it is true that the practice of the Brahmo Sabha, its form of corporate worship, took on some trappings of a Christian service: Adam wrote of 'chanting in the cathedral style'.[45]

Roy's innovatory role was equally significant in the social and political field. He was the forerunner of that whole moderate tradition of Indian nationalism, one that ascribed a providentialist role to British rule, though, in time, this was to be an approach branded as mere political mendicancy. If Roy did not adopt any radical critique of caste and was far more the opponent of the servile status of women, and if his was but a guarded critique of Company Raj, here were the vital beginnings of that social and political content to Indian religious reform movements. Sivanath Sastri's assessment of his career, if rather grudging in its praise, is probably fair: 'his duty was that of a sturdy pioneer; working single-handed to clear away a mass of popular prejudice and prepare the way for those coming after him. His work was mainly negative and reformatory and not positive and constructive.'[46]

Keshab Chandra Sen's career as a religious leader was to take on an entirely different trajectory. Through Akshoy Kumar Dutt's powers of rationalist thought the Brahmo Samaj had narrowly escaped the trap of identifying the *Vedas* as an infallible text, a certain step towards turning the movement into a new religion or sect, whilst Devendranath as leader had displayed a masterly skill in both building on Roy's progressive social programme—he supported Vidyasagar's widow remarriage campaign—at the same time drawing the movement back into a more consciously Hindu direction. Keshab proved incapable of such shrewd compromise and introduced a quite new and more hectic approach, driven by his neo-Vaishnavism. The quarrel between Keshab and his younger contemporaries, which led to the split of 1878, owed much to his retreat from social radicalism, less over caste reform, more on his rather Victorian stance on the social role of women, but a deeper divide derived from their recognition, as Farquhar put it, 'of the extreme dangers of guruism in a modern body like the Samaj.'[47]

Keshab's was a highly charismatic personality; and if sadly this was to give way at the end to delusions of grandeur, and maybe madness, here was a figure readily assuming the mantle of guru and prophet. His indebtedness to western models, to Mission and evangelicalism, is not in dispute. Under his leadership the Brahmo Samaj became a self-conscious missionary movement. Keshab adopted Christ as a role model, though he insisted on Christ being an Asiatic and universal figure and displayed little patience with Christian sectarianism, which he believed western

Christianity to be. He was leading the Samaj into a new kind of emotional religiosity, a *bhaktism*, which owed as much to his cult of Chaitanya as of Christ. A new temple was opened 24 June 1868. Here were the beginnings of a leadership cult. Sivanath Sastri, a leading Sadharan and hence, hard-pressed to write sympathetically about Keshab, wrote of the floodgates of a new revival:

... in utter self-abasement men began to prostrate themselves at each other's feet and specially the feet of Mr. Sen, and prayers were offered to him for intercession on behalf of sinners. Men ran mad, as it were, in their spiritual agony, not knowing what they said or did.[48]

Sen reported an extreme example of a man going so far as 'to wash the feet of Mr Sen with his own hand and to wipe them with the long hairs of his wife.'[49] Was this bhaktism at work or the literal acting out of the story of Mary Magdalene? It does seem that a Protestant evangelicalism exercised a morbid influence over the Samaj: 'a vivid consciousness of sin cast a gloom over our lives. Brahmo manners became sombre, austere and puritanic.'[50] Here is clear evidence of the transition of the Brahmo Samaj from being an informed debating society on matters religious, as well as social and political, into becoming itself not just a religious movement but a new religion.

But Keshab did not jettison his links with the scientific culture of the West. Even during the days of the New Dispensation he was still searching for a hybridism of a western scientific approach with Hindu spirituality. He believed that both were driven by the same imperatives and affirmed:

Between God-vision and the spirit of modern science in the nineteenth century there is no discord, but rather concord. The scientists of the present day ardently love unity. Their very vocation is to evolve unity out of variety, method and order out of confusion and disorder. In fact science is nothing but a striving after unity, the reduction of multiplicity of phenomena into unity, the unity of law or force or whatever it might be.

Just a little disingenuously he said: 'the Darwins and Huxleys, the Tyndalls and Spencers of modern times are all engaged in the work of unification.'[51] Nor did he lose sight of a religious universalism. He lambasted his audience:

Is godliness the Hindu's monopoly? Will you have only the small and one-sided creed of your country, and refuse to enter into fellowship with the great nations of the West? Shun jealousy and narrow-minded bigotry and so enlarge and distend your hearts that not only Asia but all Europe and America may find place therein. India! absorb England. Asia! assimilate Christian Europe.[52]

To this extent Keshab remained true to the legacy of Ram Mohun

Roy. If on the Jung model he does seem to have sought self-deification, intellectually he does not seem to have broken his moorings from a scientific and rationalist approach. Together with his religious universalism, here are causes to qualify a view of Keshab as transforming the Brahmo Samaj into a religion.

His loyalty to Roy's social and political legacy is mixed. He certainly retreated from Roy's proto-feminism. Keshab exhibited a very Victorian distaste for the public role of women. But he was not afraid, as Roy had not been, to mix his rhetoric on the providentialist role of the Raj with an exposure of its racism. He attacked the way the Raj excluded Indians from administrative and political office.

In many ways Keshab emerges as the key transitional figure in the history of the religious reform movements, both looking back to a western-style reform movement, initiated by Ram Mohun Roy, and forward, to a new kind of cultural revivalism, evidenced in the lives of Ramakrishna and Vivekananda and the history of the Ramakrishna mission, in the life of Dayananda and the history of the Arya Samaj, in Madame Blavatsky, Annie Besant and theosophy, and Aurobindo Ghose. To what extent can we detect a pursuit of guru status and the makings of a cult in these revivalist movements?

RAMAKRISHNA, VIVEKANANDA AND THE RAMAKRISHNA MISSION

The most unusual and at first sight the least probable leader of a religious movement was Ramakrishna. Aurobindo put this well:

Certain men were born, men whom the educated world would not have recognized if that belief, if that God within them had not been there to open their eyes, men whose lives were very different from what our education, our western education, had taught us to admire.

He mentioned his illiteracy:

He was a man who had been what they call absolutely useless in the world. He was a man who lived what many call the life of a mad man without intellectual training, a man who lived on the alms of others, such a man as the English educated Indian would ordinarily talk of as one useless to society. But God knew what he was doing. He sent that man to Bengal and set him in the temple at Dakshineswar in Calcutta.

Educated men . . . came to fall at the feet of this ascetic.[53]

Ramakrishna's was to be a long period of spiritual growth, of *sadhana*, a protracted emergence as a spiritual leader, one in which he acquired knowledge of *tantrism* and *shaktism* from a wandering nun, Bhairavi; of

Vaishnavism from one Vaishnavasharan; of Vedantism and the *jnana* path from a member of the Puri sect, Tota Puri; and an existential discovery, of other faiths and their prophets, Buddha, Christ and Mohammed. In this eclecticism and universalism are grounds for arguing that Ramakrishna did not set out to found another exclusive religion. Ramakrishna exhibited certain key features in the emergence of the guru, with the bereavement of his father when he was aged but eight and the even more traumatic death of his brother, thirty-one years older and a father surrogate. There followed a desperate search for a personal encounter with Kali, one which even his family recognized as a kind of insanity. Sudhir Kakar sees in it 'the signs of a full-fledged depression'.[54] Here was, in Storr's sense, a 'creative illness'.

This prolonged religious evolution turned Ramakrishna into an immensely subtle and persuasive leader, one well able to win disciples over to his own vision of the divine, where God could be worshipped both with and without form. This was dramatically demonstrated by his winning over two erstwhile strong believers in God without form, Keshab Chandra Sen and Vivekananda, to his worship of Kali. Both had sought a personal encounter with God and here was a man who claimed a direct experience of him through *samadhi*, on an almost daily basis. It was not surprising that at a time of cultural revivalism a man who laid claim to the knowledge of the divine, and whose claim was authenticated by the religious experts of his day, should be recognized as an *avatar* and should exercise an exceptional spell over his contemporaries. Vivekananda said of Ramakrishna that 'he himself would never be addressed as Guru or teacher;' but 'that long before anybody knew him' he foresaw 'that he had many disciples who would come to him shortly'.[55] There seems, therefore, to be no cause to doubt that Ramakrishna was a self-conscious religious leader.

But we need a careful sociology if we are to account for the appeal of an illiterate Ramakrishna to the *bhadralok*, so essentially rational and literate an elite. Through an analysis of his followers we can best understand how Ramakrishna became a guru with a cult following. It is not so difficult to see how Keshab Chandra Sen, with his own religious universalism and his reverence for Christ, if but two years his junior, should have become besotted with Ramakrishna. But why did so many younger members of Calcutta's urban elite subscribe to Ramakrishna's rejection of 'women and gold'? Sumit Sarkar has the fascinating explanation that Ramakrishna spoke to their alienation from the constraints of a business and colonial culture, to a world of strict routine, henpecked by their wives to keep up the mark set by these dictates of *chakri*. His was a kind of spirituality, the homespun rural wisdom of a naïve man, that allowed them to escape these pressures and one that encouraged a retreat into their own rural roots. The 1880s were also, in Sarkar's understanding, a period of abeyance of political nationalism, a kind of Chekhovian absorption in the merely domestic, and the apolitical. Ramakrishna spoke to that mentality.[56] This makes Ramakrishna's conversion of Vivekananda all the more significant, for it was he who led the Ramakrishna movement towards the social and, if less obviously so, to the political as well.

Vivekananda underwent a profound crisis of cultural and religious identity before finding any kind of spiritual equilibrium. The continuing uncertainties in the choice of his own personal direction, in turn made him a domineering and often intolerant leader. Yet, he was never quite the forceful leader many took him to be. Adverse family circumstances following his father's death in 1884 led to a 'period of painful tension between reason and faith',[57] accompanied by two breakdowns. These breakdowns, it could be argued, were bouts of 'creative illness'.

The tension marking this period was resolved by Ramakrishna's winning him over to the worship of Kali, an extraordinary surrender by a former Sadharan Brahmo. In turn, this convert to Ramakrishna's movement was to impose on it a radical change of direction. It might by argued that Ramakrishna chose Vivekananda just because he saw in him a man with a flair for the practical, which he himself did not possess, and one who might realize Ramakrishna's deeper purposes. This does not, however, answer the charge that Vivekananda reoriented Ramakrishna's vision in a social direction. In George Williams' account he converted 'a traditional localized ascetic group of bhaktis dedicated to devotion for their guru and Kali'[58] into a monastic order of in-the-world ascetics, karma yogis, dedicated to humanitarian social service. But there always remained a conflict in Vivekananda's make-up between, in Sumit Sarkar's language, 'a supremely self-confident activism and an inward-turning world-weariness.'[59] This underlying pessimism led him in his last years once again to seek *moksha,* or release. He was never quite the dynamic prophet-patriot that a later *Swadeshi* generation made him out to be. If he assumed, however distastefully and reluctantly, guru status, should he be seen as the initiator of a religious cult?

Vivekananda worked a bold synthesis of West and East. If through his education he had read widely in the eighteenth and nineteenth-century literature and philosophy of the West, it was an encounter, to quote Tapan Raychaudhuri, 'overshadowed by his conviction, based on his life experience, that in his chosen endeavour he had nothing to learn from the dominant culture of his day.'[60] Only the Hindu tradition promised ultimacy: 'its promise of spiritual realization was, in the last analysis, to him man's only worthwhile goal.'[61] But Vivekananda wedded the sanatana dharma, the eternal principles, to the liberal tradition of the Brahmo Samaj. It is through the way he brings into his philosophy both a scientific approach, the Vedanta itself seen as scientific, together with the social radicalism of the Sadharan Brahmos, that Vivekananda steps back from introducing a mere sect or new religion, though we cannot deny the Ramakrishna movement a description as a religious movement. And Vivekananda did try to contain any Ramakrishna cult.

But the real originality of Vivekananda lay in his social utopianism and his covert political radicalism. It is open to debate whether his monasticism and his commitment to work owes more to western influence or to the Swaminarayan movement. But here was a vision of a caste-free society, of a revolutionary Sudra movement, of the uplift of women, and through mass education a raising up of the whole of society to a knowledge of Vedanta. (There are echoes here of aristocrat and populist, Alexander Herzen, with his dream of a levelling up of Russian society.) If the early Mission under Vivekananda's direction adopted a public apolitical stance— he knew that his fledgeling movement could not have withstood the bullying of the colonial state—in private Vivekananda shared the nationalism of the Congress Extremist faction. Sister Nivedita had to leave the movement on account of her open support for Aurobindo's nationalist and revolutionary group. Aurobindo claimed to be inspired by Vivekananda, whose voice he heard in 1909 in Alipore jail, though this points to the ambiguity of Vivekananda's political message, for it was at that stage that Aurobindo diverted from political activism to yoga.

If both Ramakrishna and Vivekananda emerged as gurus in the Ramakrishna movement, the movement itself appears too flexible, pragmatic and universalist to warrant a description as a cult movement.

DAYANAND SARASWATI AND THE ARYA SAMAJ

The Arya Samaj owed much of its organizational structure to the Brahmo Samaj and did not wholly escape the fatal fissiparous tendencies of that model, but in Dayanand Saraswati it possessed an authoritative leader the Brahmo Samaj never had. Arvind Sharma writes: 'the man and his message were not merely original but perhaps unique.'[62] Aurobindo made exceptional claims for Dayanand: he wrote of 'this formidable artisan in God's worship'. He emphasized his practical side, that 'master-glance of practical intuition', 'the secret of a pure unspoilt energy, the sign that a man has not travelled far from nature', and Dayanand the cultural revivalist: 'to seize on a vital thing out of the past and throw it into the stream of modern life is really the most powerful means of renovation and new creation'.[63]

Dayanand has all the appearance of the paradigmatic guru. There was to be a prolonged *sadhana* or spiritual training before he took on the role of teacher or guru. There were certain classic features of the guru in his background, with an early bereavement of a younger sister—'it was my first bereavement and the shock I received was indeed great'[64]—and an angry rejection of his parents, in part through his alienation from their Shaivite faith, more through his refusal to marry. There followed an extraordinary odyssey through the sacred landscape of north India in search of *moksha* or release by the mastery of yoga. Through western eyes this might be seen as a period of 'creative illness'; against an Indian cultural background, it would be seen as a normative spiritual quest. In 1860 Dayanand changed direction, in Arvind Sharma's words, from being 'a private spiritual aspirant' to becoming 'a public religious crusader'[65] when he adopted the blind eighty-one-year-old Virajananda of Mathura as a guru and himself became an expert on Sanskrit grammar. This was the basis for his subsequent career, from 1867, for Dayanand only slowly saw his way to this new role as a teacher.

Crucial for the formation of the Arya Samaj was Dayanand's meeting with the Brahmo leaders in Calcutta in 1872, further evidence of Keshab's key role as the transitional figure in the history of the new religious movements. Dayanand then turned his line of fire away from the orthodox priesthood and towards the anglicized elite. He taught in Hindi rather than Sanskrit. The first branch of the Arya Samaj was set up in Bombay in 1875. The key text, *Satyartha Prakash*, first appeared in 1874 and a second edition in 1883, shortly before his death by poisoning. Subsequently the militant wing of the Arya Samaj in the Punjab had no hesitation in looking on Dayanand as a *rishi* and the *Satyartha Prakash* as a sacred text. The moderates, however, preferred to look on him merely as a great reformer.[66]

A test of the cultist character of a movement lies in whether or not it parts company from a rationalist or scientific frame of thought. Here the attitude of Dayanand is surprisingly ambiguous. Making exclusive claims for the *Rigveda Samhita* as the sole revealed text, he resorted to 'violent methods of interpretation'; and in Farquhar's words 'no Hindu ancient or modern ever taught what he teaches'.[67] He asserted extravagantly that all of western science was already contained in this Vedic text. Farquhar postulates that so great was Dayanand's admiration for western science that in order both to give it status and to win over his audience to a scientific approach, he ascribed infallibility to the *Rig Veda*. Indeed, for someone apparently so little exposed to western influence as Dayanand, the strength of his commitment to natural law was a little strange. It led him to reject all miracles, all conceptions of incarnation, all notions of the forgiveness of sins. So tough was his monotheism that he rejected the basic Vedantist belief in the oneness of *atman* and Brahma in favour of a dualist separation of the soul from God. Aurobindo was not convinced by this curious claim to a prior knowledge of western science: 'here we have the sole point of fundamental principle about which there can be any justifiable misgiving.'[68]

Dayanand's was an embattled faith. But again he rejected any charge of exclusivism. He believed that he was driven by a pursuit of the truth and was universalist in outlook. At the time of the Delhi Durbar in 1877 he sought out the leaders of other faiths, in particular Sir Syed Ahmed Khan, to hold some interfaith conference. Clearly, the influence of Mission had rubbed off on Dayanand. Farquhar wrote that an Arya Samaj meeting he attended 'was just like a Protestant service and totally unlike any Vedic observance.'[69] If in *Satyartha Prakash* his was a clearly adversarial relationship with other faiths, he was equally hostile to Hindu sects. But the Suddhi or reconversion movement had dangerous communal implications and here are grounds for ascribing cultist features to the Arya Samaj.

The huge paradox of the Arya Samaj was its radical social agenda with its view of caste as the base for a meritocratic society rather than an ascriptive phenomenon. This was to make the Samaj peculiarly attractive to upwardly mobilizing castes. But Dayanand, despite his cultural revivalism—and clearly he was a cultural nationalist—was to be curiously muted in his actual critique of the colonial state, probably on much the same grounds as Vivekananda, out of a wish to protect a still vulnerable new organization. The most he seemed ready to do was flirt with some idea of a princely federation.

It seems fair to look on Dayanand as a self-conscious guru, one somewhat reluctant to fill this role, but to recognize some ambiguity in whether or not the Arya Samaj was a cult. Is there, however, a paradigm shift on moving on to the study of theosophy and Aurobindo, given their rejection of any account of themselves as a religion and their insistence that theirs was a pursuit of spirituality? Should we conclude from the split between the Arya Samaj and the Theosophical Society that they were radically different movements?

MADAME BLAVATSKY, ANNIE BESANT AND THEOSOPHY

The Theosophical Society, with its foreign origins—it was set up in New York in September 1875—and its largely foreign leadership, seems the odd one out in this story. Yet it acquired a quite extraordinary following in India. Indians, badly bruised by hostile, above all by missionary criticism of their faiths quickly responded to outsiders who defended those religions and attacked those western critics. Here were answers to feelings of cultural inadequacy. Farquhar, a missionary himself, puts this in a predictably ironic way: 'the depths to which Mrs Besant descends in defending Hinduism will hardly be believed. There is scarcely an exploded doctrine, scarcely a superstitious observance, which she has not defended with the silliest and most shameful arguments.'[70] Can a case be made for Blavatsky and Besant as religious leaders?

It may as well be conceded at the outset that Madame Blavatsky was an impostor but on a scale that required real talent. Richard Hodgson, dispatched in 1884 by the Society for Psychical Research to investigate charges of fraud against her in Madras, reported: 'we think that she has achieved a title to permanent remembrance as one of the most accomplished, ingenious and interesting impostors of history.'[71] Farquhar's lengthy and triumphalist exposure of her many frauds no longer seems relevant in assessing her appeal and significance. Even he is forced to recognize her 'genius to will and to rule', her 'great energy and industry'.[72] Noll sees her as 'the single most influential woman in occultist circles' and in many ways, arguably, 'the most influential woman in America and Europe at the time'.[73] Can a case be sustained for seeing her so-called lost years, 1849 to 1872 as her sadhana, a period of preparation as a religious leader? It is a story where notoriously fact and fiction elide.

Probably the earlier Russian years meant the most to Blavatsky. It was always in Russia that she most eagerly sought an audience. Born August 1831 into an aristocratic family, hers was a troubled childhood, with the death of a younger brother and mother when she was but ten, but also through the grip of those intense psychical powers that haunted her till she was sixteen. At the age of nine she went to live in Saratov, home to the Kalmuch Buddhists, with nothing but the great plains between Saratov and Tibet. Was this the seedbed for her fascination with Tibetan Buddhism? In 1846, then sixteen, she found herself in Tbilisi, and there she was to immerse herself in her great-grandfather Prince Golitsyn's library. To quote one biographer: 'in the light of her later career it would seem that the hours spent in the library were the most important influence on HPB's conception of the Masters,'[74] the crucial intermediaries between her and the secret doctrine. Here she read deeply into the literature of Russian Rosicrucianism, with 'its legend of a worldwide network of Masters and a secret link with Tibet.'[75] If Blavatsky never lost contact with Russia, in 1849, following a fairly disastrous marriage with Nicephore Blavatsky (both Blavatsky and Besant were to acquire through marriage far more charismatic names than their maiden of von Hahn and Wood, respectively), she escaped to Constantinople. And now begins the mystery.

Blavatsky always insisted that she spent seven of those missing years in Tibet, the required period of apprenticeship into esoteric mysteries. It was a shrewd choice for, as Peter Washington points out, Lhasa had replaced Jerusalem as the religious centre of gravity. If she failed to penetrate east Tibet in 1854-5, though she may have entered west Tibet, there seems to be some evidence that she succeeded in 1868 and stayed nearby the Panchen Lama's great monastery Tashilunpo, close to Shigatse. She never claimed to have reached Lhasa. A later text, *Voice of the Silence*, is cited as evidence that she had studied Tibetan Buddhism.[76] Blavatsky claimed to have been instructed in the ancient wisdom by the Masters, in particular Masters Morya and Koot Hoomi. There has since been considerable speculation whether these were Blavatsky's mentally abstracted vehicles of this doctrine or real persons Blavatsky had met.

Another account of her sadhana emphasizes instead her Middle Eastern travels. There were her contacts with intellectuals in Cairo, her exposure to Sufism and to other cults. Johnson writes: 'the Theosophical historian's duty however is to admit cheerfully that he is dealing with as complex and mysterious person as ever lived and to embrace any new information which becomes available.'[77] He explores a case for both Paolos Mamon and Jamal ad-din al-Afghani as the original for Master Serapis Bey. Madame Blavatsky herself wrote: 'I have lived with the whirling dervishes, with the Druids of Mount Lebanon, with the Bedouin Arabs and the marabouts of Damascus.'[78]

This does not exhaust the possibilities in locating the origins of her ideas. Washington emphasizes her indebtedness to the novels of Bulwer Lytton, above all, *Zanoni*: 'it would not be unjust to say that her new religion was virtually manufactured from his pages.'[79]

Another possible source as Master was Mazzini. Was he the inspiration for Master Morya? Certainly in Constantinople Blavatsky was to befriend a Mazzinian, Agardi Metrovitcch, who became a long-term friend, and one always has a sense of Blavatsky as being on the fringes of Europe's left-wing intelligentsia in the mid-nineteenth century. Did she indeed fight at the battle of Mentana in 1867? She sported a Garibaldi redshirt. It is not too difficult to imagine her as one of those dispossessed intellectuals in the novels of Dostoyevsky.

Only with her arrival in America in 1873 and her involvement in its craze for spiritualism are we on firmer ground. Twice over, with her flirtation with spiritualism and her tactical alliance with the Arya Samaj, Blavatsky was to display considerable opportunism in advancing her cause. In fact, she rather despised spiritualism, mere chatterings with the dead as she saw it. But she herself possessed strong powers as a medium; and it was her inability to let go of her experiments with the phenomenon that in the end proved her undoing in both America and India. For all her flirtation with magic, however, Blavatsky did believe that she had access to an altogether more serious form of knowledge.

Her Russian contemporary, V.V. Solovyoff, probably got as close as anyone else to grasping the contradictions of her make-up. She confessed to him: 'why, suppose my books and *The Theosophist* had been a thousand times more interesting and more serious, do you imagine I should have had any sort of success anywhere, if behind that had not been the "phenomena". I should have done simply nothing.'[80] Solovyoff saw in her a shameless cynicism about the gullibility of human nature. He believed that the secret of her success lay in her manipulating human relationships. When he caught her red-handed over the manufacture of the Mahatma letters, she feared he would despise her, but his reply was:

Why so. There is deceit and deceit and there is trickery and trickery. To play the parts you play, to make crowds follow you, to interest the learned, to found societies in distant lands, to start an entire movement—good gracious. Why, it is all so out of the common, that I am enraptured at you against my will. In all my life I shall never meet another. I admire you as a real mighty Herculean force.[81]

This is the point: Blavatsky displayed exceptional powers as a spiritual leader.

One who succumbed to those powers was Annie Besant, becoming the real force in theosophy after Blavatsky's death. Did she become a religious leader in her own right? Hers is a beguiling story of a constant reinvention of herself, and her biographers are faced with the quandary of deciding whether she was a chameleon or if there was an underlying consistency in these multiple personalities. But a case can be made that hers was a constant religious quest, that hers was also a sadhana, that behind her phases of atheism and socialism lay a deeply religious personality and that her pathway to theosophy was marked by continuity rather than hiatus.

Hers was a troubled life, with the near death of her children and her divorce, the early death of her mother at the age of fifty-eight, almost certainly advanced by all the stresses in her daughter's life. Ann Taylor, Besant's biographer, suggests that she never came to terms with being a social outcast.[82] Joining the Theosophical Society was like coming home.

Blavatsky had her sights on Besant as early as August 1882, writing warmly of her in *The Theosophist*. Subsequently Besant speculated: 'had I met her then or seen any of her writings I would have become her pupil.' But she concluded otherwise: 'I fear not. I was still too much dazzled by the triumphs of western science.' And there was to be a socialist phase: 'I needed to sound yet more deeply the depths of human misery.'[83] But both Bradlaugh and the Fabians took an interest in spiritualism. Besant attended seances. She wanted to know just what had happened at the exact moment of the death of Bradlaugh's wife, Alice. Reviewing Blavatsky's *The Secret Doctrine* for the *Pall Mall Gazette* was a revelation: 'I was dazzled, blinded by the light in which disjointed facts were seen as part of a mighty whole.'[84] In the spring of 1889 a socialist, Herbert Burrows, introduced her to Blavatsky, and she became a convert. Washington sees Blavatsky's appeal—'oh my dear Mrs Besant if you would only come among us'—as a psychological masterstroke.[85] Besant acknowledged that something more than socialism was required to realize the brotherhood of man: 'there was some hidden thing, some hidden power, and I resolved to seek until I found.'[86] She brought remarkable oratorical and organizational skills to the movement. She was always the activist, the karma yogi, with a deep wish to serve humanity. 'Looking back at life' she wrote, 'I see that its keynote—through all the blunders and the blind mistakes and clumsy follies—has been this longing to sacrifice to something felt as greater than the self.'[87] Ann Taylor sums her up well: 'Anne was one of those rare persons who desire the mystic's inward-looking life at the same time as they pursue worldly success.'[88] Hers was not so strong a presence as Blavatsky's—'I have ever been the queerest mixture of weakness and strength'[89]—but there was enough charisma to turn her into a religious leader in her own right.

Did theosophy become a cult? To pursue her war with the Spiritualists, Blavatsky had, in Washington's words, 'to write her own bible and found her own church';[90] the Theosophical Society and her *Isis Unveiled* (1875). Between 1888 and 1892 she published the even more baffling *The Secret Doctrine*. Subsequently, in a number of writings but in her *Ancient Wisdom* in particular, Annie Besant, always a brilliant expositor of other people's ideas, expressed these texts in a rather more accessible form. Theosophy stood for three basic principles: forming a nucleus of a universal brotherhood, without distinction of race, creed, sex, caste or colour; promoting a study of Aryan and other Eastern religions but in the spirit of religious universalism; investigating the unexplained laws of nature or, in other words, the occult. This essentially speculative agenda could hardly be characterized as a religion. Its Achilles' heel was its fatal attraction for the occult. In its gnosticism it did turn itself into a cult. The real thrust of Blavatsky's ideas lay in their anti-Darwinism. Religion was polarized with science. To quote Theodore Roszak: 'it is seldom remembered that in the years following the publication of *The Origin of Species* HPB was the first person to aggressively argue the case for a trans-physical element in evolution against the rising Darwinian consensus.'[91] However Besant, in large part through attending Edward Aveling's lectures in the Science and Art Department in South Kensington became a convert to the nineteenth-century cult of science, and Blavatsky had always to be careful in her courtship of Besant to present theosophy itself as scientifically based. Maybe Besant in her own account interpreted theosophy as less an anti-Darwinian doctrine and rather the spiritual fulfilment of the claims of evolution.

Did theosophy match the other religious movements in adopting social and political causes? If Blavatsky stayed too short a time in India to identify with its future, and was to rebel at Adyar becoming its headquarters, hers was a lively and often angry reaction to India's social backwardness, especially to the low status of women: 'If the English ever did any good in India', she wrote, 'it is undoubtedly that they succeeded in suppressing if not uprooting altogether the terrible custom of infanticide.'[92] She was equally horrified at the plight of widows. Besant, more the cultural revivalist, trod more warily, and even defended caste as function. After 1913, however, she turned radical, though Farquhar attributes this to her attempt to deflect attention from the Leadbeater trial. But whereas Blavatsky had little or no political programme—like Dayanand she flirted with a princely revolt, in her case a Sikh—Besant was to make a major contribution to Indian nationalism. At first she deferred to Olcott's wishes to keep out of politics; with the setting up of her Home Rule League, she became in 1915, if briefly, a prominent nationalist.

Theosophy attracted a mass following both within and without India. As Washington explains: 'the late nineteenth century produced a large semi-educated readership with the appetite, the experience and the lack of intellectual sophistication necessary to consume such texts.'[93] The fierce infighting within the movement is characteristic of struggles for dominance within a cult. Through her organizational flair Besant did much to give a church-like feel to theosophy, together with the cult of the future world spiritual leader, Krishnamurti. His rejection of the role, however, proved the undoing of the movement in the 1930s.

AUROBINDO GHOSE

Aurobindo rediscovered India through his western education on his return in 1893 and his sadhana, or yogic quest, took a different path from that of Dayanand or Vivekananda. Beginning fitfully, it took a radically political direction, and became the one most highly politicized.

If his biographer, A.B. Purani, dates his awareness of Vedantism to his English years—and he did at the time read Max Müller's translations of the *Sacred Books of the East*—only on his joining the Baroda administration do we see the beginning of a spiritual quest. In the 1890s there were 'spontaneous spiritual experiences'; by 1901, Aurobindo saw himself as more Hindu than Brahmo, and expressed the conviction that the Vedanta 'would save India from plunging into the vortex of scientific atheism and the breakdown of moral idealism which is engulfing Europe.'[94] Aurobindo's sadhana proper, however, began only in 1904 after he consulted a Swami Brahmananda in Chianod, a temple town some twenty miles from Baroda, about *pranayama*, the control of breath. The results were startling: I 'felt an electric power around my head. My powers of writing were nearly dried up; they revived with a great vigour. I could write poetry with a flow.' But Aurobindo's use of yoga was to master energy for India's political struggle, not for moksha; as he put it, 'mine was a side-door entry into religious life.'[95] By August 1905 Aurobindo had, however, moved from purely psycho-physical techniques of yoga to spiritual. It was possible to know God. Through his brother, Baren, he had met another guru, Bhaskar Lele, in Baroda in December 1907. Aurobindo proved a natural at meditation; within three days he reached the state of consciousness known as 'silent brahma' or *nirvana*. As Heehs puts it: 'from this point on Aurobindo was primarily a yogi. He regarded his work and his writings as the expressions of a higher will.'[96] To his wife he wrote: 'I no longer am the master of my own will. Like a puppet I must go wherever God takes me. I am no longer free.'[97] But when Bhaskar Lele came to Calcutta and warned Aurobindo that his brother's revolutionary activities were 'asuric', Aurobindo dropped him as a guru: 'I then received the command from within that a human guru was no longer necessary.'[98] In many ways Aurobindo's yogic path matched Freud's exceptional one in psychoanalysis, that the subject can know itself as object. Following a mystical experience in Alipore jail in 1909, in Purani's words, Aurobindo 'decided to dedicate himself entirely to the spiritual life and his outer life thenceforward became a part of his sadhana and its result.'[99] In his historic Uttarpara speech, 30 May 1909, he spoke of a sadhana of the *Gita*, a freeing himself from 'repulsion and desire', a recognition of the claims of the sanatana dharma: 'it is a thing that has not so much to be believed as lived.'[100] There was to be a crucial rephrasing of priorities: 'I say no longer that nationalism is a creed, a religion, a faith; I say that it is the Sanatan Dharma which for us is nationalism.'[101]

Here there is no space to follow Aurobindo's later metaphysical speculations. On 24 November 1926 he claimed a direct experience of the overmind. His so-called supramentalism has curious Nietzschean overtones. Aurobindo remained a this-worldly figure, both mystic and humanist. His political charisma was simply redeployed and, however vigorously Pondicherry ashramites deny that he set up a religion, he was clearly a self-conscious religious leader. But had he turned nationalism into a religion?

There was an underlying Darwinism in Aurobindo's concept of nationalism. He favoured an organic view of society. Unless organisms adapt, they die. Cultural survival lies in the capacity to absorb foreign influence. India, he said, 'has always done this with all outside forces which sought to find entry into her silent and meditative being. She has suffused them with her peculiar individuality so completely that their foreign origin is no longer recognizable.'[102] India had done so with Islam but she lacked the energy to absorb occidentalism. If there were faint stirrings in this direction, India had to draw on new energies or shakti: this was the significance of his 1905 vision of the Bhawani temple. In his cult of the Mother or Kali, Aurobindo began to write wholly in that nineteenth-century European tradition of messianic nationalism. 'India', he asserted, 'is the *guru* of the nations, the physician of the human soul in its profounder maladies; she is destined once more to new-mould the life of the world and restore the peace of the human spirit.'[103]

His was an extraordinary political reformulation of Vedanta: 'we are all Gods and creators because the energy of God is within us.'[104] Passive resistance was a form of sadhana. 'Nationalism', he declared, 'is immortal; nationalism cannot die, because it is no human being. It is God who is working in Bengal. God cannot be killed, God cannot be sent to jail.'[105] There was a social dimension here, a selflessness, he believed, that would rise above the divisions of caste. But his was essentially a political vision, with the nation as God. He preached:

Swaraj is the fulfilment of the ancient life of India under modern conditions, the return of *satyayuga* of national greatness, the resumption by her of her great role as teacher-guide, self-liberation of the people for the final fulfilment of the vedantic ideal in politics, this is the true Swaraj for India.[106]

On this kind of evidence it would be difficult to deny that Aurobindo had made a cult of Indian nationalism.

CONCLUSION

Definitions of and differentiations between such concepts as religious movement, religion, sect and cult remain slippery and are unlikely ever to be hard-edged. The assumption underlying this essay is that when a religious movement becomes a religion, sect or cult there is a falling away; there is an off-putting exclusivism. For a religious reform movement, it is perfectly possible to remain within the parameters of a scientific, rationalist, even Enlightenment tradition and likewise to remain open to religious universalism. Equally, it can manifest a tendency to deteriorate into the merely revelatory or the occult. This is not a peculiarly Indian trait; there was a similar tendency in the psychoanalytical movement, which broke its moorings from the scientific tradition in which it began. We have, however, to distinguish between the 'new age', more self-advertising style in the role of guru in a western context from the more traditionalist, more sober, arguably more self-effacing role in India's ancient culture. There seems little cause—with the exception of the early Brahmo Samaj leaders, Ram Mohun Roy and Devendranath Tagore—to deny the title of guru or self-conscious religious leader to the leaders of religious movements under review. Only a few of them—assuming Noll's account to be fair—followed Jung's example of self-deification. Keshab Chandra Sen implausibly, Ramakrishna more plausibly claimed avatar status: some thrust godhood on Dayanand.

At the same time, there was an interdependence, often almost morbid, between guru and his followers, which gave the movements the appearance of a cult. Intellectually, however, they often remained on this side of scientific or rational world-view, whatever their claim to spiritual insight. To allocate responsibility between guru and disciple for this cultish tendency is difficult: it is an area for further research.

NOTES

1. J.N. Farquhar, *Modern Religions Movements in India*, London, 1918.
2. Kenneth W. Jones, *Socio-Religious Reform Movements in British India*, Cambridge, 1989.
3. Robert Baird (ed.), *Religion in Modern India*, New Delhi, 1981.
4. Frank E. Manuel and Fritzie E. Manuel, *Utopian Thought in the Western World*, Oxford, 1979, remains the classic text on this theme.
5. K.W. Jones, *Socio-Religious Reform Movements*, p. 179.
6. Gavin Flood, *An Introduction to Hinduism*, Cambridge, 1996, p. 258.
7. Anthony Storr, *Feet of Clay, A Study of Gurus*, London, 1996, p. 208.
8. Ibid., pp. 210–11.

9. Raymond B. Williams, *A New Face of Hinduism. The Swaminarayan Religion*, Cambridge, 1984, p. 61.

10. A. Storr, *Feet of Clay*, p. xi.

11. Ibid., p. xii.

12. Ibid., p. 87.

13. Much of what Storr has to say on Freud is indebted to Richard Webster's *Why Freud Was Wrong: Sin, Science and Psychoanalysis*, London, 1995.

14. A. Storr, *Feet of Clay*, p. 43.

15. Ibid., p. 81.

16. Ibid., p. 112.

17. Ibid., p. 97.

18. Ibid., p. xiii.

19. Ibid., p. 117.

20. Ibid., p. 63.

21. Ibid., p. 136.

22. Ibid., p. 120.

23. Ibid., p. 121.

24. Richard Noll, *The Jung Cult*, Princeton, 1994. My references are to the Fontana paperback edition, London, 1996.

25. A. Storr, *Feet of Clay*, p. 96.

26. Ibid., p. 27.

27. Schwabing was Munich's Bohemian quarter, Ascona a village in Switzerland, home to neo-pagan cults.

28. R. Noll, *The Jung Cult*, p. 187.

29. Ibid., p. 199.

30. Ibid., p. 194.

31. Ibid., p. 254.

32. Ibid., p. 219.

33. Ibid., p. 224.

34. Ibid., p. 281.

35. Ibid., p. 279.

36. Ibid., p. 276.

37. A. Storr, *Feet of Clay*, p. 96.

38. At least one recent biographer, Frank McLynn in his *Carl Gustav Jung*, London, 1996, is equally critical.

39. R.B. Williams, *A New Face of Hinduism*, p. xii.

40. For a brief exploration of the Proustian account of love, see Antony Copley, *Sexual Moralities in France 1780–1980*, London, 1989, pp. 170–3.

41. See Antony Copley, diary entry for 1 November 1991, from, 'In Quest of Indian Religions: A Journey to India 1991', in the *Indo-British Review*, xx (I), pp. 217–18.

42. For a recent account of this conflict, see Antony Copley, *Religions in Conflict: Ideology, Cultural Contact and Conversion in Late Colonial India*, Delhi, 1997.

43. R. Baird, *Religion in Modern India*, p. 23.

44. *Bande Mataram*, 2 May 1907, in Sri Aurobindo. *On Nationalism, Selected Writings and Speeches*, Pondicherry, Sri Aurobindo Ashram, 1996, p. 179.

45. Quoted in R. Baird, *Religion in Modern India*, p. 5.

46. Sivanath Sastri, *History of the Brahmo Samaj*, Calcutta, 1911. Here the reference is to the 1993 reprint edition, p. 49.

47. J.N. Farquhar, *Modern Religious Movements in India*, p. 50.

48. S. Sastri, *History of the Brahmo Samaj*, p. 114.

49. Ibid., p. 146.

50. Ibid., p. 132.

51. Keshab Chandra Sen, *Lectures in India*, 1954 edn, Calcutta, p. 386.

52. Ibid., p. 450.

53. Sri Aurobindo, *On Nationalism*, pp. 254–5.

54. Sudhir Kakar, *The Analyst and the Mystic. Psychoanalytic Reflections on Religion and Mysticism*, New Delhi, 1991, p. 13.

55. Quoted in J.N. Farquhar, *Modern Religious Movements in India*, p. 195.

56. Here I am summarizing Sumit Sarkar's *An Exploration of the Ramakrishna Vivekananda Tradition*, Shimla, 1993.

57. This is Tapan Raychaudhuri's paraphrase of Brajendra Nath Seal's description. See, *Europe Reconsidered: Perceptions of the West in Nineteenth Century Bengal*, Delhi, 1988.

58. R. Baird, *Religion in Modern India*, p. 60.

59. S. Sarkar, *An Exploration of the Ramakrishna Vivekananda Tradition*, p. 77.

60. T. Raychaudhuri, *Europe Reconsidered*, p. 120.

61. Ibid., p. 242.

62. R. Baird, *Religion in Modern India*, p. 291.

63. Sri Aurobindo, *Bankim-Tilak-Dayanand*, Pondicherry, 1940 (5th edn), pp. 45, 48–9.

64. Yadav, *Autobiography of Dayanand Saraswati*, Delhi 1976, p. 27.

65. Ibid., p. 293.

66. See K.W. Jones, *Socio-Religious Reform Movements*, pp. 97–8.

67. J.N. Farquhar, *Modern Religious Movements in India*, p. 116.

68. Sri Aurobindo, *Bankim-Tilak-Dayananda*, p. 57.

69. J.N. Farquhar, *Modern Religious Movements in India*, p. 123.

70. Ibid., pp. 287–8.

71. Quoted in Peter Washington, *Madame Blavatsky's Baboon*, London, 1993, p. 83.

72. J.N. Farquhar, *Modern Religious Movements in India*, p. 265.

73. R. Noll, *The Jung Cult*, p. 63.

74. Paul Johnson, *In Search of the Masters. Behind the Occult Myth*, South Boston, 1990, p. 12. ·

75. Ibid., p. 115.

76. Sylvia Cranston, in *The Extraordinary Life and Influence of Helena Blavatsky: Founder of the Modern Theosophical Movement*, makes a case for this Tibetan

residence. But the strongest is made by Jean Overtone Fuller, *Blavatsky and her Teachers: An Investigative Biography*, London, 1988.

77. P. Johnson, *In Search of the Masters*, pp. 23–4.

78. Quoted in S. Cranston, *The Extraordinary Life and Influence of Helena Blavatsky*, p. 43.

79. P. Washington, *Madame Blavatsky's Baboon*, p. 96.

80. Quoted by V.S. Solovyoff, *A Modern Priestess of Isis* (trans. by William Leaf), London, 1895, p. 156.

81. Ibid., p. 254.

82. There are several biographies of Besant but here I shall just refer to that by Anne Taylor, *Annie Besant. A Biography*, Oxford, 1992.

83. Annie Besant, *An Autobiography*, Madras, 1893 (3rd edn, reprinted 1995), p. 254.

84. Ibid., p. 310

85. P. Washington, *Madame Blavatsky's Baboon*, p. 98.

86. A. Besant, *An Autobiography*, p. 309.

87. Ibid., p. 43.

88. A. Taylor, *Annie Besant*, p. 179.

89. Ibid., p. 66.

90. P. Washington, *Madame Blavatsky's Baboon*, p. 49.

91. Quoted in S. Cranston, *The Extraordinary Life and Influence of Helena Blavatsky*, p. xxii.

92. Madame Blavatsky, *From the Caves and Jungles of Hindostan*, p. 232.

93. P. Washington, *Madame Blavatsky's Baboon*, p. 53.

94. Quoted by Peter Heehs, *The Bomb in Bengal: The Rise of Revolutionary Terrorism in India 1900–1910*, Pondicherry, 1993, pp. 70–1.

95. Quoted by A.B. Purani, *The Life of Sri Aurobindo*, Pondicherry, 1958 (4th edn), pp. 58–9.

96. P. Heehs, *The Bomb in Bengal*, p. 132.

97. In a letter, 17 February 1908, quoted in A.B. Purani, *The Life of Sri Aurobindo*, p. 106.

98. Quoted in ibid., p. 104.

99. Ibid., p. 110.

100. Quoted in ibid., p. 118.

101. Quoted in ibid., p. 122.

102. 'The One Thing Needful', *Bande Mataram*, 25 April 1908, Sri Aurobindo, *On Nationalism*, p. 317.

103. 'Swaraj and the Coming Anarchy', *Bande Mataram*, 5 March 1908, ibid., p. 272.

104. 'Bhawani Mandir', 1905, ibid., p. 70.

105. 'The Present Situation', Speech, Bombay, 19 January 1908, ibid., p. 252.

106. 'Ideals Face to Face', *Bande Mataram*, 1 May 1908, ibid., p. 328.

The Brahmo Samaj

Educating Women, Educating a Daughter: Babu Navincandra Rai, *Lakṣmī-Sarasvatī Samvād* (1869), and Hemantkumari Chaudhurani

ULRIKE STARK

'ONE OF THE MOST IMPORTANT figures in the new educated elite of the Punjab',[1] Babu Navincandra Rai (1838–90) has generally been regarded as the foremost Brahmo Samaj leader of the Punjab, an active social reformer and educator. Those concerned with Hindi literature may know him as one of the 'pioneers of modern Hindi prose',[2] whose role in the propagation of Hindi in the Punjab has been compared to that of his contemporary Raja Shivaprasad in the North-Western Provinces and Oudh.[3] Like Raja Shivaprasad, Navincandra Rai was a civil servant working for the British colonial administration; and like him, a prolific writer and author of a number of school textbooks in Hindi. These writings, which include a number of Sanskrit and Hindi grammars, have, however, hardly received any scholarly attention.[4] Among them *Lakṣmī-Sarasvatī Samvād* (Lahore 1869) stands out as a particularly interesting work: under cover of a seemingly religious title is an unusual textbook for girls which combines traditional moral instruction with topics of knowledge in the modern European sciences, mainly geography. By taking a closer look at *Lakṣmī-Sarasvatī Samvād* and at Navincandra's life and activities, as well as the education and career of his daughter Hemantkumari Chaudhurani, this essay aims at tracing Navincandra's dual role as promoter of Hindi and pioneer of female education in the Punjab. It attempts to show how almost a decade before the Arya Samaj emerged as the champion of female education, Navincandra was concerned with imparting a modern education to Punjabi girls and women through the medium of Hindi.

NAVINCANDRA RAI (1838–90)

Concluding his short account on Navincandra Rai, Sivanath Sastri in his *History of the Brahmo Samaj* states, 'A good biography of him should be written by some one from amongst his admirers, for such a life certainly needs commemoration.'[5] No one seems to have taken up this task, for information on the life of the most eminent pioneer of the Brahmo Samaj in the Punjab is still hard to come by. Navincandra Rai hailed from a Bengali Brahmin family of humble origins, but was born outside Bengal, in the town of Meerut, on 20 February 1838.[6] Little is known about his childhood and education: his father, Pandit Rammohan Rai, died when Navincandra was still an infant. The plight of his widowed mother must have left a lasting impact on the young boy who at an early age had to leave school to support the family. At the age of thirteen Navincandra found a job at a monthly salary of Rs 16 in the nearby town of Sardhana. Despite the difficult circumstances of his youth, it seems that on the strength of his own assiduity he not only managed to educate himself in Hindi, Sanskrit, and English but also got some training in civil engineering, presumably at the Lahore School of Engineering.[7] In 1863, at any rate, he was recruited for government employment by the Punjab Public Works Department in Lahore and given the post of assistant accountant in the Controller's Office of the Public Works Accounts Department. During the following years he was successively promoted to accountant, second class, and accountant, first class, his salary increasing steadily from an initial Rs 200 to Rs 430 in 1874.[8] Subsequently, he acquired the important position of paymaster of the North-Western Railway.

In 1863 Navincandra Rai together with six other Bengalis and a small group of Punjabi Hindus founded the first Brahmo Samaj of the Punjab in Lahore.[9] As a dynamic missionary, powerful speaker and prolific author,[10] he soon became the most prominent spokesman of the Brahmo Samaj in the Punjab, thus counting among the foremost Bengali Brahmos who 'provide the missing link in the diffusion of the Bengal renaissance from Calcutta to Western India'.[11] In this role he helped establish further branches of the Samaj in the Punjab, entered into a number of religious disputes with *sanātanī* Hindus,[12] and lectured in places as far away as Bombay. When in 1873 the Lahore Brahmo Samaj opened its first *mandir*, he became its minister.

By then, Navincandra's various activities in the field of education, of which more will be said later, had made him a valuable collaborator in the Punjab government's efforts at promoting education. His growing influence with the colonial educational administration is attested by the fact that in 1870 he was appointed a member of the Senate of the Punjab University College and in 1871 was selected as one of the three Indian members of a committee which was to draw out the scheme for the college examinations.[13] In 1873 he became a member of the Punjab Textbook Committee, a body consisting of ten prominent British and Indian citizens who were to examine and improve the textbooks in use in the province.

In 1875 Navincandra was transferred to Agra. By then, he must have been well off for on leaving Lahore he made over his house and a piece of land to the Brahmo Samaj. In Agra, he continued working for the cause of the Samaj with the same reformist zeal; he revived the defunct Agra Brahmo Samaj and became its minister. In February 1877, he opened an asylum for orphans and destitute children, which provided shelter and basic vocational training to a number of young boys.[14] An important event simultaneously taking place in his private life sheds a less favourable light on the social reformer: after the early death of his first wife, Navincandra married again in 1875, his second marriage presenting a curious and quite unbecoming act for a progressive Brahmo—at the age of 37 he married the fourteen-year-old Hemlata Chaudhuri, daughter of the late Bireshvar Chaudhuri, a head-clerk of a military pay office.[15] This marriage to a much younger girl who, it must be stressed, was not a child widow, seems all the more surprising in the light of events that followed: when in 1878 the marriage of Keshab Chandra Sen's not yet fourteen-year-old daughter to the young maharaja of Cooch Behar created a stir and eventually led to the second major schism in the Brahmo Samaj, Navincandra counted among the eminent opponents of the marriage and became a member of the General Committee of the newly formed Sadharan Brahmo Samaj. Soon after, he went on a two-year furlough to realize a long cherished project, i.e. the establishment of a Brahmo colony in the Hoshangabad district of the Central Provinces. He founded a village called Brahmo Gram, inviting 'such Brahmos as are excommunicated and houseless and wish to settle somewhere'[16] to help him form 'the nucleus of a little model Brahmo community with its own church, own schools, own institutions, where there will be no caste, no early marriage and no idolatry'.[17]

Navincandra could not stay in Brahmo Gram for long. By 1881, he was back in Lahore, where he obtained the joint position of Assistant Registrar of the Punjab University College and Superintendent of the Lahore Oriental College.[18] In this influential position, he temporarily acted as officiating principal of the Oriental College when its principal, G.W. Leitner, was on leave in 1883-4. As Superintendent of Studies and

Translations, Navincandra was especially concerned with the production of textbook material, including the translation of English or Bengali books into Hindi. His own contribution consists of a number of Hindi translations of English textbooks on civil engineering.[19] Of greater consequence was his role in organizing and providing the main leadership for the Lahore Students Association, which was modelled after the Students' Association of Bengal and founded in connection with the Punjab University question in 1881. Navincandra managed to mobilize the local students' support in the joint agitation of the Lahore Indian Association, Brahmo Samaj and Arya Samaj against the government's educational policy and its plans to raise Punjab University College to the status of a university.[20] According to Nazer Singh, 'Its [i.e. the Lahore Students Association] organizer, Nobin Chandra Roy became popular with them so much that all the students of Medical College, Lahore "joined en masse" the Punjab Brahmo Samaj on December 9, 1881.'[21]

As an educator as well as in any other field, Navincandra was a man of action. His dynamic leadership particularly appealed to the liberal and progressive forces within the Punjabi intelligentsia, attracting many of them into the folds of the Brahmo Samaj. In the words of his contemporary, Bhagat Lakshman Singh, Navincandra was

an intellectual man of a unique personality. By his learning and scholarship and by his wide and liberal sympathies, he had made the Samaj a centre of attraction for all young men who were for harmony and accord and who had no faith in the efficacy of the attempts for the regeneration of India by the building of a national creed on the debris of the dead and decadent ancient beliefs, mostly based on superstition and idolatrous rituals. The Brahmo Samaj stood for this liberalism. Hence to belong to the Samaj or to rank amongst its sympathizers was to belong to the intellectual aristocracy of Lahore. The Brahmo Samaj Mandir was, thus, the only place where one could hope to meet Indians of advanced views on religion and social reform.[22]

Navincandra retired from public service and left Lahore some time after 1886 to spend his last years in Brahmo Gram. He died in Calcutta on 28 August 1890.

NAVINCANDRA RAI AND HINDI

When the Hindi–Urdu controversy began to spread from the North-Western Provinces to the Punjab in the 1860s, Navincandra Rai was among the first to advocate the greater use of Hindi and the Nagari script, stressing its role as the cultural link language of north India. Hindi was to be further encouraged so that it could bring forth a modern literature and contribute to the progress of the Indian nation.[23] He publicly voiced his opinions in 1865, in one of the first publications of the Anjuman-i Punjab, a society established under the patronage of G.W. Leitner which aimed at the 'diffusion of useful knowledge, the discussion of subjects possessing literary and scientific interest, and [. . .] the free expression of native opinion on questions of social and political reforms.'[24] An excerpt from Navincandra's statement quoted by the French oriental scholar Garçin de Tassy in his annual lecture of 1865, shows him initially pleading for the encouragement of both Hindi and Urdu:

The century we are living in is a century of progress: each enlightened nation advances in civilization. Does it befit us to stay behind? How much longer shall we allow our country to be deprived of the benefits that other nations are enjoying? It is not too late. Let us join together and encourage our habitual literature, let us translate into Hindi the finest works of the Sanskrit language, and let us at the same time enrich it [i.e. Hindi] with scientific and philosophical works of European origin. Muslim compatriots, may the encouragement that you give to Urdu not make you forget the rights of Hindi. We must consider these two dialects as twin brothers and mutually assist each other in fostering their culture.[25]

Even though Navincandra in a conciliatory manner referred to Hindi and Urdu as 'twin brothers' and pleaded for the encouragement of both, the passage can hardly conceal his pro-Hindi bias and the opinion that Urdu was, actually, the language of the Muslims. Before long he became more outspoken, if not polemical, in his support of Hindi when during a subsequent session of the Anjuman in 1866 a dispute arose over the language issue. In refutation of the pro-Urdu speech given by one member, Navincandra defended the cause of Hindi in a much more aggressive way, voicing opinions that were to become stock arguments against Urdu:

The people living in this country will not profit from the spread of Urdu because this language is specific to the Muslims. The Muslims have unnecessarily loaded it with many Arabic and Persian words. Also, Urdu is not suitable for verse or metrical composition. It is the duty of the Hindus to continue working towards the progress of their traditional language. Apart from love lyrics, Urdu does not have the power to express any serious subject.[26]

While Navincandra subsequently lost no opportunity to argue the cause of Hindi,[27] the most comprehensive testimony of his views on the language question is provided by a statement he submitted to the Education Commission of 1882 on behalf of the Punjab Brahmo Samaj.[28] His list of arguments in favour of making Hindi the medium of primary instruction not only indicates a shift from the ideological to a more 'rational' and 'utilitarian' kind of argumentation, but also depicts a language markedly influenced by nationalist discourse:

The system of primary education in this province is far from being based on a sound basis. *First,* because the medium of instruction is a language which is neither the national language of the people, nor such as is calculated to raise the nation, intellectually and morally, to a level with other civilized nations, for it does not possess those facilities which other national languages of India do. It is based on *two* foreign classics, and is written in characters which are most difficult and imperfect. *Second,* because a great portion of the time of the students is wasted in acquiring knowledge, up to a very high standard, of a foreign language, as Persian is, which hardly possesses any material for enlarging the objective knowledge, or cultivating the mental faculties of the students. The compulsory learning of this language, not only in the high and the middle schools, but also in the primary schools at the sacrifice of more useful knowledge, is the greatest drawback in the system of popular education of this province. *Third,* because, for the above reasons, there is a great waste of time in receiving primary and secondary instruction through the Urdu and Persian languages. The same amount of real or useful knowledge which is now gained in eight years could be gained in three years if it were imparted through the Hindi Bhasha and the Devnagari characters. *Fourth,* because, for the above reasons, there is a great waste of educational funds: for the same amount of instruction could have been imparted on three-eighths of the present amount of expenditure by making Hindi the vehicle of instruction. *Fifth,* because the present curriculum of studies does not include practical subjects, such as agriculture, book-keeping, land-measuring, laws of health, and sanitation, &c., nor lessons on the principles of ethics. *Sixth,* because the real object of primary instruction is entirely ignored both by the parents of the students and the educational authorities. The present system serves the only purpose of training up a large number of *Munshis* for Government service instead of making the students better cultivators, artizans [*sic*], traders, and enlightened·members of society, depending more upon self-exertion than upon Government patronage.[29]

While Navincandra, thus, regarded Urdu as conducive to producing 'hawkers after government service' but not suited to the education of the masses in the Punjab, he also pleaded against Punjabi which with its Gurmukhi script was not able to fulfil the function of a national link language in the way Hindi could. In this context, it is interesting to note that Navincandra had earlier been among the founder-members of the Lahore Sat Sabha, an organization dedicated to social reforms and education founded in 1866. Although structured like and ideologically close to the Brahmo Samaj, it worked solely through the medium of Punjabi and rejected the use of Hindi in the field of education.[30] It appears that its secretary and leader, Lala Bihari Lal, fell out with the Brahmo Samaj mainly over the language issue.

By the time Navincandra submitted his statement to the Education Commission, Hindi had already made some headway as the medium of instruction among the Hindu women of the Punjab. Applying his arguments in favour of Hindi equally to the context of female education, Navincandra was not blind to the anomalous linguistic situation this created in Punjabi Hindu circles.[31] The remedy he provided for it was in accordance with his principles:

We are glad to observe that Hindu girls, unlike Hindu boys, are taught through the medium of Hindi and the Deva Nagari characters. This is as it should be. But as the instruction to boys is given through a different medium, the two sexes cannot co-operate with or assist each other in matters of education. The sooner this defect is remedied by making Hindi compulsory (and Urdu optional) for Hindu boys, the better.[32]

The chief support in the language controversy was to come from the Arya Samaj with whom the Brahmo Samaj had for some time maintained friendly ties.

Navincandra also worked for the propagation of Hindi in his role as the editor of a reformist journal. He had already gained some experience in journalism by editing several issues of the *Punjab University Intelligencer*, the English organ of the Anjuman-i Punjab,[33] when in 1866 or 1867 he started his own monthly journal called *Jñānpradāyinī Patrikā*, 'Journal for the Increase of Knowledge'.[34] A bilingual in Hindi and Urdu, it was published by the Mitra Vilas Press which also published the *Akhbār-i Anjuman-i Punjāb*. Apparently, the Urdu portion was dropped by 1868, *Jñānpradāyinī Patrikā* thus becoming the first Hindi journal in the Punjab. With its dual purpose of increasing general knowledge and propagating the views of the Brahmo Samaj it contained news, articles on education, science, philosophy and morality, but also excerpts from the Vedas, prayers, etc. It seems that *Jñānpradāyinī Patrikā* was temporarily disconti-nued and then revived after Navincandra's return to Lahore. From April 1882 to 1886, it was re-edited as a monthly, its initial circulation amounting to two hundred copies.[35]

NAVINCANDRA RAI AND FEMALE EDUCATION

One of Navincandra's main concerns as a Brahmo and social reformer was the situation of women, their social uplift and education. His activities in the field of female education, though less acknowledged, to some extent mirror those of the famous Brahmo leader Keshab Chandra Sen, who in 1870 initiated the Indian Reform Association and established a Native Ladies' Normal School in Calcutta. Navincandra's views, however, were of a far more progressive kind. He regularly donated money to the so-called Female Improvement Section of the Calcutta Indian Reform Association, thus contributing to its aim of promoting 'the intellectual, moral and social improvement of native women'.[36] His own activities were naturally centred on Lahore and the Punjab. The Lahore Brahmo Samaj soon set up its own Indian Reform Association modelled after the Calcutta organization.[37]

Even prior to the establishment of the female normal school by Keshab Chandra, Navincandra had devoted his time and energy in support of a similar institution in Lahore. At a time when the Punjab government took no initiative in training female teachers, leaving the task entirely to private enterprise, the Lahore Female Normal School had been established by the Local Committee of Instruction in 1864-5.[38] Navincandra voluntarily engaged himself in the tuition of women in the Hindi department of the school. In this, he was joined by Lala Bihari Lal, the aforementioned secretary of the Lahore Sat Sabha. The two gentlemen's efforts were favourably noticed by the government, earning them the Lieutenant-Governor's recognition for their 'enlightened cooperation in the matter of female education'[39] in 1869. Two years later, the *Punjab Education Report* again mentions Navincandra as one of the 'native gentlemen whose exertions are worthy of distinct recognition'.[40]

Navincandra's approach to the question of women's education was very progressive and simultaneously pragmatic. He was of the opinion that an essential prerequisite for the expansion of female primary education was the availability of well-trained female teachers, hence his own engagement in the female normal school of Lahore.[41] In this kind of institution Navincandra also saw an opportunity to provide a solution to another main issue on the Brahmo agenda, the situation of widowed women. Inspired by Ishvar Chandra Vidyasagar, he was himself an advocate of widow remarriage,[42] but was aware of its limited acceptance in Punjabi Hindu society. If not remarriage, at least education would improve the widow's fate. Expressing his dissatisfaction with the prevailing state of female education in his statement to the Education Commission (see above), he suggested the following measures:

Girls' schools, chiefly on grant-in-aid principles, have been established in some principal districts, but they are not enough: such schools should be established in every district, even where they cannot secure private contributions. The instruction imparted in the girls' schools has not yet attained to a higher standard than that of the lower primary schools for boys. The reason is that girls are generally married at a very early age. But there are many girls who have become widows at an early age, and, as widow-marriage is prohibited among Hindus, they can continue in the schools for any length of time, provided they receive some subsistence allowance. We would recommend that every widow should receive a stipend of Rs 2 to 5 per mensem, provided she bind herself to remain in the school until she has attained to the highest standard up to which the school can impart instruction. [. . .] The best method of providing teachers for girls is the establishment of normal schools of widows in every district, on stipends ranging from Rs 5 to 10 per mensem. Hindu widows will seldom be able to go to distant places on service as teachers; hence the necessity of having a female normal school, or a female normal school class, in every district.[43]

The expansion of primary education and broader support for normal schools, however, was not enough. Taking a more radical stance, Navincandra advocated equal educational opportunities for boys and girls, which ultimately meant equal syllabi and higher education for girls. While this was a controversial issue within the Brahmo Samaj itself,[44] in the more conservative setting of the Punjab it constituted a near-revolutionary approach not likely to meet with much official support. For instance, the Anjuman-i Punjab, where Navincandra voiced his opinions, was divided on the question of female education. While some of its members were categorically opposed to it, Navincandra argued boldly that 'female education should be as general as the education of the other sex, for the one helps the other, and that Government should give *equal* encouragement to the education of *both* sexes, not only on moral grounds, but also from an economical point of view, for educated mothers will eventually lessen the amount of state expenditure on primary education' (emphasis in the original).[45] That in his case words were matched by personal practice will be shown in the following sections dealing successively with his major written contribution to female education, *Lakṣmī-Sarasvatī Samvād*,[46] and the education of his daughter Hemantkumari.

LAKṢMĪ-SARASVATĪ SAMVĀD (1869)

In the history of nineteenth-century literature for women, the year 1869 is marked by the publication of one of the most influential books on female education, Nazir Ahmad's novel *Mirāt-al 'Arūs*.[47] Published in the same year by the Mitra Vilas Press in Lahore, *Lakṣmī-Sarasvatī Samvād* (hereafter *LSS*) shared some of the former's objectives but was a very different kind of book directed to a different kind of readership: the Hindu girls and women of the Punjab. While the idea of writing a textbook for girls may have sprung from Navincandra's experience as a Hindi tutor in the female normal school, it certainly reflects, as will be shown, his active membership in the Anjuman-i Punjab, a proclaimed aim of which was the diffusion of European science through the medium of the vernacular languages of the Punjab.[48]

The original version of *LSS* consisted of two parts, the first comprising twenty, and the second forty-four pages. A second edition was to follow in 1873. Surprisingly, it was only a decade later that *LSS* was officially approved as a textbook and incorporated into the syllabus for Hindi primary schools by the Punjab Textbook Committee in 1883.[49] A decisive step in the wider diffusion and popularization of the book, however, was made earlier, when in 1881 a new edition of *LSS* was published by the famous Newal Kishore Press in Lucknow.[50] *LSS* remained in demand for quite some time: the Newal Kishore Press published a second edition of it in 1886 and a third edition in 1906.

As indicated by its title, *LSS* consists of a dialogue between Laksmi, the goddess of wealth, and Sarasvati, the goddess of learning. To model his textbook on the classical standard form of moral instruction, the question–answer dialogue between guru and *śisya*, was a clever move on Navincandra's part: Not only did it give the textbook the sanction of tradition, but also used a narrative pattern well familiar to both literate and illiterate women through their acquaintance with *vrat-kathās* and similar religious texts.[51] Moreover, with instruction coming straight from the mouth of the goddess of learning and Laksmi assuming the role of the pupil, the textbook made education an all-female affair. At the same time it conveyed a clear message: wealth and prosperity depended on and could only be achieved through knowledge and learning, an idea reiterated by Navincandra Rai in the programmatic preface to his book.

With its adroitly built-up argument for the necessity of female education, this preface deserves further comment. Navincandra sets out by establishing the supremacy of the intellect (*buddhi*) among the human faculties and, having illustrated man's various achievements on the basis of his intellect, states that without knowledge (*vidyā*) the intellect is as devoid of power as a king without his army. The truly learned will feel a natural inclination to share their knowledge with others, including women:

> Only the learned realize the beauty of knowledge. Those who consider themselves learned but are too dull to spread their knowledge among their own families and women have not tasted the fruit of learning, nor have they known the natural substance of knowledge. He who has seen the light of knowledge will never wish to keep his sons, daughters, and women surrounded by the darkness [of ignorance].[52]

The author goes on to observe that people are generally more concerned about their women's outer adornment than their inner embellishment: 'Many adorn their women with various kinds of jewels, but deprive them of what is the most precious jewel—knowledge as a means to attain salvation and higher wisdom. Such is not the behaviour of compassionate and discriminate men.'[53] Having the conservative Hindu's reluctance to female education and his fear of its harmful effects in mind, Navincandra refrained from resorting to the social reformers' standard argument that in a rapidly changing world women had to be turned into fit companions of their educated husbands and that education was 'to bridge the mental gap between husbands and wives, mothers and sons'.[54] Instead, he sought to establish the necessity of female education on religious grounds, making the acquisition of learning (*vidyā*) a prerequisite for the attainment of higher knowledge (*jñān*) and salvation (*mukti*) for men and women alike. Navincandra obviously did not differentiate between men and women when it came to the pursuit of higher spiritual goals and regarded a woman's claim to knowledge and spiritual emancipation just as valid as a man's. 'The only means to attain higher knowledge is learning. Therefore, whether woman or man, all must strive to acquire learning,'[55] he stated categorically. Hence female education could not be limited to the basic skills of reading and writing alone but demanded instruction of a more pervasive kind. 'As long as there is no discernment of righteousness and evil, no discrimination between virtue and vice, as long as the mind is not freed from lower worldly emotions, we cannot call it acquisition of learning.'[56]

What follows in the preface is an elaborate description of the metaphorical tree of knowledge with its many branches consisting of disciplines such as natural sciences, astrology, geography, politics, medicine, literature, philosophy and economics, its roots consisting of the study of texts, its essence of writing, its innumerable leaves of learned books, and so forth. Having established the equal right to knowledge for both sexes, Navincandra was fully aware of the vast differences in actual opportunities and means to attain it. Anticipating the objection that girls hardly had a chance to study the variety of subjects described by him, he pointed out that just as someone desirous of picking a fruit from the tree of knowledge could obtain it by climbing two or three branches only and did not have to climb the whole tree, a girl could attain the kind of learning that would ultimately give her access to higher knowledge by unrestrained (*anargal*) reading and full comprehension of a book written by a learned person. This reference to 'a book written by a learned person' need not be taken literally but as a metaphor, for he goes on to argue that, while most men and women spent their entire lives in trivial pursuits, how could four or five years devoted to the attainment of knowledge as a pathway to the next world be too much? This idea also forms the basic content of Navincandra's appeal at the end of the preface to those responsible for female education: 'I entreat the gentlemen promoting female education and the girls' parents to accomplish the great task in which they are engaged in a proper fashion, that is to not give up after making the girls taste but a little of the *rasa* of knowledge, but fully work towards realizing the object of their attainment of higher knowledge.'[57] How he proposed to contribute to this goal himself will be shown in the following content analysis of *LSS*.

In accordance with the popular notion that moral instruction should come first in the education of women, the first part of *LSS* is devoted to *nītiśikṣā*, 'education in moral conduct'. In it, Sarasvati advises Laksmi in proper conduct for females and relates a number of exemplary moral tales which successively illustrate the most important virtues expected in a girl: truthfulness, honesty, compassion, modesty and respect towards her elders, loving devotion towards her husband. As stated on the title-page, Navincandra had composed the book for the sake of 'the benefit of all householders through female education'.[58] Accordingly, the focus was clearly on the girl's or woman's familial roles. In a very conventional way and with the obligatory references to the *śāstras* her duties as daughter, wife, and daughter-in-law were emphasized. Thus, there is nothing particularly new about this part of *LSS* which is at its most interesting when Sarasvati turns to the female virtue of zeal to offer concrete advice on how a girl should make the best use of her time. According to the text, twenty-four hours of the day should be divided in the following manner: four hours for study, four hours for crafts and needlework, six hours of sleep, two hours for bodily hygiene and eating, eight hours of leisure to be spent with female companions in play, conversation or physical exercise. A slightly different time-schedule was proposed for the married woman, taking into account her particular needs and duties: one hour for bodily hygiene and prayer (*pūjā*), four hours for cooking and eating, three hours for the various household chores, two hours of study, two hours for craft and needlework, four hours for social visits to family members and friends but also for the instruction of children, seven hours of rest and sleep. It is interesting to note that Navincandra not only tried to strike a balance between leisure and learning in the girl's case, but also made sure that women's learning did not end with marriage. The amount of time accorded to study may have been reduced, but still features as a separate category in the married woman's life. Moreover, she was accorded a share in the responsibility for her children's intellectual progress by supervising their reading and writing. Evidently, Navincandra's time-schedule could apply only to the upper-class girl or woman from a well-to-do background. Even in their case he may have been conscious of its limited practicability, for Laksmi's spontaneous objection, that nobody would be able to stick to such a tight schedule, is met with the reply that it was merely meant as a guideline as to how an *intelligent* woman would make use of her time.

The real interest in Navincandra's textbook lies in the second part of it, which Garçin de Tassy, who described *LSS* as 'anecdotes et préceptes moraux pour les femmes',[59] obviously never got to read. Indeed, there is a noticeable discrepancy between the two volumes of the book, with neither the preface nor the first volume preparing the reader for what is to follow. The second part of *LSS*, twice as voluminous as the first one, is devoted to 'Accounts of the earth, the atmosphere etc.' (*bhūgol aur vāyumaṇḍal prabhṛti vṛttānt*), i.e. to 'modern' European knowledge in the disciplines of geography and meteorology. This particular kind of knowledge is, as Sarasvati explains to Laksmi, of a superior kind and of foremost importance since it helps to understand God's marvellous creation. This, however, is as far as the allusion to religion goes. Navincandra takes an entirely scientific approach to acquaint his female readers with a host of facts and phenomena of modern empirical science: the shape, circumference, and diameter of the earth, gravity, lunar and solar eclipses, the depth of the oceans, volcanism, earthquakes, the composition of the atmosphere, the colour, weight and chemical composition of air, lightning and electricity, the stars and meteors. In describing all these, more specifically scientific topics like the working of a compass, a theodolite quadrant and a hypsometer(!),[60] the calculation of degrees of longitude and latitude, Greenwich mean time, etc., are explained. While this may have sounded pretty abstract for a nineteenth-century female readership, in the process the textbook also provides answers to basic questions such as why the earth revolves around the sun, why day is followed by night, why the colour of air appears to be blue, why there are several colours in a rainbow. A quaint reminiscence of traditional logical debate between guru and *śiṣya* is Laksmi's constant demand for proof (*pramāṇ*)—the answers she gets, however, are entirely taken from modern European science. The proposed scientific objectivity of the book is underlined by the fact that it sticks to empirical facts, supported by quantities and numerical data wherever appropriate. With all his pretensions to empiricism and scientific accuracy, Navincandra kept his readership in mind: to facilitate comprehension of the sometimes quite complicated matters in question, illustrations are inserted into the text and explanations are generally given by means of examples taken from the girl's own sphere of experience: the shape of the globe and gravity, for instance, are explained through the example of an ant walking on the surface of an orange without falling off.

A major portion of the book is directed to the description of the surface of the earth with its various oceans, continents, countries and geographical regions. This part takes the form of a rather tiresome enumeration of the names of islands, mountains, rivers, lakes, gulfs and peninsulae in the various parts of the world. To memorize these names, Sarasvati explains, is important for 'they frequently come up in historical and old accounts, in biographical writing, travel accounts, newspapers and so forth'.[61] The girl should be able to recognize and place them in the right context, and no longer fall a prey to someone giving her inaccurate or wrong information. Thus, an awareness of the larger world and a certain amount of intellectual independence was certainly called for.

Since Navincandra does not name his source(s), it is difficult to assess his own contribution in the composition of *LSS*. In the light of latter-day textbook writing, his textbook is remarkable for its global approach, not putting any special focus on India or, for that matter, South Asia, as well as for its total absence of patriotic undertones or attempts at instigating national pride. But most of all, it is remarkable for the seemingly natural fashion in which it combines traditional moral instruction based on ancient Hindu values with modern European science. One may wonder whether Navincandra, by using a traditional narrative pattern and presenting his reader with a first part perfectly acceptable to even the most orthodox, sought to consciously entice him into acquiring a book he might have rejected altogether had he been confronted directly with its second part. Whether the content of *LSS* was suited to the Punjabi girl's mind remains open to discussion and can only be assessed properly through a comparison with other textbooks of the period. Much of the factual information given in *LSS* may not have related directly to the Punjabi woman's life; however, the textbook certainly served to create a greater awareness among women regarding both their immediate surroundings and the world beyond it. In counteracting ignorance and superstition by providing scientific explanations of natural phenomena, it may have even created a desire to learn more. The various editions of *LSS* point to the success of Navincandra's approach. Ironically, perhaps the biggest concession this staunch supporter of Hindi had to make to the reality of the Punjabi girl's life was on the level of language. 'It was my desire that in this book Sanskritic Hindi should not be mixed with vocabulary from any other indigenous language such as Persian etc.; but on the appeal of some friends, currently used Urdu words have been inserted here and there for the sake of facilitating the girl's comprehension',[62] he stated in his preface. Navincandra took the objections of his friends seriously: the first part of *LSS* abounds in Urdu words[63] while there is a conspicuous absence of Sanskrit loanwords. Only in the second part, obviously addressed to a more advanced readership, is this pattern reversed.

One of the girls to certainly have read *LSS* was Navincandra's only daughter, Hemantkumari, to whom we shall turn next.

HEMANTKUMARI CHAUDHURANI (1868–1953)[64]

It is little known that Navincandra Rai had a daughter who, following in her father's footsteps, was herself an advocate of female education and author of a number of Hindi books for women. As father and daughter, Navincandra and Hemantkumari illustrate the significant shift taking place in women's education in the second half of the nineteenth century, from being an almost exclusive concern of male social reformers to constituting an issue in which women themselves participated and became actively engaged.

Hemantkumari was born in Lahore on 1 September 1868. Since her mother died when she was very young, Navincandra had to bear the entire responsibility of seeing to her education. He made sure he provided her with the best possible schooling, which at that time inevitably meant sending her to a mission school.[65] The mission schools found favour with Navincandra not only for their superior quality of instruction. He was also reported to think 'that Government schools and colleges have atheistical tendencies. He prefers mission schools and colleges though he is of the opinion that the best institutions are those where neither sectarian religions are taught on the one hand nor ethics omitted on the other.'[66] This, of course, was far removed from the general policy prevailing at the mission schools. Indeed, the compromise of ensuring that his daughter had a good education based on a sound moral footing, even at the risk of exposing her to Christian indoctrination, seems to have been a problematic one. Hemantkumari was initially admitted to the Roman Catholic Convent School at Agra. It has been claimed that on noticing that she was becoming too imbued with Christian ideas, Navincandra removed her from the school.[67] Whether this is true cannot be said. Her departure from the convent school might as well be attributed to the family's return to Lahore in 1881, for in Lahore she was again admitted to a mission school, the Lahore Christian Girls School which was run by the American Presbyterian Mission and open to both European and 'native' girls. At the same time, Navincandra himself took charge of Hemantkumari's religious instruction at home, thus counterposing any unwanted influence.

For her higher education Hemantkumari was sent to the prestigious Bethune College in Calcutta, a model institution for female education which was popular with Bengali *bhadralok* and progressive Brahmos and gained distinction for producing the first woman graduates in the entire British Empire in the persons of Kadambini Basu and Chandramukhi Basu in 1882.[68] After her graduation and return from Calcutta Hemantkumari was married to Rajacandra Chaudhuri, the Secretary of the Sylhet Prarthana Samaj, on 2 November 1885. The marriage was conducted according to Brahmo Samaj rites. In 1887 her husband was transferred from Sylhet to the princely state of Ratlam in central India. Not one to waste her time sitting idly at home, Hemantkumari became private tutoress to the Maharani of Ratlam state. She also edited a monthly magazine for women called *Sugrhini*, perhaps the first Hindi journal ever edited by a woman. *Sugrhini* was apparently published from Lahore by her father. Hemantkumari ran the journal successfully for about two years but had to stop it when her husband was transferred back to Sylhet in 1889.[69]

In Sylhet, Hemantkumari not only joined her husband in running the activities of the local Brahmo Samaj,[70] but continued her active engagement for the uplift of women. She founded a women's association called *Mahilā samiti* and obtained permission from the Chief Commissioner to open a *pāṭhśālā* for girls. She also resumed her journalistic activities, publishing a women's monthly magazine in Bengali entitled *Antahpura*. Apparently, Hemantkumari had to leave Sylhet due to health problems. She returned to the Punjab where in December 1906 she took up the post of superintendent at the newly opened Victoria Girls School in Patiala, a middle school providing instruction in both Hindi and Punjabi. While working at the Victoria Girls School she gave lectures on women's topics in Hindi,[71] wrote a number of books for women, and took an active part in the Hindi literary scene, for instance as one of the female delegates and speakers at the Hindi Sahitya Sammelan held in Indore in 1918 where 'Literature suitable for women in the Hindi language' was discussed.[72]

The titles of the books authored by Hemantkumari point to more traditional concerns—*Ādarś mātā, Mātā aur kanyā, Narī puṣpāvalī*.[73] She also authored two instructional works, *Hindī banglā pratham śikṣā*, a Hindi-Bengali primer, and *Navīn-śilpamālā* (Patiala 1925), a richly illustrated instruction book on knitting which—if the author is to be believed—was the first of its kind in the Hindi language.[74] *Navīn-śilpamālā*, which to a modern observer might seem too 'trivial' to be included in a list of publications, served a serious purpose for Hemantkumari who was inspired by Gandhian ideas. The book was not only to provide poor women with a tool to learn knitting and thus contribute to their livelihood, but also, in the true nationalist spirit of the age, appealed to the women of India to stop buying foreign goods and produce their own woollen clothes instead.[75]

Nothing is known about Hemantkumari's later life and activities. She died in 1953.

CONCLUSION

Among the early reformers in the Punjab, Navincandra Rai stands out as one whose contribution to education and social reform in the Punjab, especially the uplift of women, has been considerable. As a dynamic Brahmo Samaj leader, radical in thought but pragmatic in approach, he doubtless played a major role in paving the way for future reformist endeavours; however, with the Brahmo Samaj being 'too eclectic, too tolerant and at the same time too socially radical to win widespread acceptance in the Punjab',[76] it was left to the Arya Samaj to gain popular support for the two main issues Navincandra had devoted himself to, the propagation of Hindi and the spread of female education. The individual contribution of this one man who has been called 'the life and soul of the Brahmo Samaj Movement in the Panjab',[77] has been largely eclipsed by the activities of both the prominent Brahmo Samaj leaders of Bengal and the Arya Samaj leaders of the Punjab. As a figure somewhat neglected by modern research his case may well be taken to illustrate the fate of other progressive Brahmos in the Punjab who, according to David Kopf, 'after having achieved much, watched their accomplishments crumble against the overwhelming success of the Arya Samaj among the masses.'[78]

NOTES

1. Kenneth W. Jones, 'The Bengali Elite in Post-annexation Punjab: An Example of Inter-regional Influence in 19th century India', *Indian Economic and Social History Review* III. 4, 1966, 380. I wish to thank Harald Fischer-Tiné for directing my attention to a number of important articles on the historical and socio-cultural background of the period and for his comments on an earlier draft of this paper.

2. Sisir Kumar Das, *1800–1910. Western Impact: Indian Response* (A History of Indian Literature, vol. VIII), New Delhi, 1991, 468.

3. Ramcandra Shukla, *Hindī sāhitya kā itihās*, Kāśī v.s. 2051, 242.

4. These are: *Saral vyākaran saṃskṛt kā hindī bhāṣā meṁ*, Lahore: Mitra Vilas

Press, 1865 (²1870–2); *Navīncandrodaya arthāt hindī bhāṣā kā vyakaraṇ,* Lahore: Punjab Economical Press, 1868 (²1869); *Śabdoccāraṇ,* Lahore 1870; *Laghu vyākaraṇ,* Lahore, ²1878.

5. *History of the Brahmo Samaj,* 2nd edn, Calcutta, 1974 (¹1911–12), 323.

6. For the following cf. S. Sastri, ibid., 322 and Kṣemacandra 'Suman', *Divaṅgat hindī sevī,* vol. 1, Delhi, ²1983, 277–8.

7. Next to the Thomason Engineering College in Roorkee, the Lahore Engineering School, established in February 1853 and maintained by Colonel Napier, Chief Engineer of the Punjab, was the only other training institution for civil engineers in north India at the time.

8. Cf. *Thacker's Directory for Bengal, the North-Western Provinces, The Punjab, The Rajpootana States, Oude, and British Burma,* Calcutta, 1864–74.

9. David Kopf, *The Brahmo Samaj and the Shaping of the Modern Indian Mind,* Princeton, New Jersey, 1979, 320.

10. Navincandra's writings on Brahmo themes in Hindi include: *Ācārādarś arthāt brāhma smrti hindū vaṃśīya brāhmagaṇ ke nimitt,* Lahore, 1868; *Vidhvā vivāha vyavasthā,* Lahore: Mitra Vilas Press 1869; *Dharm dīpikā,* Lahore, 1873; *Brahmadharm ke praśnottar,* Lahore: Mitra Vilas Press 1880 [¹1863]; *Tattvabodh,* Calcutta, 1874; *Saddharm sutram,* Bombay: Eagle Printing Press 1878; *Upaniṣad sār,* Calcutta, 1876; *Vaidik siddhānt,* Lucknow: Sukh Sambad Press 1888; *Saddharmī log vedoṁ ko kaise mānte haiṁ,* Lucknow: Sukh Sambad Press 1888; as well as a number of smaller tracts or pamphlets such as *Bhojanbicār, Brahma upanayana paddhati, Brahma vivāh paddhati, Brahma antyeṣti aur śraddhā paddhati,* and *Prārthana pustak* (all before 1879).

11. D. Kopf, *The Brahmo Samaj and the Shaping of the Modern Indian Mind,* 320. For the activities of the Lahore Brahmo Samaj, see also K.W. Jones, 'The Bengali Elite', 377ff.

12. See, for example, Navincandra's only substantial work in Urdu, *Dharma rakṣā satīk,* Calcutta, 1877, a 280-page rejoinder to a work entitled *Dharma rakṣā* by the orthodox Hindu Pandit Sraddha Ram Phillauri, itself published in response to a lecture by Navincandra; see Jones, *Arya Dharm,* 28.

13. Chhaju Ram, 'Western Education and its Social Impact on the Punjab: 1849–1904', University thesis (unpublished), Panjab University 1992, 202 and 222.

14. *The Brahmo Year-Book for 1879,* ed. by Sophia Dobson Collet, London, 1879, 90.

15. 'Brahmo Marriage Register from July 1861 to August 1879', ibid., 50. A comparison with the other entries in the register shows that such a large difference in age was, indeed, unusual.

16. Ibid., 91.

17. Ibid.

18. Initially an oriental school founded by the Anjuman-i Punjab, the Lahore Oriental College was from 1870 maintained by and subordinate to the Punjab University College. Apart from arts and oriental languages, professional courses

in medicine, engineering and law were taught. The college had a school department attached to it, where oriental languages were taught at a lower level. Classes in English language and literature were introduced in 1875. For further details, see Navincandra Rai's yearly report of 1881-2 in G.W. Leitner, *History of Indigenous Education in the Panjab since Annexation and in 1882* (Calcutta 1882), reprint Languages Department Punjab, 1971, pt II, 102–19.

19. His three works published by the Punjab University College in 1882 are *Nirmān vidyā* (an elementary course of civil engineering in three parts), *Sthiti tattva aur gati tattva*, and *Jal sthiti, jal gati aur vāyu kā tattva*. The latter was favourably reviewed by F. Pincott:

Navina Chandra Rai's book is a translation of Chamber's English treatise on the subject, and it is very well done. It proves the author to be both a learned and a pains-taking scholar. For example, it requires more than a mechanical acquaintance with the terms 'oxygen' and 'hydrogen' to enable Navina Chandra Rai to translate them into Hindu [*sic*] by *amlajan* and *toyajan* respectively. These Hindu words mean 'acid-generating' and 'water-generating' and are good translations of the Greek terms.

Cited in S.D. Collet, *The Brahmo Year-Book for 1882*, London, 1883, 77.

20. The protest focused on the government's plans to introduce the vernacular as the medium of instruction in the Punjab University, which was taken as a conscious attempt to deprive the students of high education in English and impair their career chances. For a more detailed account on the Punjab University controversy, see Nazer Singh, 'Notes on the Anjuman-i Punjab, Aligarh Movement, Brahmo Samaj, Indian Association, Arya Samaj and Singh Sabha in the context of colonial education in the Punjab, 1865–1885', *The Panjab Past and Present*, vol. xxvi(1), 1992, 54–9. See also *Papers connected with the Punjab University question, collected and published by the Executive Committee of the Indian Association*, Lahore: Tribune Press, 1881. The relationship between Navincandra and G.W. Leitner, who was at the same time his immediate superior, co-member in the Anjuman-i Punjab, and main opponent in the Punjab University controversy, would require further study. There is a surprising claim, for instance, that Navincandra started an Urdu weekly called *The Reformer* for the alleged purpose of 'refuting attacks made on Dr. Leitner in other newspapers'; see N. Gerald Barrier and Paul Wallace, *The Punjab Press, 1880–1905*, East Lansing, Michigan, 1970, 120–1.

21. Nazer Singh, 'Notes on the Anjuman . . .,' 59.

22. *Bhagat Lakshman Singh: Autobiography*, ed. and annotated by Ganda Singh, Calcutta 1965, 40–1. For the influence of Navincandra and the Brahmo Samaj on later Arya Samaj leaders, see also V.C. Joshi (ed.), *Story of My Life. Lala Lajpat Rai*, reprint, New Delhi, 1989, 24–9.

23. For Navincandra's role in propagating Hindi in the Punjab, see R.S. McGregor, 'Bengal and the Development of Hindi 1850–1880', *South Asian Review* 5(2), 1972, 140–1. McGregor has also pointed out that Navincandra was

among the first to refer to Hindi as a potential national language, cf. *Hindi Literature of the Nineteenth and Early Twentieth Centuries*, Wiesbaden, 1974, 74, footnote.
24. C.W. Leitner, *History of Indigenous Education in the Punjab* . . ., v. The aims of the Anjuman were

to establish a National University in the Punjab, to promote the diffusion of European science as far as possible through the medium of the Vernacular languages of the Punjab, to improve and extend Vernacular literature generally; to afford encouragement to the enlightened study of Eastern classical languages and literature; and to associate the learned and influential classes of the Punjab with the officers of the Government in the promotion and supervision of popular education.

Y.B. Mathur, 'Development of Western Education in the Punjab: 1849-75', in Verinder Grover (ed.), *The Story of the Punjab. Yesterday and Today*, New Delhi, 1995, 143; see also Nazer Singh, 'Notes on the Anjuman . . .', 35-41.
25. My translation from the French original. J.H. Garçin de Tassy, *La langue et la littérature hindoustanies de 1850 à 1869*, 2nd edn, Paris, 1874, 293-4.
26. 'Urdū ke pracalit hone se deśvāsiyoṁ ko koī lābh na hogā kyoṁki vah bhāṣā khās musalmānoṁ kī hai. Usmeṁ musalmānoṁ ne vyarth bahut se arbī farsī ke śabd bhar diye haiṁ. Padya yā chandobaddh racan ke bhī urdū upayukt nahīṁ. Hinduoṁ kā yah kartavya hai ki apnī paramparāgat bhāṣā kī unnati karte caleṁ. Urdū meṁ āṣikī kavitā ke atirikt kisī gambhīr viṣay ko vyakt karne kī sakti nahīṁ hai.' Cited in R. Shukla, *Hindī sāhitya kā itihās*, 242-3. In the light of this and later polemical statements against Urdu, it seems difficult to agree with McGregor when he argues that

It is clear that Navincandra, despite of his use of the now emotive expression 'national language' at least three years earlier, was not in any sense embarking on a crusade in advocating greater use of Hindi, but was merely urging what seemed rational in the light of the predominance of persianised Urdu; for there was, indeed, other support at that time for a move away from persianised Urdu in the Panjab.

'Bengal and the Development of Hindi' 141. For Navincandra's argument see also Jürgen Lütt, *Hindu Nationalisms in Uttar Pradesh*, 1867-1900, Stuttgart, 1970, 42.
27. See, for example, the preface of *Navīncandrodaya arthāt hindī bhāṣā kā vyākaran*, Lahore, 1868.
28. See, *Appendix to Education Commission Report. Report by the Panjab Provincial Committee*, Calcutta, 1884, 490-5.
29. Ibid., 490-1.
30. 'So close were the two societies in form that initially the Sat Sabha was taken to be a branch of the Brahmo Samaj.' Jones, *Arya Dharm*, Delhi, 1976, 24.
31. The resulting 'communication gap' has been beautifully described by Prakash Tandon:

Literacy among our Hindu women thus began with Hindi, and this created some amusing situations, because in my mother's generation there were many women who could not communicate with their husbands when they were away from each other, as they could only write in Hindi and their husbands only in Urdu or English. In our generation the same problem was solved by the middle class girls learning English. At home, like their parents, they spoke Punjabi with their husbands, but their correspondence was in English. The girls were in fact trilingual as they spoke Punjabi, wrote in Hindi to their mothers, and in English to their fathers and husbands.

Punjabi Century 1857–1947, Berkeley and Los Angeles, 1984, 67.

32. *Appendix to Education Report*, 494.

33. Nazer Singh 'Notes on the Anjuman', 38.

34. R. Shukla, *Hindī sāhitya kā itihās*, 242, gives March 1867 as the date of first publication, probably referring to an earlier version of the journal called *Jñānapradāyinī*, which Garçin de Tassy also mentions (See *Littérature hindouie et hindoustanie*, vol. II, Paris, 1870, 411).

35. *Report of the Administration of Oudh, for the year ending 31 March 1883*, 282; N.G. Barrier and P. Wallace, *The Punjab Press 1880–1905*, 53.

36. Prosanto Kumar Sen, *Biography of a New Faith*, vol. II, Calcutta, 1933, 277.

37. D. Kopf, *The Brahmo Samaj and the Shaping of the Modern Indian Mind*, 321.

38. Y.B. Mathur, 'Development of Western education in the Punjab', 141.

39. *Report on Popular Education in the Punjab and its Dependencies*, for the year 1868–9, Lahore, 1869, vi. It is interesting to note that in subsequent reports growing objection to the presence of male teachers at the Female Normal School was raised.

40. *Report on Popular Education in the Punjab and its Dependencies*, for the year 1871–2, Lahore, 1872, 50.

41. For female normal schools and the problem of procuring female teachers, see Madhu Kishwar, 'The Daughters of Aryavarta', *The Indian Economic and Social History Review* 23(2), 1986, 165–7.

42. Navincandra's work *Vidhvā vivāha vyavasthā* (1869) was based on Vidyasagar's writings.

43. *Appendix to Education Commission Report*, 494. The very same solution to both the problem of scarcity of female teachers and the widow question was later on put forward by the Arya Samaj, see Kishwar, 'The Daughters of Aryavarta' 174–5.

44. Cf. D. Kopf, *The Brahmo Samaj and the Shaping of the Modern Indian Mind*, 36–41, and Malavika Karlekar, 'Kadambini and the Bhadralok: Early Debates over Women's Education in Bengal', *Economic and Political Weekly* xxi(17), April 1986, WS 25–6. For the controversy over the same issue within the Arya Samaj, see Madhu Kishwar, 'Arya Samaj and Women's Education: Kanya Mahavidyalaya, Jalandhar', WS 10–11.

45. 'Answers to questions of the Education Committee drawn up by the

select committee of the Anjuman-i Punjab', *Appendix to Education Commission Report*, 514.

46. Navincandra was also the author of a more conventional Bengali tract called *Nārī dharm*, which was not available to me.

47. See A.S. Kalsi, 'The Influence of Nazir Ahmad's *Mirāt-al-'Arūs* (1869) on the Development of Hindi Fiction', *Annual of Urdu Studies* 7, 1990, 31–44.

48. Y.B. Mathur, 'Development of Western Education in the Punjab', 143.

49. *Report on Popular Education in the Punjab and its Dependencies* for the year 1883-4, ap. F.

50. Founded in 1858 by Munshi Newal Kishore, the Newal Kishore Press turned into the biggest printing press and publishing house in nineteenth-century India. It became famous for publishing high-quality, yet low-priced editions of works in Arabic, Persian, Sanskrit, Urdu and Hindi, and had a near-monopoly of printing and publishing vernacular textbooks in the North-Western Provinces and Oudh. All ensuing citations from *LSS* are taken from the 1881 Newal Kishore Press edition.

51. *A vratkathā* ('story of a votive observance') generally exemplifies and illustrates the meaning and story of a *vrat* by means of a dialogue. See Mary McGee, 'Feasting and Fasting. The Vrata Tradition and its Significance for Women', Ann Arbor, Michigan: University Microfilms 1989, 225–34. For *vrats* as avenues of female socialization, see Poromesh Acharya, 'Indigenous Education and Brahminical Hegemony in Bengal', in Nigel Crook (ed.), *The Transmission of Knowledge in South Asia: Essays on Education, Religion, History, and Politics*, Delhi: Oxford University Press, 1996, 111–6.

52. 'Bidyā ke saundaryya ko vidvān hī dekh saktā hai dūsrā nahīm. Parantu jo log yah jānte haim ki maim vidvān hūm athavā svajan kutamb aur striyom mem vidyā pracār karne mem kunthit hote haim; unhomne vidyā kā phal āsvād nahīm kiyā hai, na vidyā ke prakṛt tatva ko unhomne jānā hai. Jisne vidyā ki jyoti dekhī hai vah apne putrakanyā athavā striyom ko andhakārāvṛt nayan rakhne kī icchā kabhī na karegā'. *LSS* 1, 2–3.

53. 'Bahut log apnī apnī striyom ko nānā vidhi ratnālankārom se bhūsit karte haim, parantu mukti aur jñān ka sādhan vidyā rūp paramratna unko vañcitā rakhte haim. Yah dayālu aur vivecakom ka kām nahīm hai.' Ibid., 3.

54. M. Kishwar, 'Arya Samaj and Women's Education . . .', WS–10.

55. 'Jñān prāpti kā upāya ek vidyā hī hai is kāraṇ kyā strī kyā puruṣ sabko vidyopārjan karna cāhie'. *LSS* I, 4.

56. 'Jab tak dharmādharm kā parijñān na ho, sat sat kā vivek na ho ātmā sāmsārik tucch bhāvom se bimukt na hom, tab tak usko vidyā prāpti nahīm kah sakte.' Ibid., 3.

57. '[. . .] strī śikṣā pravartak mahāsayom se aur kanyāom ke mātāpitāom se prārthnā hai ki ve jis mahatkaryya mem pravṛtt hue haim, usko samyak prakār sampūrṇ karem, arthāt bālikāom ko svalpamātra bidyārasāsvad karāke hī nirast na hovem, parantu unkī jñān grahinīvṛtti ko sampūrṇ rūp caritārth karem.' Ibid., 5.

58. 'striyoṁ ke śikṣā dvārā sarvv gṛhasthoṁ ke lābh ke artth.'

59. *Littérature hindouie et hindoustanie*, vol. II, Paris 1870, 411.

60. That is, 'An instrument for measuring altitudes, esp. one consisting essentially of a delicate thermometer, by which the boiling point of water is observed at particular elevations.' *Shorter English Oxford Dictionary*.

61. 'Itihās, purākṛt, jīvan vṛttānt, bhramaṇ vṛttānt, samācār patr prabhṛti ye sab nām bahudha avemge.', *LSS* II, 29.

62. 'Meri icchā thī ki is pustak meṁ saṃskṛt mūlak hindī bhinn aur kisī deśiya bhāsā arthāt fārsī ityādī śabd na milāye jāveṁ; parantu kisī kisī bandhu ke anurodhānusār kanyāoṁ ko arthāv gati kī sugamtā ke nimitt kahīṁ kahīṁ pracalit urdū bhāsā ke śabd vyavahṛt hue haim.' *LSS I*, 5.

63. From a linguistic point of view, it is interesting to note which are the common Urdu words used in lieu of their Sanskritic Hindi equivalents. Among them are, for example, *nasīhāt, naf'ā-nuqsān, etmād, manzūr, kamvāqif, fareb, asbāb, musībat, mājrā, dagābazī, munhasir, mohtāj, mulāyam, ahvāl.*

64. The scant information available on Hemantkumari was collected from Ved Pratap Vaidik (ed.), *Hindī patrakāritā: vividh āyām*, New Delhi, 1976, 729; Kṣemacandra 'Suman', *Divangat hindī sevī*, Delhi,²1983, vol. I, 698–9 and Ganeśbihārī Miśra et al., *Miśrabandhuvinod*, vol. 3–4, new revd and amended edn; Haiderabad, 1972, 327.

65. For the superior quality and efficiency of mission schools as compared to government schools, see M. Kishwar, 'Arya Samaj and Women's Education', 162–4.

66. 'Answers to questions of the Education Committee drawn up by the select committee of the Anjuman-i Punjab', *Appendix to Education Commission Report*, 512.

67. Kṣemacandra 'Suman', *Divangat hindī sevī*, 698.

68. Bethune School was founded in 1849 by John Drinkwater Bethune, President of the Council of Education, and supported by some eminent Bengali gentlemen, among them Ishvar Chandra Vidyasagar. It was taken over by the government in 1856. As a model institution it received the support of educated Bengalis and became the preferred choice for *bhadralok* girls after its amalgamation with the Banga Mahila Vidyalaya, a higher English boarding school, in 1878. With the opening of a collegiate section in 1879, Bethune School became Bethune College, soon afterwards affiliated with Calcutta University. In 1895, 29 out of the total of 44 students on the rolls of the college hailed from progressive Brahmo families. See D. Kopf, *The Brahmo Samaj and the Shaping of the Modern Indian Mind*, 40–1 and 127. For a more detailed account of Bethune school, see Malavika Karlekar, *Voices from within. Early personal narratives of Bengali women*, Delhi 1993, 154–75. For Kadambini Basu, see idem, 'Kadambini and the Bhadralok . . .', WS 25–31.

69. To my knowledge no copies of Sugṛhini exist.

70. S. Sastri, *History of the Brahmo Samaj*, 514.

71. *Miśrabandhu vinod*, 327.

72. See, Vir Bharat Talwar, 'Women's Journals in Hindi, 1910–1920', in Kumkum Sangari and Sudesh Vaid (eds), *Recasting Women*, Delhi: Kali for Women, 1989, 210.

73. No copies of these works were available to me, nor could I find out their dates of publication. For *Ādarś mātā* Hemantkumari received a prize of Rs 200 from the Panjab government.

74. A copy of *Navīn-śilpamālā* is preserved in the India Office Library, London.

75. Hemantkumari stated in her preface:

It makes me very angry and ashamed to see that our Indian markets are full of Japanese and foreign woollen hats, socks, gloves, sweaters, mufflers and the like items for everyday wear. And that we buy these foreign clothes at a price four times as high when within a year they become useless for wear. If the women and girls of our country were taught how to knit these indispensable items, they could make them themselves at a trifling expense and thus contribute to the gain and happiness of their families the way that European women do (my translation from the Hindi original).

76. K.W. Jones, 'The Bengali Elite . . .', 382.

77. Suniti Kumar Chatterji, *Indo-Aryan and Hindi,* revd and enlarged 2nd edn Calcutta, 1960, 326.

78. D. Kopf, *The Brahmo Samaj and the Shaping of the Modern Indian Mind,* 331.

The Ramakrishna Mission

Swami Akhandananda's *Sevavrata* (Vow of Service) and the Earliest Expressions of Service to Humanity in the Ramakrishna Math and Mission

GWILYM BECKERLEGGE

SERVICE TO HUMANITY IN THE RAMAKRISHNA MATH AND MISSION: A CHARACTERISTIC OF A 'REFORM MOVEMENT'?

POSITIONING THE RAMAKRISHNA MATH and Mission (henceforth, the Ramakrishna movement or the movement) within the elastic structure of Hinduism has long been a source of much careful deliberation and at times controversy among scholarly observers. Not so, in the main, for adherents to the Ramakrishna movement. Put simply, the view generally perpetuated within the publications of this movement is that Ramakrishna represented the fulfilment of the Hindu tradition and that Swami Vivekananda, his closest disciple, faithfully translated the admittedly unsystematized teaching and aspirations of his master into an organized form that would be sustained by an energetic and no less conscientious social institution, the Math and Mission.[1] Few, if any, devotees of Ramakrishna would dispute the first of these claims, but from the time of Ramakrishna's death a strand of dissent surfaced among Ramakrishna's earliest monastic and lay followers as Vivekananda established his leadership over them. The picture is somewhat confusing because the conviction that Ramakrishna had marked out Vivekananda to succeed him seems to have been generally accepted, although this is not confirmed in Mahendranath Gupta's record of Ramakrishna's dialogues. Nevertheless, Mahendranath himself, although he too was less than wholehearted in his support for Vivekananda's promotion of service to humanity, appears to have subscribed to this view.

The issue that divided Vivekananda and some of Ramakrishna's other intimate disciples was the extent to which Vivekananda seemed set on a course different from that of Ramakrishna and thus, by implication, earlier Hindu tradition. As Swami Yogananda poignantly expressed it: 'I confess that doubts sometimes arise in my mind . . . and I ask myself if we are not straying from the path chalked out by him [Ramakrishna]'.[2] The interactions and exchanges between Ramakrishna's first disciples after his death reveal that both the major initiatives most associated with Vivekananda were contentious; namely, the creation of the Math and the promotion of organized service to humanity, responsibility for which increasingly fell upon members of the Math.[3]

In this instance, therefore, the preoccupation of scholars outside the membership of the Ramakrishna movement with questions about the relationship between Vivekananda, the movement he created, Ramakrishna, and earlier Hindu tradition is an expansion of a critical agenda already written by personalities directly associated with the birth of the Ramakrishna Math and Mission. Having said that, this critical agenda has not been overtly pursued within the publications of the Ramakrishna movement, but it has given direction to studies undertaken by those outside the membership of the movement. Pursuing this agenda prompts questions concerning the status and significance of the mature Ramakrishna movement's commitment to organized service to humanity. Is this practice part of the authentic legacy of Ramakrishna as the reputed link between the organization that took his name and the Hindu tradition? What does the adoption of this practice tell us about the character of the Ramakrishna movement? Was the movement's early adoption of organized service to humanity a characteristic of a commitment to reform, and, if so, were the sources of this commitment found within the legacy of Hinduism or were they external to it? Clearly, the way in which these questions are answered will substantially shape judgements on the position of the Ramakrishna Math and Mission in relationship to Hinduism and its status as a 'reform movement'.

T. Ling has noted that the Ramakrishna movement has been variously interpreted as an agent for *religious reform, religious renaissance, and religious revitalization*. Ling favours the *revitalization* interpretative option and in his review makes the point that even what is conservative in intent may prove to be innovative in its outcome.[4] This passing reference to conservative tendencies is significant because, although some commentators have cast Ramakrishna and Vivekananda as 'purifiers', 'modernizers' and 'reformers', others have stressed that, in many respects, Ramakrishna and Vivekananda were far more concerned with upholding and defending aspects of the Hinduism they inherited than certain leaders of the Brahmo Samaj, for example.[5] In terms of the concerns of this volume of essays, this in turn begs the question of what is meant by 'reform' when applied to Hindu movements, including the Ramakrishna Math and Mission, that originated in nineteenth-century India then in the throes of a vast cultural interaction with western thought and institutions.

To speak of nineteenth-century Hindu 'reform movements' seeking to change, and, in their own terms, to 'purify' the expression of their inherited religious traditions is incontrovertible but hardly discloses the distinctive character of these movements when considered separately. For, their spokespersons often evinced markedly different degrees of willingness to replace fundamentals of their received religious tradition in order to secure transformations of society in the here-and-now and the promotion of the unadulterated truths held to comprise the religious ideal. To paraphrase J.N. Farquhar, not all so-called Hindu reform movements were in pursuit of 'serious' or 'vigorous' reform, if that meant the abandonment of the most generally shared and authoritative assumptions of Hinduism.[6]

In embarking upon a discussion of the Ramakrishna Math and Mission's practice of seva, service to humanity, within a volume of essays on Hindu *reform* movements, it is important, therefore, to recognize at the outset that the application of the designation 'reform movement' is potentially contentious. Critical judgements on the sources of the practice of seva adopted by the mature Ramakrishna movement under Vivekananda's guidance, in fact, must play a central role in any attempted resolution of the ongoing and wider debate about the position of the Ramakrishna movement in relationship to Hinduism, including its status as a 'reform movement'. For example, scholars who have been insistent that the Ramakrishna movement is either a most unrepresentative or even inauthentic expression of Hinduism have tended to hold that the movement's commitment to service to humanity was imported from alien western religious and social theory.[7] On this understanding, fired by European and Christian paradigms, Vivekananda may be seen as having turned his hand to the reform of Hinduism, but the very influences absorbed by the organization he created as the agent of reform disqualified it from being counted as a *Hindu* reform movement for it had abandoned the fundamentals of Hinduism. For other scholars, however, what has been significant is the manner and extent to which Vivekananda *blended* strategies designed to ameliorate social conditions in India of his day with a strong dose of traditionalism that upheld the basic structures of

Hinduism.[8] There was change and synthesis of value but the strongest constituents remained Hindu.

Questions concerning the relationship of the Ramakrishna movement to earlier and other forms of Hinduism, the origins of the movement's commitment to service to humanity, and its status as a 'reform movement' are thus closely interrelated and complex. They touch on problems that cannot be fully addressed, far less resolved, within the scope of a single chapter. In this chapter, which is but one in a series of attempts on my part to engage with the problems central to a critical reconstruction of the historical relationship between the teachings of Ramakrishna and Vivekananda,[9] I intend to consider the origins of seva within the Ramakrishna Math and Mission from a different angle; namely, from the perspective of insights provided by the autobiographical recollections of Swami Akhandananda, Vivekananda's *gurubhai* (brother disciple).

SWAMI AKHANDANANDA'S INDEPENDENT PERSPECTIVE ON THE DEVELOPMENT OF SERVICE TO HUMANITY IN THE RAMAKRISHNA MOVEMENT

Born into a strict Calcuttan brahmana family in 1865, Swami Akhandananda (Gangadhar Gangopadhyaya) first saw Sri Ramakrishna Paramahamsa in 1877. Attracted to a life of austerity, he had already undertaken an extended pilgrimage by the time he joined Ramakrishna's band of young disciples in 1883. It was Ramakrishna who encouraged the young Akhandananda to seek out the company of Narendranath Datta, later Swami Vivekananda. After the death of Ramakrishna, Akhandananda became the first *gurubhai* to become immersed in the delivery of organized service to humanity. During 1894–5, he undertook educational initiatives on behalf of low-caste boys in Khetri with the financial support of the Maharaja of Khetri.[10] In 1895, Swami Akhandananda was instrumental in feeding deprived Bhils, starting more schools and religious discussion groups. On his return to the Alambazar Math at the end of 1895, he ventured forth to nurse cholera victims. In 1897, it was Akhandananda who became the spearhead of the newly formed Ramakrishna Mission Association's first systematic attempt at famine relief and orphan care in Murshidabad.

Yet, in spite of Akhandananda's pioneering role, his contribution to the growth of service to humanity within the early Ramakrishna movement has been virtually ignored in critical studies that have concentrated on the relationship between Ramakrishna and Vivekananda for clues as to the origins of this practice. In exploring the background to Akhandananda's 'vow of service', I shall argue that a proper understanding of

Akhandananda's role throws a different light on the nature of Vivekananda's contribution to the Ramakrishna movement's adoption of seva and thus on the critical debates outlined in the first section of this chapter. I shall also illustrate the way in which later members of the movement have subordinated the contribution of Swami Akhandananda to this enterprise by enhancing the roles of Vivekananda and Swami Brahmananda, the first president of the Ramakrishna Math.

In view of his commitment to the practical delivery of service to humanity and his personal devotion to Vivekananda, it might be supposed that Akhandananda held ideas very close, if not identical, to those of Vivekananda. Yet, it was Akhandananda who resisted pressure from Vivekananda and Brahmananda to publicize reports of the relief work at Mahula in the newspapers.[11] Akhandananda also relates how he refused the entreaties of a patron who offered to build a temple to Ramakrishna in Gujarat, fearful of the householder's attachment and of the risk of himself becoming attached. On hearing of this, Vivekananda commented, 'You should have accepted the offer. We could have had a nice institution there.'[12] Such independence of mind enhances the value of Akhandananda's own recollections as a source of information about the origins of the earliest recorded examples of organized service to humanity within the Ramakrishna movement.

VIVEKANANDA IN GUJARAT AND THE INCEPTION OF SWAMI AKHANDANANDA'S VOW OF SERVICE AT JAMNAGAR, GUJARAT

Speaking of his time spent with Ramakrishna, Akhandananda made no reference to any incident or teaching associated with Ramakrishna that led him to adopt a life of service to others. Like Vivekananda, the immediate impact of his encounter with Ramakrishna appears to have heightened Akhandananda's desire for solitary pilgrimage, which only in time gave way to a life centred on altruistic service. Both Akhandananda and Vivekananda reached the point in their lives when they made a commitment to the service of humanity during much the same period. It is more than probable that both were forced to reflect upon the social conditions in India during their extended pilgrimages, which took place during a period of considerable social and economic change.[13] If this 'awakening' appears to parallel that of the legendary confrontation of the Buddha with the hallmarks of existence, this may not be inappropriate, given that Akhandananda shared with Vivekananda a profound reverence for the Buddha.[14]

Although Swami Gambhirananda emphasizes in his standard history of the Ramakrishna movement that 'Swami Akhandananda had lived in personal touch with Swami Vivekananda for a long time before the latter sailed for America', it is difficult to know the exact extent of what passed between Vivekananda and Akhandananda before Akhandananda started work in Khetri.[15] Vivekananda's early letters (1890) to Akhandananda speak of exchanges largely confined to their shared interest in the Buddha and other matters relating to personal spirituality and meditation.[16] Their paths did cross in Gujarat in April 1892. There are risks of oversimplification, if it is assumed that the development of ideas can be reconstructed neatly from references, or absence of reference, to these ideas, in surviving correspondence and autobiography. But such is the importance attached in Akhandananda's autobiographical recollections to the time he spent in Gujarat that we have little reason to doubt the profound and lasting effect of this period upon his eventual adoption of a life of altruism.

The fact that both Vivekananda and Akhandananda spent approximately a year in Gujarat is of additional interest because it opens up the possibility of their acquaintance with the Swaminarayan tradition in which *sannyasin*s had played an active part in the practical delivery of service to the *satsanga*. These activities had included building wells and offering famine relief.[17] Vivekananda, for example, spent time in Ahmedabad, Junagadh, Bhuj and Nadiad (formerly Nariad), all of which were major centres of Swaminarayan activity. He also visited Kathiawar where, during the famine of 1813–14, Swaminarayan ascetics had been active in organizing famine relief.[18]

Unlike the early Ramakrishna movement, the Swaminarayan satsanga had its origins in a part of India where British influence only gradually began to increase during the closing years of the life of its founder, Sahajanand Swami (1781–1830). Critical explanations of the Swaminarayan commitment to the forms of organized seva encouraged by Sahajanand Swami, therefore, tend to point to precedents within the Vaishnava tradition rather than to western and particularly Christian paradigms. In spite of its practice of organized seva, the Swaminarayan satsanga is not usually placed within the category of nineteenth-century Hindu 'reform movements'.[19]

Somewhat frustratingly, it is not possible to gauge with any certainty what effect, if any, a knowledge of Swaminarayan practice might have had upon Vivekananda's understanding of the scope of Hindu philanthropy during the formative period of his own thinking about service to others. His extended and repeated stays in known centres of Swaminarayan activity, however, make it seem unlikely that a person of his curiosity and personal magnetism would not have acquired some degree of knowledge of the Swaminarayan tradition. When we turn to Swami Akhandananda, however, although once again no certain link with Swaminarayan practice can be established, he was unequivocal in his testimony to the influence of one Gujarati philanthropist upon his subsequent life.

After a period of no more than a fortnight together, Akhandananda and Vivekananda parted company by the end of April 1892. Akhandananda went to Jamnagar where he stayed for a year.[20] In his account of his time in Jamnagar, he wrote, 'The Sevavrata (vow of service) had its inception at Jamnagar; it had its evolution at Khetri in Rajputana, and its development and maturity in Murshidabad'.[21]

Swami Akhandananda spoke with particular warmth of his relationship with Jhandu Bhat, an Ayurvedic healer and philanthropist, whom Vivekananda had also met at Jamnagar. On the basis of this acquaintance, Vivekananda declared, '. . . nowhere have I seen a generous man like Jhandu Bhat Viththalji.'[22] Akhandananda himself determined to study Ayurvedic medicine and opened a feeding-house. He also resolved to improve the quality of Vedic education in the area. On the occasion of the publication of a biography of Ishvar Chandra Vidyasagar, which Akhandananda does not identify, Jhandu Bhat insisted that a copy be purchased and that Swami Akhandananda should read it to him daily.[23]

Swami Akhandananda recalled in particular a certain verse that was constantly on the lips of Jhandu Bhat: 'I do not hanker after that heaven of Vaikuntha where I may not have an opportunity to serve or do good to a man.'[24] The edited volume of Swami Akhandananda's recollections refers to Pandit Hathibhai Sastri of Jamnagar who identified the verse in question as one attributed to Rantideva, described in the *Mahabharata* as a pre-eminent provider of charity. The Pandit added, 'Swami Akhandanandaji took this verse as a motto. It clearly revealed his pity for suffering humanity and his desire for removing their distress.'[25] Swami Tapasyananda remembered Akhandananda writing to the movement's publishing house, Advaita Ashram, in the month before his death '. . . for a verse that he had come across in the *Prabuddha Bharata* some time back.' The verse is identified as one from the *Srimad Bhagavatam*, which tells of Rantideva being tested by God as he was about to take food at the end of a forty-eight day fast. Having given away his food and water to a series of human and animal guests sent by God, Rantideva uttered the verse: 'I do not desire for kingdom, heaven or even liberation. My one desire is to relieve the sufferings of the distressed.'[26]

Swami Akhandananda stated that, when he repeated Jhandu Bhat's verse as he remembered it to Vivekananda, it brought tears to the latter's eyes. Whether Vivekananda recognized the original source of the verse is not disclosed. Vivekananda certainly did not include Rantideva in his list of paradigms of compassion and charity from the earlier Hindu tradition. For Akhandananda, of course, it was not the example of Rantideva but that of Jhandu Bhat that came to hold such importance. Summarizing the impact the meeting with Bhat had upon his life, Swami Akhandananda declared, 'The best thing in a man's life is to serve man and to love man—the life of Bhatji brought home this truth to me.'[27]

In terms of possible connections to be made with the Swaminarayan presence in Gujarat, the source of the Rantideva verse, the *Srimad Bhagavatam* is one of the eight scriptures from the extensive Vaishnava Hindu tradition that were adopted by Sahajanand Swami, the founder of the Swaminarayan movement. The version of the Rantideva verse Swami Akhandananda recalled being on the lips of Jhandu Bhat made reference to not hankering after 'that heaven of Vaikuntha.' In addition to being a designation for the mythological paradise of Vishnu, Vaikuntha also had a particular meaning in the Swaminarayan strand of the greater Vaishnava tradition as the residence of Rama and one of a hierarchy of states culminating in *akshardham*, the heavenly abode of the Supreme Being. The sentiment underlying the verse associated with Jhandu Bhat by Swami Akhandananda is very close in substance to the two boons said to have been requested by Sahajanand Swami on his installation as acharya; namely, that any miseries destined for members of the satsanga should be borne by Sahajanand himself, and that Sahajanand should bear any scarcities of food or clothing in place of other members of the community.

Resemblances between Swami Akhandananda's recollections of Jhandu Bhat and aspects of Swaminarayan tradition, intriguing though they are, do not constitute evidence that links Jhandu Bhat to the Swaminarayan tradition. Nor do they establish any proof of an influence exerted by the earlier Swaminarayan satsanga upon the embryonic ideas developed by pioneers in the Ramakrishna movement. The apparent similarities that have been identified, however, do indicate the existence of common underlying sentiments that could prompt individuals in different regional traditions to undertake substantial and organized philanthropic activity beyond the limits of conventional almsgiving. If Vivekananda and Akhandananda indeed encountered such ideas during their extended stay in Gujarat, they may well have recognized these as part of the common heritage of the wider Hindu or even Indian religious tradition, including Buddhism.

Swami Akhandananda's own account of his time in Gujarat, therefore, suggests that the source of his commitment to service to humanity cannot be explained adequately either with reference solely to the influence of Ramakrishna or in terms of direction provided by Vivekananda and by other followers of Ramakrishna. The fact that it was Jhandu Bhat, and neither Ramakrishna nor Vivekananda, who is said to have been the immediate trigger behind Akhandananda's resolve to adopt a life of service, is a further example of the independence of the account given by Akhandananda of the way in which he came to a life of service to others.

THE EVOLUTION OF AKHANDANANDA'S VOW OF SERVICE AT KHETRI

Swami Akhandananda learnt of Vivekananda's departure from Bombay for the World's Parliament of Religions at Chicago some weeks after 31 May 1893. Having been summoned to a meeting at Abu Road station, Akhandananda received the news from Swamis Brahmananda and Turiyananda.[28] Akhandananda states explicitly that he had been ignorant of Vivekananda's intention to travel to the West in order to find the resources with which to combat India's poverty until this was disclosed to him during the meeting at Abu Road station.[29] This was the same meeting-place where, just before leaving for the United States, Vivekananda had spoken to Swami Turiyananda of the expansion of his heart through compassion for humanity.[30]

According to the biography written by Vivekananda's Eastern and Western Disciples, Vivekananda's reflection on his widening compassion was shared with Swami Turiyananda. No mention is made of Swami Brahmananda having been party to it, although he had accompanied Turiyananda to Abu Road station. In Swami Nikhilananda's later and more conflated version, no separation is made between Turiyananda and Brahmananda, and Vivekananda is also depicted as seizing the occasion to tell both about his plan to visit the West.[31] In the earlier account, it is implied that Turiyananda and Brahmananda had hurried to Abu Road station, having heard about Vivekananda's plans while passing through Khetri, which Vivekananda had already visited. This difference may be due to no more than a compression of the narrative, yet one outcome of Nikhilananda's condensation is to keep Brahmananda firmly in the centre of the story. Swami Gambhirananda appears to have followed the earlier version provided by Vivekananda's Eastern and Western Disciples.[32]

News of the forthcoming World Parliament of Religions is said to have reached Vivekananda in Gujarat and probably at either Junagadh or Porbandar early in 1892.[33] According to his biographers, Vivekananda decided to attend the Parliament of Religions while at Khandwa some time between the end of April (after he had parted from Akhandananda).

and 15 June 1892, by which date he was *en route* for Bombay.[34] Apart from Vivekananda's attempts to distance himself from his gurubhais before 1893, the rapidity of the events that took him to the United States lends credibility to the profound impression made upon Swami Turiyananda by Vivekananda's words and to Swami Akhandananda's profession of ignorance of Vivekananda's plan. If, in fact, Vivekananda had only learnt of the Parliament on his return visit to Porbandar and Junagadh after separating from Akhandananda, this would make Akhandananda's ignorance of a plan, then unforeseen even by Vivekananda, entirely consistent with this order of events.

Swami Gambhirananda states that, after the meeting at Abu Road station, '. . . it was at Swami Brahmananda's advice that Swami Akhandananda went to Khetri . . . which place thus became the first field of his activity.[35] Writing about the service that Akhandananda undertook at Khetri, Swami Gambhirananda declares, 'There can be no doubt that the inspiration came from Swami Vivekananda.'[36] Akhandananda was 'impelled to action' by Vivekananda's words and by what he saw.[37] By linking Akhandananda's journey to Khetri with Brahmananda's advice, which is presented almost as an appendage to the report of Vivekananda's reasons for going to America, Gambhirananda's account enfolds the beginnings of Akhandananda's preoccupation with seva within an envelope of influence and direction emanating from Brahmananda. Akhandananda's own account states, however, that persisting ill-health induced him to follow Brahmananda's advice and move to Khetri to recuperate under the patronage of the Raja of Khetri, a disciple of Vivekananda.[38]

Taking Gambhirananda's explanation of the circumstances that took Akhandananda to Khetri with Nikhilananda's inclusion of Brahmananda in all the exchanges with Vivekananda at the Abu Road station meeting of 1893, there are signs that later members of the Ramakrishna Math may have tended, even if unconsciously, to enhance the role of the early movement's leaders in shaping initiatives that promoted the earliest practice of seva. Akhandananda's own account of his adoption of seva is fuller than that found in the later, standard 'insider' histories of the movement, and it sheds a different and very illuminating light on his relationship with Vivekananda during the period in which the possibility of offering service at Khetri was being considered.

When Swami Akhandananda proceeded to Khetri on the suggestion of Swami Brahmananda in order to recuperate, he took with him the vivid memories of his recent encounters with philanthropic impulses in

Gujarat, and most notably with Jhandu Bhat. On arrival in Khetri, Akhandananda initially resided with the Raja, where he had an opportunity to read 'all the works of Theodore Parker' in addition to improving his grasp of Hindi.[39] Then reference to Parker is of interest, given Parker's role as shaper of the Unitarian 'social gospel', which had such a profound effect upon Brahmo philanthropy. Then followed a period when Akhandananda travelled extensively through the region and witnessed the huge disparity between the lives of the rich and their tenants; 'I exercised my mind as to how to alleviate the sufferings of the poor tenants. I felt it to be the most sacred duty of a man and took a vow to do it.'[40] Akhandananda did not relate his decision to any specific change wrought by learning from Brahmananda of Vivekananda's reason for travelling to the West.

The order of events thereafter is clear. Akhandananda wrote a letter to the Raja about the plight of his subjects that virtually amounted to a treatise on the duty of the ruler, couched in terms of traditional notions of *rajadharma*. Having been recalled to Khetri, Swami Akhandananda then '. . . wrote a letter to Swamiji in America, giving a graphic description of the misery of the poor tenants . . . I wanted to know whether I was right in taking the vow of relieving the distressed people'.[41] The eventual outcome of Akhandananda's action was the educational initiatives that marked the acknowledged beginning of the Ramakrishna movement's first forays into service to humanity. In a series of conversations with Swami Niramayananda, recorded between 1935 and 1937, Swami Akhandananda made a mention of how he broached the matter of service with Vivekananda:

I began to count the days in expectation of a reply, and thought of many things that Swamiji might write. If he were to write: 'you are a Sannyasin. Why bother your head with mundane problems? Remain satisfied with your scriptures, spiritual practices and travels', I would have left India, crossed the Himalaya . . . from which I had been called back by Swamiji himself.[42]

The uncertainty voiced by Akhandananda about the outcome of his approach to Vivekananda would suggest that, by early 1894, even a disciple so close to Vivekananda, one who had shared pilgrimage with him and who was beyond doubt motivated to undertake service to humanity, was not certain whether Vivekananda would regard a life of service as compatible with the discipline of sannyasa. This in turn implies that the way in which Akhandananda came to learn of Vivekananda's reason for journeying to the West had not set down a blueprint for action clear enough to assure him that he would have Vivekananda's support.

Vivekananda's reply to Akhandananda's letter arrived a 'couple of months' later.[43] In this letter, assigned by the publishers to March or April 1894, Vivekananda instructed Akhandananda to '... develop spirituality and philanthropy . . . in Rajputana' and to 'Go from door to door amongst the poor and lower classes . . .' in order to provide both religious and general education.[44] If Akhandananda's account is correct, Vivekananda's letter of March/April 1894 must be read as a confirmation of the rightness of the decision already taken, in effect, by Akhandananda when he challenged the Raja of Khetri and not as an instruction that instigated this initiative. The published, edited form of Vivekananda's letter to Akhandananda, while including an acknowledgement of the receipt of Akhandananda's letter but omitting reference to its substance, makes the instruction to develop philanthropy appear unrelated to the very purpose of Akhandananda's letter.[45]

In a human and revealing postscript, Swami Akhandananda reflected that, after the receipt of Vivekananda's letter,

. . . I would always ask myself whether he had chosen me alone for this task. How was it that my other Gurubhais enjoyed the bliss of meditation and worship, while I alone should go about with the burden of other people's misery on my head? What a joy would it be if he set all of us to this task! Sometime before I left Udaipur, I got a postcard written by Swami Ramakrishnananda from our Math. He informed me that all of my Gurubhais had been urged by Swamiji to engage themselves in the service of man.[46]

The message to which Swami Ramakrishnananda alluded is presumably Vivekananda's letter to the Alambazar Math assigned by the publishers to the summer of 1894.[47] It would appear that, from this point in Vivekananda's thinking, service to humanity was no longer regarded as a matter of personal conscience and as a personal response to what lay before the eye of the performer. Rather, it became a matter of (inescapable?) religious responsibility and took on the shape of an appropriate and systematic response to the recognition of widespread social need. Yet, it would seem from Swami Akhandananda's 'confession' that even such an ardent servant of humanity as he continued to discriminate between the life of meditation and worship and carrying 'the burden of other people's misery'. The possibility of fierce resistance from those less sympathetic than Akhandananda may have affected both the manner and the pace at which Vivekananda chose to disclose his strategy for the provision of organized *seva*. Vikekananda may have privately determined at an early stage that this would be a central feature in his strategy but thought this to be potentially too contentious a proposal to publicize in his absence. Akhandananda's declared doubts about the substance of Vivekananda's reply, however, make this seem unlikely, unless Vivekananda had kept his cards very close to his chest even in his dealings with the gurubhai most willing to undertake service to humanity.

Early hints of Vivekananda's plan to gather resources appeared in newspaper reports in the United States in 1893 shortly after his arrival there.[48] From August 1893, Vivekananda also began to share his ideas about service in letters to his closest Indian householder followers in Madras and, in particular, with Alasinga Perumal.[49] Yet, it was only in a letter of 1894 to his gurubhai, Ramakrishnananda, that Vivekananda retrospectively disclosed the vision of activist sannyasins that he declared had gripped his imagination at Kanya Kumari towards the end of 1892.[50] This, according to Vivekananda, was the point at which his plan came together, shaped by the legacy of Ramakrishna and his own experiences of the poverty of the Indian masses. It does appear, therefore, that the strategy for householder and monastic *sevakas* (those offering seva or service) was revealed progressively to each faction in the period August 1893 to the summer of 1894.

The fact that Vivekananda ultimately instructed members of the Alambazar Math to take up organized seva in the summer of 1894, while still abroad and with no immediate intention of returning to India, further undermines the view that this was a long-held plan that he had kept to himself until in a position to supervise its implementation in person. The pattern of Vivekananda's correspondence in the first half of 1894 suggests instead that this period marked the point at which, having resolved an uncertainty or even an internal conflict over his strategy for and the role of the sannyasin, he felt able to make this known and to encourage his followers to adopt his plan. It is worth considering, therefore, what impact, if any, Akhandananda's own initiative in Khetri might have had upon Vivekananda. For example, if it could be established that Vivekananda's reply to Akhandananda was written before the letter of March 1894 to Ramakrishnananda, it would suggest that considerable weight should be placed on the interchange with Akhandananda in shaping Vivekananda's own ideas about the role of the sannyasin in the provision of organized seva.

A letter of 24 May 1894, from Vivekananda to one of his earliest American patrons, Professor Wright, refers to enclosures, including a letter from the Maharaja of Khetri.[51] In this letter of 7 April 1894, the Maharaja mentioned an earlier letter from Vivekananda, dated 28 February 1894, in which it seems that Vivekananda had reproached the Maharaja for failing to write. Correspondence with Mary Hale, dated 30 March 1894, however, indicates that Vivekananda had received recent communications from the Maharaja, for Vivekananda expressed pleasure at receiving a letter from the Maharaja of Khetri.[52] Having defended himself against the charge of failing to write, the Maharaja concluded his letter of 7 April 1894, as follows: 'Swami Akhundanandaji [sic] is here now-a-days. He has written a separate letter to your holiness enclosed with this.'[53] It would appear that the full exchange of letters during this period between Vivekananda and the Maharaja of Khetri has either not survived or has not been made public because Vivekananda's letter of 28 February 1894, to which the Maharaja refers, does not figure in the *Complete Works of Swami Vivekananda*. It is also evident that mail could take between six weeks to two months to reach Vivekananda.

It is reasonable to assume that, in his letter of 7 April, the Maharaja was passing on fresh news of Akhandananda's return to the palace, which presumably took place after the dispatch of the Raja's earlier letter to which Vivekananda referred in his correspondence with Mary Hale. The evidence, such as it is, tends to point to April as the time when Akhandananda would have been in a position to write to Vivekananda from Khetri, and it seems reasonable to conclude that it was this letter that the Maharaja enclosed with his own letter of April 1894. If Akhandananda's letter to Vivekananda left Khetri shortly after 7 April 1894, it is unlikely that Vivekananda would have received it in time to reply to Akhandananda during March/April 1894, the date assigned to this letter by the publishers in the *Complete Works of Swami Vivekananda*. In fact, assuming that Vivekananda was anxious to answer those critics who were undermining his support in the United States, the date of the letter to Professor Wright, in which he enclosed the Maharaja's letter as a testimony to the authenticity of his standing as a sannyasin, may provide a reliable guide to the period when the letter(s) from Khetri arrived, especially if Vivekananda chose to pass on the Maharaja's letter as a matter of urgency. Vivekananda did not write to Professor Wright until 24 May 1894.

There are good reasons, therefore, to accept that Vivekananda's letter of 19 March 1894 to Ramakrishnananda was earlier than the letter to Akhandananda, and to suggest that this latter letter was later than the March/April dating which its publishers have assigned to it, possibly being written in late May or thereafter. This implies that Vivekananda could not have had Akhandananda's letter before him when he wrote to Ramakrishnananda. Allowing for the 'couple of months' that Akhandananda had to wait before receiving his reply, which had arrived before he learnt from Ramakrishnananda that Vivekananda had also written to the Alambazar Math to encourage service to humanity, this in turn would suggest that Vivekananda's letter to the Alambazar Math may have been written well into the summer of 1894; its publishers give it as (Summer?), 1894.

Akhandananda's uncertainty over Vivekananda's response to the proposal that a sannyasin should adopt a life of service, however, remains intriguing, to say the least. It is no less striking that the letter from the Maharaja of Khetri made no mention of Akhandananda's intervention, which would have been known to the Maharaja by the time he wrote to Vivekananda. Had the Maharaja himself associated Vivekananda with a strategy of organized seva spearheaded by sannyasins, one might reasonably have expected some mention of Akhandananda's activities in the Maharaja's own letter to Vivekananda.

Taken together, Swami Akhandananda's recollections and Vivekananda's correspondence during 1894 suggest a fluid quality in Vivekananda's emergent commitment to service to humanity. Akhandananda's professed desire to adopt a life of service in Khetri may have provided Vivekananda with a timely confirmation of the rightness of the path upon which he, Vivekananda, was increasingly resolved to set the followers of Ramakrishna. Alternatively, replying to Akhandananda's letter from Khetri may have provided Vivekananda with a further opportunity to disclose a strategy that he had begun to entertain by the end of 1892, but which had not been sufficiently defined in his mind to be released with the force of a policy directive until the middle of 1894. In either case, contrary to the impression given by later writers within the Ramakrishna movement, Vivekananda did not instigate the project at Khetri; he merely put an anxiously awaited sign of approval on an initiative that had been Akhandananda's from the first.

THE DEVELOPMENT AND MATURITY OF AKHANDANANDA'S VOW OF SERVICE IN MURSHIDABAD

Once having taken his 'vow of service', Swami Akhandananda's level of direct participation and single-mindedness in the provision of service to humanity was without parallel in the early Ramakrishna Math. Even when made president, Akhandananda did not leave the orphanage he founded at Sargacchi after the Mahula famine.

In an undated encounter, which took place some time between Akhandananda's return to the Alambazar Math in 1895 and before Vivekananda's return to India, we find the Swami upbraiding Surendranath Banerjea over the gulf between the Congress movement and the village poor.[54] In his wanderings around the hinterland of Calcutta, in the districts of Tarakeshvar and Hugli, Akhandananda saw villages ravaged by malaria and hunger, and, travelling to Murshidabad in 1897, faced the famine that would draw him into relief work at Mahula. His comment on hearing of the famine from emaciated herders is interesting: 'It was from them that I got the news of famine. At the Math I had never heard of famine in Bengal.'[55] This is entirely in accord with Swami Gambhirananda's account of the movement's first involvement in famine relief, from which it is clear that it was Swami Akhandananda who again took the initiative by staying in the afflicted region and drawing the attention of his gurubhais to the local conditions and the need of the inhabitants.[56]

Yet, as with the accounts given of the beginnings of seva at Khetri, there are striking differences of detail in the versions of the initiation of the famine relief at Mahula provided respectively by Swami Gambhirananda and Swami Akhandananda. It is significant, perhaps, that Gambhirananda begins his account, 'Naturally, Swami Vivekananda played a decisive role in undertaking the work.'[57] He recounts Swami Vivekananda reacting immediately to three letters written to Swami Premananda by Swami Akhandananda, which contained a full description of the situation at Mahula. Akhandananda's own version of Vivekananda's action is then given, which records how Vivekananda immediately sent money 'from his own pocket' and two sevakas. Gambhirananda refers next to the financial support 'offered at this time' by the Mahabodhi Society, which sustained the relief for two months, and then notes the controversy that broke out between the two organizations over which should receive the credit for the relief work.[58]

According to Swami Akhandananda, however, the initial response to his letters from Swamis Ramakrishnananda and Premananda was that it was not possible for 'a mendicant sannyasi' to feed 'thousands of mouths' and that he should return to the Math. At this time, Vivekananda was in Darjeeling and he too 'inquired after' Akhandananda and directed Brahmananda to recall him to the Math. It is not clear from the account whether Vivekananda was fully aware of the situation at Mahula when he gave this instruction, or even whether this inquiry was made while Vivekananda was in Darjeeling or on his return to Calcutta. It is more than evident, however, that the first response to his three letters that Akhandananda received from his gurubhais was at least three letters from Swamis Ramakrishnananda, Premananda and Brahmananda urging him to withdraw from Mahula. Again, according to Akhandananda's own account, it was during this period of hiatus that the Mahabodhi Society, having heard of Akhandananda's 'firm resolve' from Swami Premananda, first offered financial support. At this point, Vivekananda comes fully into the picture for, by now having returned to Calcutta and in possession of Akhandananda's three letters to Premananda, he then instigated the dispatch of the money and sevakas to Mahula.[59] As in his account of the educational work at Khetri, Gambhirananda's version of the Mahula relief work places Vivekananda firmly in the centre of the stage and depicts him reacting immediately to Akhandananda's letters on return to Calcutta. Akhandananda's account, on the other hand, shows how far removed other members of the Math were from the scenes of distress in the region around Calcutta. His account also suggests that other direct disciples of Ramakrishna at this time did not regard the conditions at Mahula as lying within the power (or, possibly, even within the responsibility) of a sannyasin to address. This last observation must be balanced against a recognition of the role of fund-raisers played subsequently by both Swamis Ramakrishnananda and Brahmananda.

Akhandananda is unstinting in his acknowledgement of the moral support and practical help provided by Vivekananda but it should not be lost sight of that, as with Khetri, Vivekananda is shown once again to be reacting to initiatives taken by Akhandananda. The lack of clear evidence concerning the point at which Vivekananda inquired after Akhandananda, whether before or after he had seen the letters from Mahula, and concerning the timing of the offer of financial support from the Mahabodhi Society relative to Vivekananda's dispatch of money, make it difficult to assess the speed with which Vivekananda acted and under what pressures. It can be established from dated correspondence that funding famine relief was on Vivekananda's mind before the Mahula incident[60] and that he returned briefly to Calcutta from Darjeeling before setting off for Almora again due to poor health.[61] He would have been in a position, therefore, to take action prior to 15 May 1897, the date on which, according to Swami Gambhirananda, the work at Mahula started 'in right earnest'.[62]

CONCLUSION

The implications of the interpretation offered in this chapter of one crucial phase in the genesis of organized seva within the Ramakrishna movement yet again draw attention away from Ramakrishna himself. Swami Akhandananda's progression to a life of service is another example of the way in which the intimate disciples of Ramakrishna seemed to have needed more than solely the example of their guru to prompt them to take up this cause. Akhandananda, like Vivekananda, showed no immediate desire to plunge into a lifetime of service to others in order to live out the message of Ramakrishna. In the case of Vivekananda, as noted at the beginning of this chapter, there has been considerable debate about the extent to which western influence shaped his formulation of seva. Akhandananda, on the other hand, did not travel West. For Akhandananda, as we have seen, the decisive turning-point was his encounter with Vaishnava philanthropy in Gujarat.

It could be argued that Akhandananda had also been extensively exposed to English-language education well before his year in Gujarat, having been a student at the Oriental Seminary in Calcutta. We know, for example, that he was acquainted with the writings of Theodore Parker. Akhandananda's involvement in formal English-language education, however, was less than Vivekananda's. Although the hagiographic narratives of the Ramakrishna movement note Akhandananda's reputed powers of concentration, there is no suggestion that Akhandananda was ever a voracious assimilator of works that gave access to western thought.[63] His reading of Theodore Parker occurred after his initial involvement in philanthropy in Gujarat under the influence of Jhandu Bhat. Of strict brahmana parents, Akhandananda had undergone the sacred thread ceremony, resisted attempts to find him a wife and slipped away from the family home (much to the distress of his mother) to go on extended pilgrimage, all by the age of eighteen when he joined Ramakrishna's band of young disciples. Before giving himself up to the call of a life of renunciation that initially at least was patterned on classical Hindu ideals, Akhandananda does not appear to have experienced the youthful ambivalence that Vivekananda displayed about a worldly career. Akhandananda's route into a life of altruism, at his own speed, was one that drew heavily upon Hindu exemplars both past and present, particularly from the Vaishnava bhakti tradition.

There are evident differences in the ways in which Vivekananda and Akhandananda respectively dedicated themselves to the service of others. Vivekananda remained very much a project coordinator and fund-raiser whilst Akhandananda became a project manager and was actively involved in the delivery of service over a long period of time. These differences in outlook and practice are often overlooked because Vivekananda and Akhandananda concurred that the sannyasin should take an active role in addressing both the material and spiritual conditions of the Indian masses. In adopting this 'innovative' policy, the later Ramakrishna movement has been said to have departed from earlier Hindu principles as a result of exposure to Christian missionaries. Yet, as we have seen, both Vivekananda and Akhandananda are more than likely to have heard of, if not actually met, activist sannyasins during their extended spells in Gujarat. If the emphasis placed in this chapter upon the independence of Akhandananda's route into service to humanity is valid, it is striking that Akhandananda adopted the lifestyle of an activist at much the same time as Vivekananda was formulating a policy that would regulate the future conduct of all members of the Ramakrishna Math.

The emphasis placed on the independence of Akhandananda's route to a life of service via Jamnagar, Khetri, and finally Murshidabad, may appear to contradict the uniform insistence, among later members of the Ramakrishna movement, upon the centrality of Vivekananda's role as the instigator of organized seva within the movement. In fact, giving full weight to the part played by Akhandananda does not detract from Vivekananda's role as a coordinator of these early initiatives. It does, however, reflect more faithfully the complex interplay of influences that fed into what would become the movement's characteristic sadhana or spiritual discipline, of service to others.

Just as the causes of the growth of organized service to humanity in the Ramakrishna movement were varied and complex, so too were the motives of those committed to the promotion of seva. In many ways Akhandananda's concerns were hardly those of a reformer, if 'reform' here implies an extensive abandonment of the Hindu past. Many aspects of the present—grinding poverty, illness and widespread famine—encountered on his travels, Akhandananda found unacceptable, and he resolved to ameliorate these conditions. But in drawing inspiration from Vaishnava and Buddhist notions of service and compassion, there is little to suggest that Akhandananda had internalized a negative critique of Hinduism as the source of these present ills. Akhandananda's initial experiment with seva in Khetri was very much within the framework of traditional assumptions about rajadharma and depended heavily on the benevolence of the local ruler. Moreover, much of his energy in both Khetri and later in Murshidabad was committed to the rekindling of Vedic education. Signs of the incorporation of ideas foreign to Hinduism to act as vitalistic ingredients are far harder to find in Akhandananda's writing than in Vivekananda's. As we saw at the outset of this chapter, the loyal Akhandananda became uneasy when pressed by Vivekananda to adopt fund-raising and publicity strategies more in line with modern voluntary social service agencies. In his turn, Vivekananda was impatient of the 'hands on', day-to-day efforts that characterized Akhandananda's approach when these stopped short of a wider transformation of the outlook of villagers.[64]

Vivekananda's judgement on Akhandananda's approach to service to humanity implies the acceptance of a strategy for the delivery of organized philanthropic activity that was very different, both in form and scope, from traditional Hindu expressions of service to humanity. The synthesis of ideas effected by Vivekananda was more eclectic than that attempted by Akhandananda, immersed as the latter was in the practicalities of famine relief and the care of orphans. The experiences that Vivekananda shared with Akhandananda, contact with Ramakrishna and wandering through India, were supplemented by youthful involvement with the Brahmo tradition and, of course, years spent in the United States and in Europe. Vivekananda's commitment to service to humanity was laced with a criticism of the failure of the Hindu elite and a plea for revitalization of Hinduism that is absent from Akhandananda's autobiographical reflections. This edge to Vivekananda's public declarations has been taken as confirmation of his intention to reform Hinduism at least in part through a style of humanitarianism that was alien to Hinduism both in principle and organization. But this is where, as A. Sen has observed, '. . . the theoretical distinction so often made between the Moderate-Reformist camp on the one hand and the Extremist-Revivalist on the other . . .' requires qualification.[65]

There were clear limits to Vivekananda's radicalism. In his outlook, many conservative tendencies were revealed in his attitude to asceticism, women, caste and materialism.[66] It has been suggested that, far from being a root-and-branch reformer, Vivekananda was able to count upon the support of influential members of India's elite precisely because of the appeal of his traditionalism. On this understanding, the retention of traditional Hindu elements in Vivekananda's thought is seen as imposing a clear limit on either the extent of his commitment to reform or the effectiveness of the strategies he adopted, or both.[67] Most significantly in the context of the present discussion, even though dubbed a 'reformer' Vivekananda played no part in any campaign for social reform; neither did he formulate any clear plan of action for the achievement of social reform.[68] This last observation may sound surprising, given the foundation of the Ramakrishna movement and its commitment to service to humanity. As Vivekananda's own life progressed, however, he disengaged himself increasingly from the practicalities of promoting organized service, and many of the developments of this kind of activity in the later Math and Mission can be shown to owe a lot to policies adopted by central and state governments in India after independence.[69] In short, organized service to humanity was one of a number of innovations for which Vivekananda was indeed largely responsible but the purpose of this service, apart from the amelioration of immediate distress, was far more closely bound up with a vision of a revived and revitalized Hinduism than a thoroughgoing reform of Hindu society.

Recognizing the role played by Swami Akhandananda in the Ramakrishna movement's earliest forays into service to humanity not only gives due weight to the varied factors involved in shaping what would become the characteristic practice of this organization. It also underlines the need for caution in treating earliest expressions of commitment to seva as indicative of an underlying reformist intent on the part of the two disciples of Ramakrishna who ensured that this practice became embedded in the institutional life of the Ramakrishna Math and Mission.[70]

NOTES

1. Different views held within the Ramakrishna Math and Mission about the nature and extent of continuity between Ramakrishna and Vivekananda are discussed in Beckerlegge, 'Social Service as *Sadhana*: Different Perceptions of the Nature of the Continuity Between the Teachings of Sri Ramakrishna and Swami Vivekananda', *Religion and Society* 33(4), 1986, pp. 46–77.

2. Swami Gambhirananda, *History of the Ramakrishna Math and Mission* (3rd revd edn), Calcutta, 1983 (hereafter *HRMM*), p. 98.

3. These factions are described in more detail in Beckerlegge, 'A Study of Continuity Within the Ramakrishna Math and Mission with Reference to the Practice of Seva, Service to Humanity' (unpublished thesis), University of Lancaster, 1995, ch. 4.

4. T. Ling, 'The Ramakrishna Movement: The Question of Assessment' in Anon, *Studies on Sri Ramakrishna*, Calcutta, 1988. Cf C.R. Pangborn, 'The Ramakrishna Math and Mission', in B.L. Smith (ed.), *Hinduism: New Essays in the History of Religions*, Leiden, 1976.

5. A spectrum of opinion concerning the status of the Ramakrishna movement was established soon after the earliest independent, scholarly studies of the movement had been completed. For F. Max Müller, Ramakrishna and Vivekananda were the prime movers in an attempt to change, to 'purify', to bring Hinduism into the modern age; in short, to reform that tradition. (Müller's understanding of Ramakrishna is discussed in Beckerlegge, 'Sri Ramakrishna Paramahamsa—F. Max Müller's *A Real Mahatman*: A Study in Nineteenth Century Indology,' *International Journal of Comparative Religion and Philosophy 1(2)*, 1995, pp. 16–26.) Yet another early observer, the missionary scholar J.N Farquhar, drew a sharp distinction between movements such as the Brahmo Samaj that favoured 'serious reform' and both Ramakrishna and Vivekananda whom Farquhar cast as 'full defenders' of the 'old religion' of Hinduism (see Farquhar, *Modern Religious Movements in India* (1st Indian edn), Delhi, 1967.

6. Farquhar, ibid., pp. xiii, 29.

7. See, for example, A. Bharati, *The Ochre Robe,* Santa Barbara, 1980; P. Hacker, *Kleine Schriften,* Wiesbaden, 1978.

8. See, for example, N. Dhar, *Vedanta and the Bengal Renaissance,* Calcutta, 1972; D. Rothermund, *The Phases of Indian Nationalism and Other Essays,* Bombay, 1970.

9. In addition to references made during the course of this chapter, see also Beckerlegge, 'Human Rights in the Ramakrishna Math and Mission: For Liberation and the Good of the World', *Religion* 20, 1990, pp. 119–37.

10. *HRMM,* p. 87.

11. Ibid., p. 97f; cf Swami Akhandananda, *From Holy Wanderings to the Service of God in Man* (2nd edn), Mylapore, Madras, 1979, pp. 163–5.

12. Akhandananda, ibid., p. 53, n. 1.

13. The impact of the encounter with famine upon Vivekananda's emergent commitment to service to humanity is explored in Beckerlegge, 'Swami Vivekananda's Response to the Immorality of Modern Famine', in R.K. Das Gupta (ed.), *Swami Vivekananda: Hundred years Since Chicago—A Commemorative Volume,* Calcutta, 1994.

14. For example, Akhandananda, *From Holy Wanderings . . .,* p. 20.

15. *HRMM,* p. 87.

16. For example, *The Complete Works of Swami Vivekananda* (8 vols), Mayavati Memorial edn, Calcutta, 1973 (hereafter *CWSV*), vol. VI, pp. 224ff, 234f.

17. See R.B. Williams, *A New Face of Hinduism—The Swaminarayan Religion,* Cambridge, 1984, pp. 17f, 135f.

18. Ibid., p. 17.

19. This observation about the probable origins of the form of seva within the Swaminarayan satsanga may be contrasted with the practice fostered in the Arya Samaj. The Arya Samaj opened its first centre of service in 1877, the Ferozepore Orphanage. It is evident, however, that this example of Hindu orphan care and later provision of famine relief was stimulated at least in part by Christian philanthropic activity, and the fear that Christian missionaries were using disasters as opportunities to gather Hindu orphans as potential converts. See K.W. Jones, *Arya Dharma—Hindu Consciousness in 19th-century Punjab,* Berkeley: University of California Press, 1976, pp. 235ff.

20. Akhandananda, *From Holy Wanderings . . .,* p. 42.

21. Ibid.

22. Ibid., p. 55; cf. pp. 55–8.

23. Ibid., p. 55.

24. Ibid., p. 58.

25. Ibid., p. 58f, fn.

26. Ibid., p. ix; cf *Srimad Bhagavatam* (trans. A.C. Bhaktivedanta Swami Prabhupada), New York, 1977, p. 128 (9(21)12).

27. Ibid., p. 58f.

28. *HRMM,* p. 87.

29. Akhandananda, *From Holy Wanderings* . . ., p. 61.

30. *The Life of Swami Vivekananda*, by his Eastern and Western Disciples, Calcutta, 1779, vol. I, pp. 387f.

31. Swami Nikhilananda, *Vivekananda: A Biography*, Calcutta, 1971, p. 106.

32. *HRMM*, p. 57; cf. *The Life of Swami Vivekananda*, vol. I, p. 388.

33. *HRMM*, p. 57.

34. *The Life of Swami Vivekananda*, vol. I, p. 304; *CWSV*, VIII, p. 287.

35. *HRMM*, p. 87.

36. Ibid., p. 86.

37. Ibid., p. 87.

38. Akhandananda, *From Holy Wanderings* . . ., p. 61.

39. Ibid., p. 61f.

40. Ibid., p. 62.

41. Ibid.

42. Swami Nirmayananda, *The Call of the Spirit* (Conversations with Swami Akhandananda, a Direct Disciple of Sri Ramakrishna, as recorded by Swami Nirmayananda), Mylapore, Madras, 1984, p. 72.

43. Akhandananda, *From Holy Wanderings* . . ., p. 63.

44. *CWSV*, VI, p. 287f.

45. Ibid.

46. Akhandananda, *From Holy Wanderings* . . ., p. 70.

47. *CWSV*, VI, pp. 289–95.

48. For example, *CWSV*, III, pp. 465f.

49. For example, *CWSV*, V, p.15.

50. *CWSV*, VI, p. 254.

51. *CWSV*, VII, p. 467.

52. *CWSV*, VIII, p. 304.

53. M.L. Burke, *Swami Vivekananda in America: New Discoveries*, Calcutta, 1958, pp. 407f.

54. Akhandananda, *From Holy Wanderings* . . ., p. 81.

55. Ibid., p. 41.

56. *HRMM*, p. 96.

57. Ibid.

58. Ibid., p. 97.

59. Ibid., p. 96; Akhandananda, *From Holy Wanderings* . . ., p. 155f.

60. *CWSV*, VI, p. 388.

61. For example, *CWSV*, VIII, p. 399.

62. *HRMM*, p. 97.

63. For details of Akhandananda's life, I have relied upon Swami Annadananda, *Swami Akhandananda*, Calcutta, 1993, and Swami Gambhirananda (ed.), *The Apostles of Shri Ramakrishna*, Calcutta, 1972 (2nd imp).

64. *CWSV*, VII, p. 507.

65. A.P. Sen, *Hindu Revivalism in Bengal 1872–1905*, Delhi, 1993. p. 342.

66. Ibid., pp. 330ff.

67. See, for example, Dhar, *Vedanta and the Bengal Renaissance*, p. 147. Contributors to Anon *Swami Vivekananda Studies in Soviet Union*, Calcutta, 1987, also uniformly draw attention to the inherent limitations of Vivekananda's strategies.

68. A.P Sen, *Hindu Revivalism in Bengal*, p. 329.

69. I explore these points at length in my thesis; see note 3 above.

70. The research for this chapter was supported by a grant in 1995 from the Faculty of Arts, The Open University, UK, which enabled the writer to use the library at the Ramakrishna Mission Institute of Culture, Calcutta, and to visit the ashrama founded by Swami Akhandananda at Sargacchi.

The Ramakrishna Mission:
Its Female Aspect

HILTRUD RÜSTAU

ALL THE IMPORTANT RELIGIOUS movements which came into being in India in the late nineteenth century had certain features in common: an attempt to bring traditional values in line with changed conditions; a partial programme for social reform and a distinctive quest, compared to religious movements at other times and elsewhere, for national renewal. Not only did they draft proposals for educational reform and health-care, they founded their own schools and hospitals. They actively encouraged the industrial development of their country by setting up professional training centres, organizing exhibitions (*melas*), etc. Within this complex an improvement in the condition of women became a central part of their endeavours. No effort to bring about social change and religious reform could hope to succeed if women were excluded. But women were not merely to be the passive recipients of such an attempt at reform; they became its active participants. Their own history they were to take into their own hands.

WOMEN FROM THE WEST

Looking at the history of some of the most important religious movements at the end of the last century in South Asia, one is struck by the role European and American women played in their origin and development. Madame Helena Petrovna Blavatsky, together with Colonel Henry Steel Olcott, was to found the Theosophical Society, and Annie Besant, an even more significant figure in this context, was to turn theosophy into an Indian movement. It was the theosophy of Blavatsky and Olcott that attracted the sixteen-year-old David Hewavitarana (Hewavitharne) renamed Anagarika: in 1891 he was to be the founder of the Mahabodhi

Society. Blavatsky took him to Madras. Later, in 1893, Annie Besant introduced him to society in Britain and Chicago. But an increasing tendency in theosophy towards the mystical element in Hinduism led to a certain distancing and in 1904 the friendship was broken off.

The history of the Mahabodhi Society is, however, unthinkable without another woman. Whenever Anagarika Dharmapala was in financial trouble in his endeavour to revive Buddhist traditions, it was Mary Elizabeth Foster who gave him support. The America-born Foster, living in Hawaii, first met Dharmapala in the harbour of Honolulu on board the ship in which he returned from the Parliament of Religions in Chicago. She asked his advice in overcoming certain psychological problems. Thereafter, she became, in addition to Dharmapala's own father, the main economic resource for subsidizing his projects: educational institutions in Sarnath, the construction of Viharas in Calcutta and Sarnath and of a *dharmaśālā* in Bodh Gaya, the maintenance of the Buddhist Mission in London and the establishment of health centres and schools in India and Ceylon. Foster supported the Mahabodhi Society generously even after her death with a magnanimous endowment, deeply impressed as she was by the personality of Dharmapala and his self-sacrificing dedication to the resurrection of Buddhism. She paid deep respect to Buddhism, though nothing is known of how far she identified herself with the world-view which Dharmapala was representing, that is, whether she became a Buddhist herself.

Most striking is the active support of an Indian religious movement, the activities of Swami Vivekananda and the Ramakrishna Math and Mission which he founded in 1897, by European and American women. This is not to discount the valuable support American and English men gave to Vivekananda's work. There was, for example, J.H. Sevier, former Captain of the British Army, who first met Vivekananda in 1896 and became his follower together with his wife. There was also J.J. Goodwin, the English stenographer, who was engaged by Vivekananda's followers at the end of 1895 in New York to transcribe his lectures, important for their later publication. E.T. Sturdy, initially a follower of theosophy, who had heard of Ramakrishna and Vivekananda whilst in India, became Vivekananda's host in London in 1895 and 1896. He organized his lectures and gave important support to Vivekananda by preparing the publication of his works; it was he who started building up the London Vedanta Centre.

Just the same, women played a far more decisive role than men in the origin and development of the Ramakrishna Mission, either by giving generous financial support, or by becoming devotees of Vivekananda, or by collecting Vivekananda's sayings and speeches and by spreading his teachings in the western world, or by building up organizations in the West which, for their part, could give support to the Indian *Math* and Mission both financially and morally.

These women mainly came from two types of social background. One type came from high society, closely linked with intellectually and socially leading circles, wealthy, well educated, broad-minded, independent and with a humanistic outlook. The other type were of lower middle-class extraction, some of them unmarried teachers—a profession that allowed women from educated but not well off middle-class families to a living without compromising their gentility. Not satisfied with the narrow outlook in Christian teachings with regard to new findings in science and technology, all of them took a strong interest in anything new regarding religious and philosophical questions. Women from the second group also became followers of the Vedanta world-view and even *sannyāsinī*s of the Ramakrishna movement.

Some of the more important western women behind Swami Vivekananda will be mentioned here in chronological order. We start with Kate Sanborn, writer, acquainted with leading lights of the New York high society. Vivekananda first met her in the observation car of the Canadian Pacific train. He had taken the train after disembarking at Vancouver, on way to the Chicago World Parliament of Religions. In Kate Sanborn's house he met many influential people with whose help he could start lecturing. Most important of all, he was introduced to Dr Wright, Professor of Greek at Harvard, who acquired for him the status as official delegate to the Parliament.

Ellen Hale, another mentor, was a well-to-do Chicago matron who guided Vivekananda to the Parliament office after he had lost his way and gave him food, shelter and affection.[1] Neither Kate Sanborn nor the Hale family ever became disciples of Vivekananda, but without their support he would never have been able to participate in the Parliament, nor carry out his lecture programme in his first year in the USA.

Mrs John J. Bagley, widow of the late Governor of Michigan and one of the most influential women of Detroit, met Vivekananda at Chicago where she was one of the elected women managers at the World's Fair. Through her Vivekananda received many invitations to speak at women's meetings, which enabled him to acquire a far-reaching and influential public in USA. Though Mrs Bagley was spiritually inclined, she did not become a Vedantin.

Christine Greenstidel, who as Sister Christine became one of Vivekananda's closest disciples, first met him in 1894, while working as a teacher.

In 1902 she visited India to support Sister Nivedita in her educational work in Calcutta. Sara Ellen Waldo, called Haridasi (servant of God), dedicated her life to the Ramakrishna-Vivekananda movement but without visiting India. A distant relative of Ralph Waldo Emerson, she attended Vivekananda's lectures at the Brooklyn Ethical society in 1894 and was in charge of organizing his classes in the Vedanta Society's early activities in New York. Her dedication resulted in the book *Inspired Talks* and other publications of Vivekananda's lectures based on her notes. She also edited *Jñāna Yoga*.

Sara Bull, the wealthy widow of a famous Norwegian violinist, of Cambridge, Massachusetts, was another close follower of the Vedanta movement. She introduced Vivekananda to important people, helped him financially, and protected him from unfriendly attacks. Vivekananda, who called her Dhira Mata (the steady mother), had often been her guest, and placed the newly developed Vedanta Societies in the USA in her charge. In 1898 Sara Bull visited India, where she supported Nivedita's educational work with donations. She was 'a lavish giver'[2] who spent a great deal of money in publishing Vivekananda's works, and also purchased landed property for the Belur Math. She was, in addition, an effective organizer of the Vedanta movement, besides being a mediator, always at hand in case of need. Whereas Sara Ellen Waldo was acquainted with the Transcendental School of Philosophy, Sara Bull was already acquainted with the *Bhagavadgītā* before she met Swami Vivekananda. Though she took no vows, she called herself a servant of Ramakrishna and Vivekananda. Sarah Farmer, a friend of Sara Bull, and likewise well acquainted with the intellectual elite in USA of those days, organized the Greenacre Summer Camp which in 1894 did much to enhance Vivekananda's popularity in the USA.

Josephine MacLeod always described herself as a friend of Vivekananda, rather than his disciple. She belonged to the upper stratum of society and was closely linked not only to the American cultural and political elite but also European. She first met Vivekananda in 1895. Josephine remained a spinster and dedicated her life to spreading Vivekananda's message. Romain Rolland acquired firsthand knowledge of Vivekananda and Ramakrishna through her. Josephine had a long talk with him in French so that Rolland became interested and later put his sister to work translating Vivekananda's published works. His books on Ramakrishna and Vivekananda through their translation into many languages, exercised a great influence all over the world. Josephine arranged for and financed the translation and publication of Vivekananda's works into German and French. She donated the money for establishing the Bengali magazine *Udbodhan* and for many other things in the history of the Ramakrishna Math and Mission. Her sister Betty Leggett, very much interested in Vivekananda and the Ramakrishna movement, more or less confined her interest to giving donations. Josephine, on the other hand, was always in close touch with everything going on in Belur and abroad. She used her local prestige more than once in negotiations with the British government in India when the Ramakrishna Math was suspected of connections with seditious activities.

Charlotte Sevier met Vivekananda in 1896. After her husband's death she undertook the publication of the *Prabuddha Bharata* in Almora. Henrietta Müller, a follower of the Theosophical Society, was close to his movement for a certain time, though she never lost touch with the Theosophical Society. She partly financed the purchase of land for the Belur Math.

SISTER NIVEDITA

Most outstanding among the women from the West behind Vivekananda was Margaret Elizabeth Noble, better known as Sister Nivedita, whom Vivekananda called his spiritual daughter. She first met Vivekananda in 1895 in London and again attended his lecture course the following year. Margaret was of Irish origin, daughter of a clergyman and from a family closely linked with the Irish national movement. Her father having died early, the family lived in poverty. Margaret became a teacher, was much interested in the educational theories and in short became a recognized member of London intellectual circles. Though brought up as a pious Christian, in the light of the new scientific discoveries Margaret became dissatisfied with Christianity and was searching for philosophical answers to her questions. She was open minded but critical when she first listened to Vivekananda's lectures in 1895.

When Vivekananda returned to London for another lecture course in 1896 she attended all his lectures and became his follower. One year later Vivekananda concurred with her wish to visit India. Margaret arrived in Calcutta in January 1898. For more than four and a half years Nivedita was in close contact with Vivekananda. Though 'taken in bulk, they would not perhaps make two years in all,'[3] as she herself remarked, it was most probably the closest and most intense contact which any of Vivekananda's disciples had with him in the years after 1893. As an experienced and theoretically well-versed educationist, she was Vivekananda's choice to take over a pressing task: education of the masses, and especially the education of women. Since he believed that to fulfil this task any foreigner would have to become an Indian,[4] he took much pains to teach Margaret and to impart to her a knowledge of India, its history, philosophy, religion; in short, to give her the whole cultural background of her adopted land. He also acquainted her with the customs, manners, traditions, religious rituals, etc. of the common people, together with village life and questions of agriculture. Nivedita was taught Bengali and Sanskrit by a young brother monk of Vivekananda.

This process of 'Hinduization' or 'Indianization' was completed by Vivekananda's systematic endeavour to have her accepted by orthodox Indian society. Following her arrival, she stayed for one week in the house of Sarada Devi, widow of Ramakrishna, a Brahmin, and shared the food with the Brahmin women there.

Nivedita took pains to get a good understanding of Vivekananda's teachings. She confessed that she started to learn the worship of Kali in the same manner as learning a foreign language.[5] This enabled her in her first year in India to lecture on Kali worship. She stressed the point that the divine in Kali, both in its beneficent and terrifying aspects, was to be adored.[6]

Sister Nivedita's importance in spreading Vivekananda's thought and strengthening the Ramakrishna movement can hardly be overestimated. With her western cultural background, her ardent training in and study of Indian culture and her intimacy with Vivekananda, she gave lucid expression to his teachings (e.g. the concept of *māyā*, the dialectics of unity and diversity in Brahman and the personal concept of god and his *śakti*). She convincingly argued for the central importance of Vivekananda's appearance at the Parliament of Religions in Chicago, which in turn became of decisive effect on the development of Hinduism. Her book, *The Master as I Saw Him*, seems to have been the first attempt at writing Vivekananda's biography. Nivedita described his life and teachings in the same way as her own understanding had grown, making it easy for the readers to follow her train of thought even to the highest philosophical level.

Nivedita looked upon herself as a transmitter of Vivekananda's thoughts.[7] She explained his aim of making Hinduism assertive by means of linking traditional values with new ones. She visualized Vivekananda's aim as two-faceted: to disseminate the teachings of Ramakrishna and to strengthen his mother country. She identified herself with his country, speaking of Indians as 'we, 'us' and 'ourselves'.[8]

Immediately after her arrival in India Nivedita opened a school in Calcutta where girls and women could get an education as well as training in handicraft, housekeeping and other skills. This school still exists, though with a profile somewhat altered over time.

Two months after her arrival, on 25 March 1898 she was initiated into *brahmācārya* by Vivekananda and given the name 'Nivedita', the dedicated one. This dedication was strikingly demonstrated when a plague epidemic broke out and Nivedita did her utmost to improve the hygienic conditions and to help the sick and dying. She actively participated in all the early philanthropic actions of the newly founded Ramakrishna Mission in the case of epidemics, famines, and floods.

Besides her educational work and her lecture tours in India and abroad, Nivedita produced much published work. Two-thirds of the bulk of this was meant for the Indian public, to disseminate Vivekananda's thoughts, at giving information on Ramakrishna and Vivekananda in general and making Indians aware of their cultural heritage and historical development. Some other publications were written to provide information on Indian life and culture to people in the United States and Britain in order to attract donations for her educational programmes or to satisfy demands for certain topics. These publications were well accepted by some (Rudyard Kipling among them). Some others, including members of Ramabai Clubs in the USA, rejected them vehemently. Nivedita's writings have yet to be comprehensively analysed. Besides her contribution to the development of modern Indian aesthetics (especially painting) her thoughts on the civic ideal and the philosophy of history influenced modern Indian philosophy.

During Vivekananda's lifetime itself Nivedita started political activities, which became the seed of future conflict between her and the Ramakrishna movement. After Vivekananda's death on 4 July 1902 Nivedita was summoned by the president of the Ramakrishna Math on 10 July and, following a long talk with the Swamis Brahmananda (the President) and Saradananda she declared in public that she had dissolved all official bonds with the Ramakrishna Mission. Henceforth she called herself 'Nivedita of Ramakrishna-Vivekananda'.[9] Between 1902 and 1904 she travelled throughout India lecturing on Ramakrishna and Vivekananda as well as on different aspects of Indian culture. The stress of all her lectures was on strengthening national self-confidence so as to enable India to throw off foreign rule.

In 1902 Nivedita met Sri Aurobindo at Baroda, and in 1903 became a member of the executive committee of the Revolutionary Society in Calcutta. For this action of hers the newspaper *The Englishman* called her a traitor to the British nation.[10]

In 1898, whilst journeying with Vivekananda to the north, Nivedita wrote to her friends in England complaining of surveillance by the police. Several times later she feared imprisonment. This was not unjustified. Vivekananda's writings were well accepted by the young revolutionaries of those days and often his books were discovered in their residences during a search by the police. Vivekananda's younger brother, Bhupendranath, participated actively in the revolutionary movement, and Nivedita was in close contact with him. She also had close contact with Vivekananda's mother until her death.

Nivedita participated in 1905 in the meeting of the India's National Congress at Varanasi, where she emphatically, urged the participants not to allow a split in the Congress. She expressed her firm belief in the unity and coming national rebirth of India.

Nivedita was well acquainted with many leading lights of India's political and cultural life. Rabindranath Tagore, who wrote the introduction to her book *The Web of Indian Life*, written at the suggestion of R.C. Dutt, was much interested in her educational work, and he wrote an emotional obituary on Nivedita. It is said that his novel *Gora* was modelled on Nivedita.[11] Rabindranath Tagore was all admiration for what she did for Swami Vivekananda.[12] Besides being a friend of G.K. Gokhale and B.C. Pal, she was personally acquainted with Ramsay MacDonald, the British Labour leader, and the Russian anarchist Peter Kropotkin.

THE MONK AND THE WOMEN

Vivekananda's appeal to women for cooperation in his cause was not confined to women from the West. He proposed to Sarala Ghosal (Sarala Devi), a niece of Rabindranath Tagore, for example, that she should accompany him to the West in 1899 and teach Vedanta there. Sarala, editor of the Bengali monthly *Bharati*, wrote an editorial article on Swami Vivekananda after his return from America. They exchanged letters, in one of which Vivekananda stressed the need for the spread of education. The funds for this he expected from the West. In exchange, he said, Indian spirituality needed to be taught there by women like herself who possessed spirit, culture and knowledge of Vedanta.[13] Swami Vivekananda admired her education as being perfect, and said that every girl in India should have an education like hers.[14] Sarala Devi was an active and convinced member of the Brahmo Samaj, which probably was the reason why she did not accept his proposal though she was inclined to a life of renunciation. Sarala Devi visited Belur in 1898, and acted as the intermediary in negotiations between the Brahmo leaders and Vivekananda.

But on behalf of the Tagore family she asked him in a letter to give up the cult of Ramakrishna as a condition for their support and cooperation.[15]

One reason why so many western women were attracted to Vivekananda may be that women's education there had already reached a reasonable level, besides the increase in the movement for the equality of women. Women of the upper and middle classes had already gained some independence. As Christianity could not cope with modern science they were looking for new thoughts. They had already acquired some knowledge of ideas developed in the East, through, for example Arnold's *New Light on Asia*. Followers of the Brahmo Samaj had been lecturing in the United States and Britain; the Theosophical Movement had aroused some interest. News of the Parliament of Religions had given an impetus to this. But the Christian missionaries and the Ramabai Clubs, with their focus on the negative aspects of the Hindu way of life had stirred curiosity. And last but not least Vivekananda was a handsome young man, a brilliant orator with an excellent command of English and able convincingly to explain his world-view. His spirituality, his love for India and his encyclopaedic knowledge enabled him to participate in any discussion and made him an interesting lecturer as well as a welcome guest in many intellectual circles.

Vivekananda, on his part was a *sannyāsin*, a monk, whom Ramakrishna, his teacher, had exhorted to avoid money and women. But that did not preclude women as his followers and disciples. His relationship with them is indicated by the names he called them: mother, sister, daughter. Mainly it was the 'mother' he used to see in any female person, according to the Hindu tradition.

Different reasons may be given why Vivekananda did not differentiate between the sexes among his disciples and got along quite well with his female disciples. To begin with, Vivekananda was highly interested in women's education and their advance. He believed that the precondition for regaining India's lost greatness was to improve the condition of the common masses which, according to him, could be attained only by education, especially of women: education would give them the means to improve their condition without having to depend on others.

There are several reasons why Vivekananda was sensitive to the promotion of women's lot. First, there are the facts of his personal life. One of his uncles was a member of Bamabodhini Society, a society for the advancement of women. As early as 1856 another published a booklet, *On the Education of Hindu Females—How Best Achieved under the Present Circumstances of Hindu Society*.[16] The women of his family were well educated, and he was proud of his sisters. Therefore he suffered greatly when his favourite sister committed suicide in 1890. She was married as a child into an orthodox family and could not face up to the problems that became her lot.[17] Also, during his wanderings throughout India Vivekananda got a deep insight into the hard life of its womenfolk.

We may also recall that in 1855 the Kali Temple in Dakshineswar was built by a woman, Rani Rashmani, who had a deep understanding of Ramakrishna's spirituality and god-intoxication. Ramakrishna was not constrained by the duties of a temple priest but could become the focus of his devotees.

One of Ramakrishna's spiritual teachers was Bhairavi Brahmani, a *śakta sannyāsinī* with whom he practised *dakṣinācāra*, right-handed Tantrism for two years (1861–3), and, though he stressed the need to avoid any attachment to money and women, he had gathered a circle of women devotees and disciples around him in the centre of which was Sarada Devi, his wife, who was to play a prominent role in the origin and development of the Ramakrishna Mission. Before Vivekananda decided to travel West and participate in the Parliament of Religions, he asked his guru's widow for advice and blessings. In a letter written in Chicago he proposed to his gurubhais that first of all they should establish a women's math with Sarada Devi. When in 1898 he travelled to Kashmir with some of his western women devotees, he tried to shape this project. The Maharaja was ready to donate some land for the construction of a women's math together with a Sanskrit college. But the British Resident repeatedly rejected this project, so that finally it had to be given up.[18]

Finally, we need to take note of the belief in the divine as virginal mother, deep rooted in Bengal. Vivekananda once remarked to Sister Nivedita: 'I cannot but believe that there is somewhere a great power that thinks of Herself as feminine, and called Kali, and mother. . . . And I believe in Brahman too. . . .'[19] Time and again we meet this adoration of Kali in Vivekananda's writings, and especially in his poems it had a beautiful touch.[20]

SARADA DEVI

Today three pictures are at the centre of veneration at the Ramakrishna Mission, representing Ramakrishna, Sarada Devi and Vivekananda. This was not always so. In the report of the first convention of the Ramakrishna Mission held in April 1926, we read that in the shrine of the *pandal* where the convention took place the pictures of Ramakrishna, Brahmananda (the first President of the Ramakrishna Mission) and Vivekananda were to be seen. The importance of Sarada Devi gained greater weight after her birth centenary celebration in 1953.

In scholarly analyses of the Ramakrishna Mission not much attention has been paid to Sarada Devi, though many publications on her exist in India. Between 1948 and 1954 a series of editorials were published in *Vedanta Kesari* and after 1953 some books on her were published in Bengali and English. *Holy Mother Sri Sarada Devi* by Swami Gambhirananda is a detailed biography.[21]

Sarada was born in 1853 in a poor Brahmin family. Her father was a farmer. The goddess Jagaddhatri, being very close to Simhavahini and incorporating features of Durga and Sarasvati, was her mother's favourite deity, and Sarada Devi worshipped her according to custom.[22] At the age of five Sarada Devi was married to the twenty-three-year old Gadadhar Chattopadhyaya (Ramakrishna). The marriage was never consummated. Between 1872 and 1886 when Ramakrishna died, she lived, except for some short breaks, at Dakshineswar. A typical rustic girl, she was used to hard work. In her mother-in-law's house she learned to read, but until her later days, she was most probably unable to write. She was well acquainted with the Hindu myths and religious concepts and liked to attend *yātrās*.

Sarada Devi lived a secluded life at Dakshineswar. She cooked for Ramakrishna and looked after him and his devotees. He trained her to be his first disciple. Other devotees followed three years later (1875), when the first devotees of Keshab Chandra Sen came to Ramakrishna; from 1880 young educated boys from Calcutta also became his disciples.

After Ramakrishna's death Sarada Devi lived either in Kamarpukur, his native village, or in Jayrambati, her own, or in Calcutta, in close contact with Ramakrishna's disciples or elsewhere on pilgrimage. For some time after Ramakrishna's death she suffered from extreme poverty. Later on the Swamis and devotees took care of her. Soon she also had her own devotees and started to give initiation and was venerated by the village people. After a poor and simple life dedicated to the service of others she died in Calcutta in 1920.

Like Ramakrishna, Sarada Devi also was a bundle of contradictions: she was a married sannyāsinī, and as a widow she led a householder's life. As a sannyasini she had to be unattached to any worldly affair, but out of love she suffered greatly when others suffered. She gave *darśan* and initiation and possibly also *sannyāsa mantras*, but simultaneously, she had to tackle many problems connected with her relatives for whom she always felt responsible. She always moved around with an entourage.

She did not take to monastic life and did not found any order of nuns, and 'it is not known whether the Holy Mother ever received *sannyāsa* in the traditional way.'[23]

Sarada Devi encouraged members of the Ramakrishna Mission to engage in social service. There was a discussion among Ramakrishna's disciples whether social service should be done only after one had meditated and achieved realization. She made it clear that 'There is no greater Dharma than the service of the needy.'[24] She called the Sevashrama in Varanasi the work of Ramakrishna, who himself was present in the social service undertaken there, as she said, thus interpreting Ramakrishna's teachings definitely in favour of social service.[25]

She was hardly concerned about caste notions of physical purity. Though she did not speak against the caste system she gave initiation to people from all strata of society. One of her devotees was a Muslim dacoit.[26] She said, 'As you go on practising spiritual disciplines, you will find that He who is within me, He who is within you, is also within the carrier, the cobbler and the pariah.'[27] Since the Divine is immanent in everybody differences of caste or creed were not important. In a very unorthodox way she gave food offerings made to Ramakrishna to visitors with the remark that the Lord is within everybody and it did not matter who got the offering.[28] Her maternal feeling for everybody and her compassion led her to wish for the end of British rule in India. This she recognized as the main source of the suffering and sorrows of the people in her environment. By her practical understanding of the Advaitic point of view she was able to lay stress on the unity of the world: 'Learn to make the whole world your own. No one is a stranger . . . the whole world is your own', she said a few days before she died.[29]

Sarada Devi was all praise for Sister Nivedita's educational activities and was in close contact with the Nivedita Girls School. She stressed the necessity of education for girls, for self-development and to 'be able to help others.'[30]

Sarada Devi was entirely unassuming, living a retired life. Not much was published on her before her birth centenary. 'This is so because one does not easily dare write about her, her personality is so overpowering', as a former head of the Vedanta Society in New York explained.[31] Or, as a former President put it: '. . . when we were young people in the Order we never spoke publicly about the Holy Mother. . . . We wanted to keep her away from public gaze thinking that the public would not understand her.'[32]

The members of the Ramakrishna movement have, however, always stressed her importance for the movement.[33] She encouraged the

Ramakrishna Math: she had seen in Gaya the *āśram* of the *daśanāmi* sannyāsins and she thought of Ramakrishna's disciples who had no place to stay. She stated her opinion that whilst begging and wandering *sādhus* were numerous in India, there was a demand for sannyāsins who, in connection with meditation and *japa*, could preach and teach. She expressed her wish that Ramakrishna's disciples should live together without want for simple food, where the afflicted could come for support. With her motherly love she welded Ramakrishna's disciples together into a permanent organization. From 1890 Sarada Devi's role as a spiritual guide began increasingly to be recognized by the disciples. Though she never became a member of the math, monastic as well as lay members looked to her for guidance. She did not confer formal *sannyāsa* but gave the monastic garb to many.

ŚAKTI, THE FEMALE ENERGY

Wives had considerable importance in the life of gurus in ancient India. Sarada Devi was venerated while Ramakrishna lived, and even more so after his death.[34] Ramakrishna, we are told, was convinced of her divinity. All the twelve presidents of the Ramakrishna Mission (except the fifth, who died shortly after his election), stated explicitly that they accepted Sarada Devi as an avatāra alongside Ramakrishna. Whereas the wives of earlier divine incarnations did not actively participate in the divine mission of their husbands, the Holy Mother completed her husband's work after his death, propounding his message in a feminine body. Furthermore, it is stressed that since half of mankind comprises women, the divine appeared in a feminine body in order to be easily understood by women.

Sarada Devi was cosmic energy, śakti or māyā incarnate.[35] Brahmananda, the first President of the Ramakrishna Mission, called her Mahamaya, the divine mother who embodied herself to liberate all souls and awaken the entire womanhood of the world.[36] Vivekananda wrote: 'Mother has been born to revive that wonderful Shakti in India. . . .'[37] Ramakrishna saw her as both the all-embracing Mother Kali and also the Śakti of the tantric concept, according to which she is linked with Śiva or the primary deity on an equal footing. He also said: 'She is Sarada, Sarasvati; she has come to impart knowledge . . . .'[38]

For Ramakrishna, following a beatific vision of Kali in his early years as temple priest, she had become the Mother of the universe.[39] Though he realized god in various other forms this vision of Kali was permanently etched on his consciousness. On account of this, his world-view became a new synthesis of the tantric Kali cult, the philosophic Advaita Vedanta and the Bhakti of the Gaudiya Vaishnavas. For Ramakrishna Kali is everything—she has every attribute, bad as well as good, who is at the same time nothing but pure love. His relationship with Kali is determined by the Bhakti approach to god which has at least since the time of Chaitanya a strong footing in Bengal. It is a monistic world-view, identifying Kali with Brahman or *ātman*. Our material world is understood as non-negatively conceived māyā, because Kali is seen simultaneously as the energetic or immaterial Brahman and the material māyā. By this the Advaitic monistic view via the tantric world-view was combined with devotional Bhakti religion and took on a positive content. Śakti, the mother of the universe, was 'the inscrutable power of the transcendent Brahman, making possible Its immanence in the universe, even though It is one without a second and is devoid of any point of contact with anything . . .', a view of practical importance for 'the workaday life cannot be built upon a purely transcendental conception; and for emancipated souls too, a positive relationship with the immanent aspect of the Deity becomes a logical desideratum', as Swami Gambhirananda puts it.[40]

God, according to the tantric view, can work only with the help of his śakti, i.e. in the unity of *īśvara* and maya or *puruṣa* and *prakṛti* or Śiva and Durga/Kali. Following this understanding, Ramakrishna and Sarada Devi are both looked on as manifestations of the same divine energy which is behind the phenomenal world. From the empirical point of view Śiva and Śakti create the universe, preserve it and destroy it, time and again. From the transcendental point of view, Brahman is the only reality. According to this understanding the godhead is the efficient as well as the material cause of the universe. Śakti, the female element who projects the universe, is inseparable from the divine of which she is the earthly symbol as well as identical with it. According to Swami Nikhilananda this is the reason why every woman is entitled to a man's reverence.[41] As Lynn Gatwood has rightly put it, Kali, in the eyes of Ramakrishna, is independent, self-willed, though thought of as married. Not being dominated by her husband, the female principle is therefore elevated over the male principle.[42]

At least since 1872 Ramakrishna identified Sarada Devi with the Mother goddess, when he formally worshipped her as the Mother of the Universe in the form of Shodashi. It is not unknown in the history of Bengal to recognize the divine in one's own wife: Shri Chaitanya had installed the image of his own wife, Vishnupriya, in a shrine.

Shodasi is one of the ten Mahavidyas which, according to Hindu mythology, came into being when Śakti felt greatly insulted because her father did not invite her husband Śiva to attend his great sacrifice. She intended to disrupt the sacrifice and, when Śiva stopped her, she assumed these ten horrific forms. According to other interpretations the ten Mahavidyas, understood as personifications of Brahman's śakti, lead to the realization of Brahman, so that by worshipping them it is easier to reach the supreme wisdom. Shodasi, which means sixteen, stands for a girl of sixteen, with red complexion. She is a form of Kali.

As Ramakrishna under the guidance of the sannyāsin Tota Puri embraced monastic life he has to be looked upon as belonging to the Puri Order of the *daśanāmis*, where the deity is Sarada (the presiding deity of Sringeri with a strong tantric inclination) or Sarasvati or—as one of the Mahavidyas—Shodasi, Shri Vidya. From the point of tantric schools Shodashi comprehends Sarasvati (knowledge), Durga (action) and Kali (will).

Sri Ramakrishna as well as Sarada Devi declared to a few disciples that they were incarnations of the divine. Sarada Devi said about herself: '. . . the Master [Ramakrishna] used to see the Divine in every one. He left me behind this time for teaching the motherhood of God to humanity.'[43]

Both Ramakrishna and Sarada Devi looked upon themselves as manifestations of the same divine energy which is behind the phenomenal world—being one in two and two in one. Ramakrishna was to Sarada Devi the embodiment of all gods and goddesses, dwelling also in all the creatures and being purusa and prakrti, father as well as mother. 'If you think on him you have thought of all', she said.[44] She also identified herself with Ramakrishna: 'He who is the Master, am I',[45] having by this in mind the inseparable unity of Śiva and his Śakti. But strangely, she also called Ramakrisna 'Mother Kali' after his death: 'Mother Kali, dear, for what fault of mine have you left me?'[46]

A MATH FOR THE WOMEN

Though Swami Vivekananda already in 1894 wrote to his gurubhais in India: '. . . it is her [Sarada Devi's] Math that I want first'[47] and in the Rules of the Belur Math from 1897 it was said: 'For women too there will be started a similar Math',[48] it was only sixty years after Vivekananda's first proposal that the Sarada Math was founded on 2 December 1954. The demand for a women's math arose among educated girls from families devoted to the Ramakrishna Mission. Seeds for the math were already laid in 1931, when in the small Bengali town of Taki (24 Parganas) a Ramakrishna ashram was started where young women could lead a religious life. In 1938 this ashram was sanctioned by the Ramakrishna

Mission. In 1945 the Sarada Mahila Ashram was formed in Calcutta where female students lived together. At a Monks' Conference in 1946 the president of the Ramakrishna Mission said:

The problem of women workers has not received our due attention so long. They have not been given any appreciable scope for leading a monastic life in the Sangha as yet. There are hundreds who are ready to renounce the world and to consecrate their lives to the cause. Their demand is growing more and more. Since the institutions for such women are slowly springing up, though with little or no resources, it is high time that the case of women who earnestly desire to dedicate their lives to the Sangha should receive your careful and sympathetic consideration.[49]

One girl, encouraged by this speech, wrote an article on 'The Hindu Women's Right to Sannyasa', published in the *Udbodhan*, the Bengali magazine of the Ramakrishna Mission. In 1950 the members of the Sarada Mahila Ashram, who had already given free service in different centres of the Ramakrishna Mission, were given the opportunity to join the Ramakrishna Mission as dedicated workers, and, in the same year, a meeting of the workers of the Nivedita Girls' School and the Sarada Ashram took place. The teachers of this school played an important part in the establishment of the math, and the Headmistress of the school later on became its first general secretary. Also in 1950 the Belur Math bought a plot of land on the east bank of the Ganga, which became the site of the women's math. In 1952 the Golden Jubilee of the Nivedita Girls' School was celebrated and the memory of Nivedita and other women was revived. When in December 1953 the celebrations of the birth centenary of Sarada Devi started, brahmacarya had been granted to a group of dedicated women workers of the Ramakrishna Mission. Finally, in December 1954, the Sri Sarada Math was opened by the President of the Ramakrishna Mission and the *brahmacārinīs* ran the Math under the guidance of the trustees of the Belur Math. In December 1958 sannyāsa was given to seven *brahmacārinīs* of the Sarada Math by the President of the Ramakrishna Mission and in 1959, the trustees of the Belur Math handed over full responsibility of administration of the Sarada Math, with independent status, to its sannyāsinī trustees. Sarala Devi (Pravrajika Bharatiprana), a direct disciple and personal attendant of Sarada Devi was appointed president.

Sarala Devi (1894–1973) hailed from a Brahmin family in a Bengali village but grew up in Calcutta where she lived close to the Nivedita Girls' School. She became a student of this school. Hers was a child marriage. When her in-laws came to take her she ran away with the help of Sudhira, an Indian woman teacher of the school. Sarala Devi, who after Sarada Devi's death lived in Varanasi maintained her contact with the Nivedita Girls School.

Sri Sarada Math was 'an institution of Sannyasinis, established to help individuals to work out their own liberation and also to train them to serve the world along the lines laid down by Bhagavan Ramakrishna.'[50] It has branches in eight Indian states and one in Australia. In 1960 the trustees of the math founded the Ramakrishna Sarada Mission with the object 'of carrying on educational, cultural, charitable and similar activities among women and children, looking upon them as veritable manifest- ations of the Divine.'[51] The mission has as its main aims educational work, medical service, rural development, the spread of spiritual ideas and foreign work. It has eleven branches in India. A registered association, it is concerned mainly with welfare activities for women and children, unlike the math which emphasizes the dissemination of the religious teaching of Ramakrishna and Vivekananda by preaching and lecturing. Both institutions are, however, concerned with women and children 'irrespective of caste, creed and nationality'.[52] The governing body of the mission consists of the trustees of the math and the main workers of the mission are sannyāsiñis of the math: In 1963 the Ramakrishna Mission entrusted the Sister Nivedita Girls School to the Ramakrishna Sarada Mission.

The Sri Sarada Math and the Ramakrishna Sarada Mission have opened a new and significant chapter in the complex of new religious movements in South Asia.[53] Among the Vedic *ṛṣi*s there had been women, Gargi and other women in the Upanisadic times, who were able to discuss highly philosophical questions. In the biographies from Sankara to Ramakrishna also we meet with *yoginī*s, sannyāsinīs or *sadhvī*s. They wandered alone belonged to maths or ascetic sects of the different *sampradāya*s, the overwhelming majority of which consisted only of men. As far as we know there did not exist any math or ascetic order exclusively for women. In Buddhism, there are monasteries for nuns but the final say in every religious or worldly affair of importance is with the monks. In contrast, the Sarada Math is independent of the Ramakrishna Math and Mission.

CONCLUSION

In those different religious movements which came into being at the end of the century, in 1980 an Indian woman, Radha Burnier, took office as the seventh International President of the Theosophical Society and was re-elected twice to that office. Obviously, in this society equal chances are given independent of sex.[54]

In the Mahabodhi society the president, the secretary-general and the deputy secretary-general are traditionally from Sri Lanka. Asked about the enrolment of nuns, the residing Bhikkhu at the headquarters of the society in Calcutta, as well as the treasurer, explained that in Theravada Buddhism the tradition of Bhikkhunis had been broken off for a long time. Though there exist in Sri Lanka so-called *daśasīlmātās*, women who had pledged themselves to the ten commands, they were not nuns in the true sense of the term. The Bhikkhu did not exclude the possibility of taking nuns from Korea where the tradition was kept alive, to give again to women the chance to lead a secluded life as Bhikkunis within Theravada Buddhism.[55]

There are three main reasons why the female aspect of the Ramakrishna–Vivekananda movement assumed such importance. First is the distinctiveness of Bengal's development, which does much to explain why a certain independence for women became possible. Second was the role women from the West played in the origin and development of the movement. Last but not least, there was the widespread native belief in 'a great power That thinks Herself as feminine',[56] in the motherhood of the Divine or in the divine energy, śakti. Both the Sarada Math and the Ramakrishna Sarada Mission have to be seen as emerging from an ancient tradition. Facilitating it was the important role played by three personalities: Swami Vivekananda, the liberal minded, highly educated as well as socially and spiritually engaged monk; Sister Nivedita, with her ardent love for India and her educational work; and Sarada Devi, the married sannyāsinī, with her love of the poor and needy.

Notes

1. A loose connection of the Hales with Vivekananda and the movement started by him lasted all their lives. This can be demonstrated by the fact that in 1933 the youngest of the sisters bequeathed $78,500 to the Belur Math.

2. Pravrajika Atmaprana (ed.), *Western Women in the Footsteps of Swami Vivekananda*, New Delhi, 1995, p. 78.

3. Sister Nivedita, *The Complete Works*, vol. 1, Calcutta, 1995, p. 272.

4. Vivekananda was of the opinion that 'if European men or women are to work in India it *must* be under the black man!' (Bhupendranath Datta, *Swami Vivekananda Patriot-Prophet*, Calcutta, 1993, p. 127). Indians themselves had to spread education for in any other way the national culture would be endangered. Education amongst women had to be spread by women and since there was a

lack of educated Indian women Vivekananda thought of 'borrowing women from other nations' (ibid., p. vii), but they had to do it in the Indian way. He demanded of Nivedita to 'Hinduize' her thoughts, and even more, to forget her own past and to become a real *'Hindu brāhmin brahmacārinī'* (ibid., p. 203f). Vivekananda's brother Bhupendranath rightly called him an interpreter of Indian life to Nivedita (ibid., p. 66).

5. Sister Nivedita, *Complete Works*, vol. 1, p. 117.

6. The topic of her very first public lecture in India held shortly after her arrival was 'The influence of the Spiritual Thoughts of India in England'.

7. Sister Nivedita, *Complete Works*, vol. 1, p. 138.

8. Belarani De (ed.), *A Soldier with a Flaming Sword*, Calcutta, 1993, p. 71.

9. In the declaration of aims and objects of the Ramakrishna Mission, adopted on 5 May 1897 it is written: 'The aims and ideals of the Mission being purely spiritual and humanitarian, it shall have no connection with politics.' Swami Gambhirananda, *History of the Ramakrishna Math and Mission*, Calcutta 1983, p. 96. But that did not exclude young men, engaged in the political anarchist movement coming to Sarada Devi, Ramakrishna's widow, from paying their respects and getting initiation. Swami Vivekananda and Sister Nivedita were observed by the police as also at Sarada Devi's house in Jayrambati. See *Sarada Devi the Great Wonder*, Swami Mumukshananda, Calcutta, 1994, p. 55. Swami Shivananda, the second president of the Ramakrishna Mission, encouraged some of his disciples to devote their life to the service of their mother country and to participate in political activities as, for example, in Gandhi's salt *satyagraha*. See *Pravrajika Muktaprana*, Sri Sarada Math, Calcutta, 1994. pp. 6, 9.

10. Bhupendranath Datta, *Swami Vivekananda*, p. 64

11. Ibid., p. 227.

12. See Ketaki Kushari Dyson, *In your Blossoming Flower-Garden: Rabindranath Tagore and Victoria Ocampo*, New Delhi, 1988, p. 342f.

13. Sailendra Nath Dhar, *A Comprehensive Biography of Swami Vivekananda*, vol. 2, Madras, 1976, p. 948.

14. Ibid., p. 1148.

15. Lizell Reymond, *The Dedicated: A Biography of Nivedita*, Madras, 1895, p. 179.

16. Bhupendranath Datta, *Swami Vivekananda*, p. 71.

17. Sister Nivedita, *Complete Works*, vol. 1, p. 61.

18. Ibid., p. 94.

19. Ibid., p. 120.

20. See Swami Vivekananda, *In Search of God and Other Poems*, Mayavati, 1981.

21. Madras, 1955.

22. Jagaddhatri is the Mother of the World, fair and gentle, riding a lion. The tradition of Jagaddhatri *pūjā* continues in the Sarada Math. In 1981 the new temple of the math was consecrated on the day of Jagaddhatri pūjā.

23. *Sarada Devi the Great Wonder*, p. 449.

24. Ibid., p. 102.

25. Swami Gambhirananda, *Holy Mother Sri Sarada Devi*, Madras, 1955 p. 268.

26. Ibid., p. 272.

27. *Sarada Devi the Great Wonder*, p. 457.

28. Ibid., p. 74.

29. Ibid., p. 469f.

30. Swami Gambhirananda, *Holy Mother Sri Sarada Devi*, p. 477.

31. *Sarada Devi the Great Wonder*, p. 157.

32. Ibid., p. 175.

33. Ibid., p. 161.

34. Ibid., p. 127.

35. Cf. the *Gita*: 'Though I am unborn, of changeless nature and Lord of beings, yet subjugating My Prakriti, I come into being by My own Maya'.
Srimad-Bhagvad-Gita iv, 6 trans. by Sri Swami Swrupananda, Almora, 1933, p. 99.

36. *Sarada Devi the Great Wonder*, p. 34.

37. Ibid., p. 33. He wrote in 1894 to his gurubhais: 'You have not yet understood the wonderful significance of Mother's life. . . . Without Shakti (Power) there is no regeneration for the world. Why is it that our country is the weakest and the most backward of all countries?—Because Shakti is held in dishonour there.' Swami Vivekananda, *The Complete Works*, vol. 7, Calcutta, 1990, p. 484.

38. *Sarada Devi the Great Wonder*, p. 137.

39. Later on Ramakrishna took successfully much pains to make his disciple Vivekananda accept this belief in Kali.

40. Swami Gambhirananda, *History of the Ramakrishna Mission*, p. 21.

41. *Sarada Devi the Great Wonder*, p. 192.

42. Lynn E. Gatwood, *Devi and the Spouse Goddess. Women, Sexuality, and Marriage in India*, New Delhi, 1985, p. 172f.

43. *Sarada Devi the Great Wonder*, p. 438.

44. Swami Gambhirananda, *Holy Mother Sri Sarada Devi*, p. 451.

45. Ibid., p. 457.

46. Ibid., p. 452.

47. Swami Vivekananda, *Complete Works*, vol. 7, p. 484.

48. Swami Gambhirananda, *History of the Ramakrishna Mission*, p. 108.

49. *Pravrajika Muktaprana*, p. 13.

50. *Sri Sarada Math and Ramakrishna Sarada Mission*, Calcutta, 1990, p. 2.

51. *The General Report of Sri Sarada Math and the Ramakrishna Sarada Mission*, April 1991–March 1993, p. 6.

52. Ibid., p. 7.

53. The General Reports provide evidence of the extensive social work done by the nuns, the pravrajikas, or brahmacāriṇīs, by the novices and lay devotees.

54. At the time of writing the International Vice-President is also a woman, Mary Anderson.

55. Finally, we might look at the movement started by Sree Narayana Guru

in Kerala with the slogan 'One Caste, One Religion and One God for Men'. The Sree Narayana Dharma Paripalana Yogam (SNDP) was founded in 1903 and the Sree Narayana Dharma Sangham, an order of Sannyasins, in 1928. In December 1967, with the approval of the President of the Sree Narayana Dharma Sangham, the Shivagiri Sree Narayana Dharmasodari Matam was founded in Varkala, '. . . an organization of women founded on the lofty ideals of Sree Narayana Guru who wanted to establish a separate institution for women in this country . . .'. *Thus Spake Sree Narayana Guru*, comp. by Sannyasini Devaki Amma, Varkala, 1972, p. 19. The Matom is a registered association. This I could see from the document shown to me by some women from the governing body of the Matom. The founder of the Matom, Sannyasini Devaki Amma, died some years ago and the Sangham claims the right over the Matom's property. When I visited the Matom in March 1996 it seemed to me that there was little chance of its survival, very much in contrast to the Sarada Math in West Bengal.

56. Sister Nivedita, *Complete Works*, p. 120.

The Arya Samaj and
the Ahmadiyya Movement

'Kindly Elders of the Hindu Biradri': The Ārya Samāj's Struggle for Influence and its Effect on Hindu-Muslim Relations, 1880–1925[1]

HARALD FISCHER-TINÉ

If the Hindus were publicly to disown the followers of Dayananda, the question of the unity between Hindus and Muhammadans would become easy of solution.[2]

THE ĀRYA SAMĀJ, FOUNDED in 1875 by Dayānand Sarasvatī not only was the most influential new religious movement in late-nineteenth-century India, it was probably the most controversial as well. The above excerpt from a north Indian Muslim newspaper in 1910 illustrates that the Hindu reform 'sect' was held responsible by many Muslims for the tensions between India's largest religious communities. Sharing this view, the British administration declared the Samaj a 'seditious body' and followed its activities with suspicion.[3] Most of today's scholars seem to agree and stress the political character of the movement much more than the religious. The Ārya Samāj is generally understood as an ancestor of modern Hindu chauvinist outfits and is sometimes even described as the 'germ cell' of Hindu nationalism.[4] Not only Pakistani historians[5] emphasize the strong communal and anti-Islamic character of the Ārya Samāj ideology but even the western scholars come to a similar assessment.[6] The aim of this essay is to examine how the Āryā Samājīs actually contributed to an aggravation of communal polarization in the late nineteenth and early twentieth centuries and whether this contribution was, in fact, a result of anti-Islamic elements integral to *ārya dharm*. I try to suggest that the movement was not clearly anti-Islamic at inception but that the constant pressure of self-legitimation towards the 'orthodox' Hindu majority fostered this tendency. To verify this assumption, it is crucial to have a close look at the disputed position of the Samāj within the wider frame of Hinduism, rather than analyse it in isolation or look only at its direct interaction with Islam.

The focus will be on the *śuddhi* movement, undoubtedly the most controversial activity of the Hindu reformers. *Śuddhi* was a method of conversion (or reclamation) introduced by the Ārya Samājīs in order to provide Hinduism—traditionally a non-proselytizing religion—with an effective weapon against the onslaught of Christianity and Islam. Its application in massive reconversion campaigns amongst north Indian Muslims caused a great stir in the 1920s.

Dayānand's Ideological Legacy

Since Svāmī Dayānand Sarasvatī's ideology and the early history of the movement[7] have been examined extensively in a number of scholarly studies, I do not need to go into the details. Nevertheless, it is useful to recall some basic facts in order to be able to follow the line of argument:

The success of the Ārya Samāj was to a large extent the result of a 'collective identity crisis' of the urban Hindu middle-class intelligentsia exposed to the cultural invasion through the British colonial power and the missionaries; hence the Ārya Samāj ideology was defensive and aimed at restoring the threatened self-image and integrity.

To accomplish this task, the Samājīs tried to undertake a comprehensive reform of Hinduism. On the scriptural basis of the Vedas, the dharma of the golden age of Āryan civilization was to be restored and all later elements of corruption removed. These elements were largely identical with the 'evils of Hinduism' which had always been the target of both missionaries and the colonial administration: namely polytheism and idolatry, the injustice of the caste system, untouchability, child marriage, status of women, etc.

The reformist zeal of the Ārya Samājīs, expressing itself not only in harsh criticism of the arbitrary pandits and refutation of basic concepts of brahmanism such as the existence of avatārs and of a *varṇa vyavasthā* based on birth but also in openly breaking taboos, soon provoked a 'counter-reformation' by parts of the brahmanical 'orthodoxy'.

In order to spread their message efficiently, the Samājīs not only used traditional methods like public disputations (*śāstrārthas*), devotional songs (*bhajans*), etc., they also successfully copied western patterns and techniques of fund-raising and mobilization and built up a remarkable network of branches, sub-organizations, temples, educational institutions

(DAV colleges and *gurukulas*), well-trained preachers, newspapers and printing presses in the Hindi-speaking parts of north India.

Keeping in mind these observations, it is not surprising that the Ārya Samāj soon came under attack from both the missionaries and conservative Hindus. But how did the controversy with Islam emerge? To what extent are there anti-Islamic elements in the basic doctrines of Dayānand's *ārya dharm*? In the edition of his magnum opus *Satyārtha Prakāś*,[8] published shortly after the Svāmī's death in 1884, he uses the last four of the fourteen chapters of the book for a critique of the major non-Hindu religions. The fourteenth chapter deals with Islam exclusively.

As he does with Christianity, Dayānand looks upon Islam as a scriptural religion only and confines his analysis to a critical interpretation of the Qur'ān. Neither does he take into account the modifications in religious content and liturgy that took place during the centuries nor the fact that there were numerous regional and local variations. Instead he singles out certain isolated statements, interprets them literally and tries to falsify them.[9] Because the Svāmī had no command of Arabic or Urdū, he had a Hindī translation made especially for this purpose. Being unfamiliar with the subtleties of Qur'ānic exegesis, he looked for the help of a specialist, which he eventually found in the person of Munśī Manoharlāl from Patna.[10]

Though Dayānand dedicates about sixty pages to the *khandan* (refutation) of Islam, his critique is neither scholarly nor exhaustive; it can easily be reduced to two major points:

1. The Qur'ān is a striking example of religious bigotry since it has two completely different systems of morals: one for the followers of Islam and another for infidels.
2. Islam is an aggressive faith, which not only tolerates war and atrocities, but also makes them an integral part of its doctrine.[11]

Of course, one can also find attacks against Muhammad on a mere personal level, trying to prove that he was a man of doubtful moral principles, but that was a device frequently used in the religious propaganda at that time.[12]

In order to assess Dayānand's critique of Islam justly, it is important to note that compared to his crusade against the corruption of brahminical Hinduism (especially his rude attack of the Vallabhācāryas)[13] and his harsh criticism of Christianity his utterances about Islam are relatively mild. Also the few reported *śāstrārthas* with Islamic clergymen seem to have been less polemical and more disciplined than disputations against 'orthodox' pandits.[14] It may also be noted that Dayānand was invited by Muslims to give lectures in their houses during his first Panjab tour in 1877. Close contact with Muslims was not new to the Svāmī. Imdād Husain, a *maulvī* from Benaras had become a sort of disciple during Dayanānd's stay in the town in 1872.[15] More than five decades later he still remembered the long and friendly discussions he had with the reformer from Gujarat and stressed his openness and tolerance in religious questions.[16] From the same source we know that Muslims quite frequently attended his lectures and were treated politely even during the Svāmī's final years.[17]

Apart from these events that are closely connected with the person of Dayānand himself, we have clear evidence that even after his death sporadic cases of Muslim support for the Ārya Sāmajīs occurred. Among the first donors for the Dayānand Anglo-Vedic College were two 'Mohammedan gentlemen'[18] and several others followed their example in subsequent years.[19] Considering this we can only arrive at the conclusion that Islam did not play the role of the natural enemy in the *Weltanschauung* of the Āryā Samajīs in the early phase of the movement. If the Samāj showed open hostility towards adherents of one particular religion at that time, it was towards the Christian missionaries whose conversion activities were regarded as a vital threat. How then, did the Samāj become a symbol of communal narrow-mindedness and Hindu militancy only a decade later? One important key to the understanding of this development lies in the isolated position the Ārya Samājīs occupied within the Hindu camp.

REFORMIST ZEAL VS. PRAGMATISM: THE DILEMMA OF THE ĀRYA SAMĀJ

As already mentioned, Dayānand's radical ideas had caused a lot of protest and dissent among more traditional Hindus. The Svāmī was always aware of the danger of becoming the leader of an isolated, elitist sect and did everything he could to prevent his organization from meeting the fate of other reformist bodies like the Brahmo Samaj. In his excellent biography, J.T.F. Jordens has shown how Dayānand always tried to find an agenda for his Ārya Samājīs that could be approved by all Hindus without regard to caste, region of origin or *sampradāya* in order to broaden the basis of the movement.[20]

The first issue that brought the Samajis into the limelight was the fund-raising campaign for Munśī Indrāmanī, a prominent Hindu who had been brought before the court and fined for having published a fiery pamphlet against Islam. The Svāmī's initiative was welcomed by a large majority of Hindus despite the fact that the Munsī was a member of the Ārya Samāj.

Dayānand earned greater popular acceptance with his campaign against cow-slaughter[21] and his support for the cause of Hindī in the ongoing controversy about the administrative language in the United Provinces. His populist commitment to these issues gradually brought about a certain fame for the Ārya Samāj as a champion of Hindu interests. As this favourable reputation was an outcome of the use of symbols that had some importance for most of the traditionalist Hindus as well, the commitment to 'Hindu issues' turned out to be the most promising means of combating isolation and sectarianism. In all three cases, the short-term mobilization of Hindus of various backgrounds was achieved at the expense of offending the Muslim minority: the 'common' could only be defined against the 'other'. The deterioration of Hindu-Muslim relations was readily accepted as an inevitable side-effect.

The relationship between the Ārya Samājīs and the rest of the Hindu world continued to be fragile and complicated after the Svāmī's death. It became a difficult balancing act between the reformatory claim of the Samaj and the necessities of *realpolitik*. The pressure on the reformists increased after the emergence of counter-reformatory organizations like the Sanātana Dharm Sabhās and Bhārat Dharm Mahāmaṇḍal in the late 1880s.[22] In reaction to these developments, the Ārya Samājīs voluntarily played the role of 'watchdogs of Hinduism'[23] and drifted further towards open confrontation with the Muslims. Starting from the late 1880s the fierce quarrel between Ārya Samājīs and the followers of the Prophet was carried out publicly, with countless pamphlets and newspaper articles. Interestingly, it was not Islamic orthodoxy which became the main rival of the Samāj's *upadeśak*s (preachers, propagandists), but the reformist sect of the Ahmadiyyas.[24] One could conclude that the adherents of Mirza Ghulam Ahmad felt a similar need for self-legitimation in the Islamic camp. When Ghulam Ahmad's personal quarrel with the famous Ārya Samāj preacher Pandit Lekhrām ended with the latter being murdered by a Muslim in 1897, for a short while after the incident even non-Ārya Samāj Hindus supported the Samāj ideologically and financially.[25] The 'martyrdom' of their most aggressive upadeśak earned the reformers more sympathy than any other of their activities till then; the anti-Islamic bias became now a constant feature of the Ārya Samāj policy.[26]

A ritual of purification, obviously invented for completely different purposes, was to become the most efficient weapon of the Ārya Samāj in this controversy.

THE CONCEPT OF ŚUDDHI AND THE BEGINNINGS OF THE MOVEMENT

In the view of the Ārya Samājīs, one of the greatest deficiencies of Hinduism and a major reason for its decline since the golden age of the Vedas was the want of a ritual of conversion; active proselytization would help make the Hindus resistant against the propaganda of Christian and Islamic missionaries.[27] The problem had become acute since the 1860s, when the Protestant missionaries had a growing success with conversion campaigns among the 'untouchables'.[28] The census, carried out by the British every ten years since 1871, became an important stimulus for the formation of religious identities, with the Census Reports giving publicity to the latest trends in demography, and the gains and losses of the different religious groups being discussed and commented upon at length by the press. Especially in the Hindu camp the awareness of the rising number of 'native' Christians[29] fed the paranoia of an 'extinction of the Hindu race'. A Punjabi newspaper warned in 1895:

The Hindus should awake from their slumbers; otherwise wholesale conversions to Christianity will take place and Christianity will take as strong a hold in the Punjab as Buddhism [*sic*] once did.[30]

With the slow process of 'devolution of power', initiated by the British at the local administrative level in the 1880s, and continuing with the constitutional reforms in the early twentieth century, majorities, percentages and numbers (provided by the decennial census) had gained an enormous importance in British India. Only someone who could claim to represent a numerically important group or community had a chance to be heard by the authorities.[31] With the invention of a mode of conversion, therefore, the Ārya Samājīs could not only appropriate one of the most threatening and efficient elements of the Semitic religions, they were also in a position to present themselves as the protectors of the entire Hindu community.

The Sanskrit word śuddhi means cleansing, purity, freedom from defilement, purification.[32] In the last sense the word was used for an ancient brahminical ritual which aimed at re-creating the state of purity after polluting contact or impure activity. In the nineteenth century, it was mainly used to reintegrate Brahmins, who had crossed the *kālā pānī* (i.e. travelled abroad) into their respective *birādrī*s.[33] Dayānand gave the ritual an entirely new meaning by using it for the reclamation of Hindus who had been converted to Islam or Christianity. The concept of śuddhi, however, played only a marginal role during the Svāmī's lifetime: hardly a dozen cases of such reclamation are reported, and in his written work the new method is not mentioned.

Only in 1886, three years after his death, did some Ārya Samāj leaders recognize the unifying potential of śuddhi. An exact set of rites was elaborated and the new ceremony was declared to be authoritative.[34] In order to save the reconverted from possible restrictions by their caste clans—most of which had a very conservative outlook—the Ārya Samājīs collaborated with traditional Brahmins in the beginning. It was another seven years before they felt confident enough to carry out the reconversions according to Ārya Samāj rites exclusively. With this discarding of 'orthodox' precepts, many biradris refused to welcome the reclaimed back into their fold. Sometimes the Ārya Samājīs who had conducted the śuddhi ceremony were excommunicated as well.[35]

The split of the Panjab Ārya Samāj in 1893 over the questions of vegetarianism and the curricula for the educational institutions by the Samāj into a moderate (DAV) and a radical (Gurukul) wing[36] did not affect the pursuit of śuddhi activity. The year 1896 witnessed a decisive change in the purification movement. Whereas previously only individuals or small groups had undergone the ceremony, in that year reclamation of whole clans and villages was reported.[37] Moreover, the concept was widened in the sense that śuddhi was no longer used merely to reclaim 'apostates'; it was also employed as a means of integrating the untouchables into the varna system and so improving their lot. The DAV was active for a few years: it worked together with the reformist Singh Sabhās of the Sikhs in the Lahore Suddhi Sabha and guided several thousand untouchable śuddhis.[38] Considering that Christian and Islamic mission had always been most successful among the depressed classes, one may seriously doubt whether the Ārya Samājīs' motives were strictly philanthropic.

During the first decade of the movement, most of the reclaimed had been Christians. Thereafter, the focus shifted increasingly to neo-Muslims.[39] The first opportunity to put the new strategy to the test occurred in south India.

Suddhi as Defensive Weapon against the 'Islamic Threat'

In summer 1899, the Shanars, a caste of toddy-tappers resident in Tinnevelly in the Madras Presidency, converted to Islam. When the news reached northern India, the Ārya Samājīs were alerted. They felt the need to come forward and accomplish the task of defending Hinduism, although the incident had happened far beyond their sphere of influence, which was still largely restricted to Punjab, United Provinces and Rajputana. The *Arya Gazette* wrote:

If the followers of Hinduism do not take prompt steps to make a recurrence of such incidents impossible in the future, the day is not far distant when Hindu society will be swept off the face of the earth. The only way to avert the disaster and put an end to the internecine quarrels existing among the Hindus is to discard the Puranas and spread the light of the Vedas in the land.[40]

The Ārya Samājīs collected funds[41] and sent two upadeśaks to the 'benighted Presidency'[42] to try and persuade the disloyal Shanars to return to the Hindu fold. The operation was doomed to failure, because the local Brahmins refused to cooperate with the reformists from the north, who, in their eyes, must have been almost as suspect as the Muslims.[43] Obviously, the consciousness of supra-regional collective identity, comprising all the various shapes of the Hindu tradition, was not yet developed. But despite its futility, the Tinnevelly expedition illustrates convincingly to what extent the Ārya Samājīs had already internalized their feeling of paternal responsibility for the whole Hindu community.[44]

Only a few months later, they took a further step; in November 1899 the *Arya Gazette* published an article which amounted to an open provocation of the Muslims. The appeal postulated nothing less than the reclamation of all Muslims whose ancestors had been Hindus:

Dear parted Muhammadan brothers!

[. . .] Riches for the sake of which you have thrown away the priceless pearl of religion as valueless have bid you adieu. Unwholesome food and a rude way of living have blunted your intellect and we now feel shame in touching you. [. . .] Why do you not then cry for readmission in your old family and chauka? [. . .] It is possible, that your new companions try to make you obstinate and advise you to tread the wrong path. Nevertheless you are wanderers from the right path and the sooner you recover it, the better for you. Dear parted brothers we are willing to purify you.[45]

The article made the Muslims realize for the first time that the suddhi activity of the Ārya Samāj represented a danger to the unity of the Islamic community in India. Muslim newspapers and organizations reacted with angry protest and the editor of the *Arya Gazette* thought it prudent to distance himself from the contents of the article. The point to note is that at least one faction of the Ārya Samāj regarded śuddhi as an instrument that could be used effectively to counter the Islamic threat and did not hesitate to employ it with that objective, regardless of the possible conse-quences for Hindu-Muslim relations. Strangely enough, despite the clear hint they give of an early political instrumentalization of suddhi, neither the call to the 'parted Muhammadan brothers' nor the Tinnevelly expedi-tion have met the attention they deserve from scholars writing about the subject.[46]

As the emphasis was placed again on the role of śuddhi as a method for the uplift of the 'untouchables' (achutoddhār) in the following years, the Samājīs had to face once more the fierce resistance of 'orthodoxy'. The experience of the first twenty-five years of organized śuddhi efforts had shown that almost all of the more conservative Hindus were reluctant to accept the new ceremony as a means for effective social reform. And even worse for the Ārya Samājīs: despite the occasional cooperation in times of a real or imagined threat, only a part of them were ready to accept suddhi as a ritual for 'reclaiming the strayed sheep'.[47] In June 1909, a Sanātanī paper postulated the excommunication 'of those Ārya Samajists who are engaged in destroying the purity of Hindu blood by making converts from Christians and Muhammadans by entering into social relations with them'.[48] Some weeks later this demand was fulfilled by a Brahman Sabhā from Calcutta which declared that Hindus ought not to maintain social relationships with the reformists because of the latter's śuddhi work.[49] The Ārya Samājīs were disappointed and their newspapers were full of lament about the ungrateful behaviour of the 'purānic' Hindu majority.[50] Even a few months before the Sabhā's decision became public the Arya Gazette had expressed the ill-feeling of the Samāj towards the reaction of the conservative majority quite bluntly:

The Sanatanists resemble a foolish child who does not know what is good and what is bad for him, and who is rendered beside himself at unpleasant advice from his kindly elders or well wishers and prepares to work himself injury.[. . .] It is a mistake on the part of the Hindus that the Aryas still stand in need of protection from Hindu society. It is the Hindu baradari which have now to look up to the Arya Samaj which serves as a shield to them.[51]

In 1910 the census commissioner Gait published his famous circular, that caused a shock in the Hindu camp.[52] He advised the census workers to list the depressed classes in the approaching 1911 census not under 'Hindus', but in a separate category. For a short while it seemed that even the conservative sections of the Hindu world would become interested in the Ārya Samāj's śuddhi programme,[53] but as soon as the first excitement about the impending danger of a possible breakaway of the untouchables receded, 'orthodoxy' returned to its position of indulgence.

The rapprochement between the Muslim League and the Hindu-dominated Indian National Congress at the national level during World War I and after was probably the main reason for the indifference of the Hindu majority towards reclamation of 'Indian Muslims' during these years. Once this period of communal harmony ended and tensions reappeared more virulent than ever, the Hindu mainstream became less mistrustful of the reformers.

THE TURNING-POINT IN MALABAR

At the beginning of the 1920s, the political atmosphere in India changed dramatically. The enthusiasm for Gandhi's non-cooperation campaign, which Hindus and Muslims had fought side by side gave way to resignation and bitterness. Even before the Mahatma broke off the campaign completely, an incident in southern India had estranged the two communities from each other: the Mappila rebellion in Malabar, which started in summer 1921.

The Māppilas were descendants of Arab merchants who had settled on the Malabar coast in the ninth century and were mostly landless tenants or petty peasants.[54] They had actually been mobilized during the Khilāfat agitation but soon their wrath against the prosperous Hindu landlords and moneylenders erupted in violent outbreaks. They erected a millenarian Islamic kingdom, and many Hindus died in the riots. Looting, ravage and rape continued for months. The atrocities were reported at length by the press all over India and caused a tremendous stir in Hindu circles. Especially the news that the rebels had forced hundreds of Hindus to embrace Islam was received with horror and disgust by the Hindus of northern India. As they had previously done in Tinnevelly, the Ārya Samājīs again saw an opportunity to win prestige by acting as the defenders of Hinduism. Unlike twenty years before, the situation this time was favourable for the Samājīs, and their endeavour was welcomed by the 'orthodox' Hindus. On 16 October 1921 the Arya Pradesik Pratinidhi Sabha Panjab passed the following resolution:

Considering the state of those Hindus forcibly converted to Islam by applying atrocious means we have resolved, that this sabha shall try to organize the śuddi and help of the Hindus converted by force. The president [Lālā Haṃsrāj] has been given the authority to make a public appeal on behalf of this urgent service in order to arrange as soon-as possible for the śuddhi and relief work and raise the necessary money.[55]

In his account of the Malabar campaign Lālā Haṃsrāj mentioned three goals of the operation, leaving no doubt about where the primary interest of the organization lay. The first goal was the reclamation of the 'fallen' 'so that the opponents of Hindu dharm will realize that *no Hindu can be forced to give up his religion.*'[56] Humanitarian relief work was only secondary, the long-term aim of the Arya Samaj commitment being again to make 'the building of the Hindu society in Malabar firm and immutable'.[57]

On 1 November 1921 Pandit Rsirām was sent to Malabar. The Ārya Samāj press launched a fund-raising campaign but during the first weeks the response was somewhat disappointing. Until the end of November not more than Rs 1,739 had been donated, and due to this shortage of funds Rṣirām was instructed not to start the relief work but to spend the money solely on preparing the reconversions.[58] Here again, it becomes obvious that the whole affair was exploited for demonstrating the Samāj's efficiency as a bulwark against the enemies of Hinduism. This, of course, was nothing new. The actual sensation was that the Dehra Dun Hindū Sabhā, an 'orthodox' organization, immediately approved of the Ārya Samāj resolution and declared itself ready to actively support the plan.[59]

The Sabhā's declaration marks a crucial change in the relations between Ārya Samājīs and 'orthodoxy'. The same Sanātanīs who had proscribed the Samājīs because of their śuddhi activities now officially collaborated with them in such a campaign. The only possible explanation for this change of mind could be their sentiment that the incident in Malabar represented a menace for the whole Hindu community. Fear for the survival of the Hindus was additionally fed by certain separatist tendencies of the Sikhs and the growing self-consciousness of the *dalits* (untouchables), which occurred at the same time.[60] All these factors provoked a mental process which has been aptly described by the French political scientist Christophe Jaffrelot as a '*complexe d'infériorité majoritaire*'.[61] The repeated reappearance of this inferiority complex of the majority is one of the striking features of political Hinduism in the twentieth century.

The fact that many conservative Hindus were willing to cooperate with the reformers had not solved the problem of the appropriate conversion rites. It was well known that the south Indian pandits were very strict in terms of ritual correctness; they would never have accepted a mode of reclamation not sanctioned by the sacred texts. One could suspect then that it was not mere coincidence that, exactly at the time when the problem was discussed, the manuscript of the *Devalasmrti*,[62] an old sastra text dealing with the proper rites necessary to purify a Hindu after he had contact with *mleccha*s, was re-'discovered' by none other than the later Hindu Mahāsabhā leader B.S. Moonje.[63] It henceforth served as the main source of legitimation for the reconversions and thus paved the way for cooperation of the two groups.

Altogether, the joint venture of local Brahmins and āryopdeśaks conducted about 3,000 purifications;[64] according to R.L. Hardgrave they did not confine themselves to the victims of the forcible conversions led by the Māppiḷas but continued their śuddhi work with the clans that had embraced Islam during the reign of Tipu Sultan (1782–99).[65]

The engagement in Malabar brought about a considerable gain in popularity for the Ārya Samāj, which thus established a first bridgehead in south India. Even more important, the Ārya Samājīs and Sanātanīs had found a common *modus operandi* in the field of śuddhi. The Samājīs had succeeded in putting one of their most important issues on the agenda of important Hindu organizations such as the Hindu Mahāsabhā. This success was partly because this time, unlike twenty years before, they acted very cautiously, stressing their 'Hinduness'[66] and taking care to avoid any provocation of the 'orthodox'. As a result, their self-declared role as a unifying avant-garde now seemingly was accepted by some influential representatives of non-Ārya Samājī Hindus in the south. G. Krishnan, a leader of the Malabar Thiyya community, wrote in August 1922:

[. . .] it is no impossible task to evolve the feeling of brotherhood[,] the silken chain to bind together the various communities that fall under the common name 'HINDU'. I say again, the Arya Samaj should provide this chain, create this feeling of brotherhood, especially at this juncture, when the ground has been prepared by the rebellion to receive the seed of fundamental unity of Hindus that the Arya Samaj will sow.[67]

Tragically, once again the issue that brought them closer to the majority of Hindus alienated them from the Muslims. The disciplined and well-organized Samāj was to play more and more the role of a 'mobile task force' of Hinduism on which one could rely in times of danger from outside.

THE RECLAMATION OF THE MALKĀNĀS

This tendency reached its climax in the years 1923–6 during a huge reconversion campaign in the Braj region of the United Provinces. In the meantime the Hindu fear of being dominated and humiliated by the Muslim minority had grown because of a series of communal riots (the most serious had taken place in Multan, Sindh) in which the Hindus once again saw themselves as defenceless victims. The slogan 'Malabar and Multan', used extensively by the Hindu press, became a synonym for the perceived cruelty of Islam. More and more voices called for Hindū sangathan (union, organization) and the Hindū Mahāsabhā (HMS), which had been of minor importance since its foundation in 1915, was transformed into a vital body. In its Gaya session held in December 1922 the HMS demanded concrete steps for the 'self-preservation and religious safety of the Hindu community',[68] and explicitly declared the reintegration of apostates from Hinduism, who had undergone the śuddhi procedure, to be lawful.

The Ārya Samājīs, now backed by the 'orthodox' members of the HMS, did not have to wait long for an opportunity to start a major purification campaign. The Malkānās were a Rajput community resident around Agra, Bharatpur and Mathura. They had nominally become Muslims during the reign of Aurangzeb (1658–1707), without embracing the Islamic faith completely. Their religious practice was a curious mixture of Hindu and Muslim elements.[69] After a resolution of the Kṣatrīya Upkārini Sabhā, a Rājput caste organization, had paved the way for their integration into the jāti system, in February 1923 the Bhāratīya Hindū Śuddhi Sabhā was founded under the leadership of the Ārya Samāj. Svāmī Śraddhānand, the leader of the gurukul faction, was elected president and Lālā Haṃsrāj, a prominent Ārya Samājī of the moderate DAV wing, who had already guided the reconversion in Malabar, became vice-president.[70]

On 23 February, Śraddhānand published an article in the widely circulated newspaper *The Leader*, titled 'Save the Dying Race',[71] in which he called for financial and ideological support for the planned campaign. The first purifications took place only a few days later. In the following months the Ārya Samāj preachers and other volunteers walked from village to village trying to convince the Malkānās to return to the Hindu fold. Soon they faced the competition of Muslim propagandists desperately trying to stop the 'mass apostasy'. The whole affair was blown up to incredible proportions by the press. The Ārya Samāj newspapers and most of the Sanatānī press hailed the campaign and saw the golden future of Hinduism at hand[72] whereas the Muslim gazettes spread a hysterical fear which almost matched the 'dying race' paranoia of the Hindus. The *Milap*, for example, was sure that 'the days of Islam in India were counted' if the śuddhi, campaign was not stopped.[73] In July the Jamīat-al-Tabligh al-Islām was founded as an all-India organization for the propagation of Islam in order to counterbalance the missionary efforts of the Bhāratīya Hindū Śuddhi Sabhā.

Despite the relative success of the Malkana campaign,[74] the Ārya Samājīs soon had to bury their secret hope of creating a homogeneous Hindu front through the śuddhi movement. After a short phase of enthusiasm—which had expressed itself in generous donations from all parts of the wide spectrum of Hinduism—had ended, the old conflicts soon reappeared. The question of the exact position the reclaimed should be given in the caste system remained unsolved, and the Sanātanīs still vigorously opposed the purification of untouchable groups. Many of them even rejected the śuddhi rites of the Ārya Samāj. They founded their own organization, the Hindū Punah Saṃskār Samiti, which was not very successful. At the same time, the radicals among the Ārya Samājīs became increasingly reluctant to give up their reformist attitude completely for the sake of Hindū sangathan and severely criticized the Sanātanīs.[75] Doubtless, these internal quarrels have to be regarded as a major cause for the declining intensity of the movement after less than a year, although it continued into the 1930s. Frustrated at the uncompromising stance of the Sanātanīs, Svāmī Śraddhānand declared in early 1925 that the majority of the Hindus were obviously not yet ready for change, and so a comprehensive reform of Hinduism had to be preceded by a further strengthening of the Ārya Samāj.[76] Consequently he concentrated his efforts on his own organization and resigned from his posts in the Bhāratīya Hindū Śuddhi Sabhā and the HMS. His book *Hindu Sangathan: Saviour of the Dying Race* (published in 1926 but written in 1924) is full of reproaches of the Hindū Mahāsabhā. The svāmī doubted the organization's ability and willingness to fulfil the task of Hindū sangathan which, in his opinion, could not become a reality without serious steps towards comprehensive social reform, including the abolition of caste barriers and a full integration of the untouchables:

The Hindu Mahasabha has passed a lengthy resolution purporting to deal with the problem of untouchability, but it has resulted in confounding confusion worse [. . .] the climax is reached, when, after allowing all the above mentioned privileges, the Hindu Mahasabha lays down the authoritative dogma, that 'initiating the untouchables with the sacred thread, teaching them the Vedas and to interdine with them is against the Shastras and custom according to the Sanatan Dharma.'

To get rid of this rigmarole and to root out [. . .] untouchability and exclusiveness, there is only one sovereign [*sic*] remedy and that is the resuscitation of the ancient Aryan 'Varna-dharma'.[77]

Although the assassination of the svāmī by a Muslim fanatic in December 1926 provided the śuddhi movement with a martyr and caused much uproar throughout the Hindu camp,[78] it could not stop the decline of the campaign. The incident occurred at a time when it was already evident that the vision of the Ārya Samājīs of transforming Hinduism into a united entity by playing the role of a pugnacious avant-garde had failed. Organizations like the Hindū Mahāsabhā and the Rāṣṭrīya Svayamsevak Sangh (RSS, founded in 1925), that were not hindered by a religious *mission civilisatrice*, proved much more adept at fulfilling that role.

CONCLUSION

In this essay I have challenged the widespread assumption that the undeniable contribution of the Ārya Samāj in aggravating the communal tensions in late-nineteenth- and early-twentieth-century north India was a direct outcome of the militant and anti-Islamic outlook of the reform movement. Instead, I have emphasized an aspect hitherto neglected, by showing how the Ārya Samājīs were partly pushed into, and partly deliberately adopted, the role of 'watchdogs of Hinduism', because of the isolated role they were playing within the Hindu world. Under the given circumstances of a devolution of power by the British administration and a collective identity-formation along religious lines catalysed by the Census, this necessarily led to open conflict with Islam. Svāmi Dayānand, the founder of the Ārya Samāj, had already recognized that for an organization which aimed at reform of Hinduism and consequently provoked rejection by the Hindu mainstream, it was crucial to prove its usefulness to the majority.

I have chosen the śuddhi movement—the most controversial of all Ārya Samāj activities—to show that the same strategy was used by the Samājīs through the following decades. The Ārya Samāj gradually internalized a self-perception as paternal guides of the backward Hindu majority, steeped in ritualism and irrationality, and took every opportunity to act as its defender. The majority, however, responded only in times of an external threat perceived as vital to the iconoclastic Ārya Samāj's offer of protection. The changing attitude becomes clear if we look at the two expeditions to south India launched by the followers of Dayānand. As early as 1899 śuddhi was instrumentalized as a defensive weapon against Islamic missionary activities in Tinnevelly, but at that time the 'puranic' Hindus were not ready to accept the initiative of the reformers. Only in times of a supposedly mortal danger could they forget their scruples regarding the Ārya Samājīs.

For this very reason, the Malabar rebellion in 1921 brought about a decisive change in the relations of Ārya Samāj and Sanātanīs. The fear of being marginalized and humiliated by the Muslim minority pushed the 'orthodox' to cooperation with the Samāj, which, due to its high degree of organization and its śuddhi know-how, indeed provided an effective 'mobile task force'.

But before long, hardliners in both camps gained momentum and the incompatible positions on the matter of untouchability put an end to a durable alliance. While even the most conservative pandits now seemed ready to accept śuddhi as a method of 'reclaiming the strayed sheep', thereby countering the (largely imaginary) threat of Islam, the 'orthodox' section remained fiercely opposed to accepting it as a means of internal reform through the uplift of untouchables (*dalitoddhār*). Since social and religious reconstruction still was the main concern of the Samāj, and its leaders and adherents were not willing to give up their reformist policy, the organization slowly lost influence in subsequent years. Gradually, new movements like the RSS filled the gap left by the Ārya Samājīs. To the latter's disappointment, the Sanatani Hindus remained ungrateful towards their 'kindly elders'.

NOTES

1. I dedicate this essay to the memory of Professor K.W. Jones, who passed away in September 1996. It draws partly on my article 'Die Reformorganisation Arya Samaj und die Hindu-Moslem-Beziehungen 1875–1926, in: C. Weiss et al. (eds), *Religion-Macht-Gewalt. Religiöser Fundamentalismus und Hindu-Moslem-Konflikte in Südasien*, Frankfurt a.m., 1996, pp. 71–97. The title refers to the quotation of an Ārya Samāj newspaper given in full length on p. 115. I am grateful to Christoph Schmutz, John Zavos and Ulrike Stark for reading an earlier draft of this paper and making valuable suggestions for its improvement. Special thanks to Christina Oesterheld for helping with the Urdu sources.

2. *Watan*, 30 September 1910, *Selections from the Native Newspapers Published in the Punjab* (henceforth *SNNP*), 1910, p. 891.

3. Cf. the 'Note on the Arya Samaj' prepared by the Criminal Intelligence Office, Calcutta on 20 December 1909; in Home Department Proceedings, Political, April 1912, no. 4, pp. 1–22 [National Archives of India].

4. Cf. K. Malik and V.B. Singh, *Hindu Nationalists in India. The Rise of the Bharatiya Janata Party* (Neudr.), New Delhi, 1995, p. 29, and C. Jaffrelot, 'Emergence des nationalismes en Inde. Perspectives théoriques; *Revue Française de Science Politique* 38(4), 1988, pp. 55–75, p. 573. Most explicit is the same author's essay 'The Genesis and Development of Hindu Nationalism in the Punjab: From the Arya Samaj to the Hindu Sabha', *Indo-British Review. A Journal of History* 21(1), 1994, pp. 3–39.

5. See, for example, A. Hakim, 'Hindu Reformist and Revivalist Movements', in M. Husain et al. (eds), *History of the Freedom Movement*, vol. II, pt. 2, Karachi, 1961, pp. 390–414, esp. p. 402.

6. N.G. Barrier observes, for instance, that 'Militantly anti-Muslim, the Arya Samaj inculcated visions of a Hindu nation among its members . . .'; see 'The Punjab Government and Communal Politics, 1870–1908', *Journal of Asian Studies* (henceforth *JAS*) 27(2), 1968, pp. 523–39, p. 528. For a similar view, see G.R. Thursby, *Hindu-Muslim Relations in British India. A Study of Controversy, Conflict and Communal Movements in Northern India 1923–28*, Leiden, 1975, pp. 10ff.

7. The most reliable still are: K.W. Jones, *Arya Dharm. Hindu Consciousness in 19th Century Punjab*, Berkeley, 1976; J.T.F. Jordens, *Swāmī Dayānand Sarasvatī. His Life and Ideas*, Delhi, 1978; the same author's *Swāmī Shraddhānanda. His Life and Causes*, Delhi, 1981, and J.R. Graham's unpublished PhD dissertation, 'The Arya Samaj as a Reformation of Hinduism with Special Reference to Caste', Yale University, 1943.

8. The second edition, published shortly after his death, is regarded as authoritative and has since then been reprinted continually and translated several times.

I refer to the following edition: D. Sarasvatī, *Satyārth Prakāś* (repr. of the 2nd edn, ed. by the Ārya Pratinidhi Sabhā), Naī Dillī, 1993.

9. Dayānand uses a similar technique in his chapter on Christianity. Cf. H.G. Coward, 'The Response of the Arya Samaj,' in idem (ed.), *Modern Indian Responses to Religious Pluralism*, New York, 1987, pp. 39–64, esp. pp. 45–8.

10. Cf. J.T.F. Jordens, *Dayānanda Sarasvatī*, pp. 248 and 268f.

11. D. Sarasvati, *Satyārth Prakāś*.

12. See N.G. Barrier, *Banned. Controversial Literature and Political Control in British India 1907–1937*, Columbia, 1974, ch. III.

13. Cf. J. Luett, 'From Krishnalila to Ramarajya: A court case and its consequences for the reformulation of Hinduism', in V. Dalmia, and H.Y. Stietencron, *Representing Hinduism. The Construction of Religious Traditions and National Identity*, New Delhi, 1995, pp. 142–53, p. 148f.

14. Cf. J.T.F. Jordens, *Dayānanda Sarasvatī*, p. 167f. For a detailed account of Dayānand's śastrārthas see Bh. Bhāratīya, *Ārya Samāj ke śāstrārth mahārthī*, Ajmer, 2041 vs [1984], pp. 5–15.

15. I. Vidyāvācaspati, *Ārya Samāj kā itihās*, vol. I (repr.) Dillī, 1995, p. 230.

16. Cf. I. Husain, 'Mukhtasar ḥālāt svāmī Dayānand Sarasvatī', in H.B. Sarda (ed.), *Dayananda Commemoration Volume*, Ajmer, 1933, pp. 407–14. Husain does not give an exact date for the incident. But several details he mentions clearly indicate that it happened during Dayānand's stay in Benaras during March and April 1872. See also H.B. Sarda, 'Dayanand's Itinerary' in S.P. Sarasvati (ed.), *Dayananda Commemoration Volume, Mahārṣi Dayānand nirvāṇ śarti smṛti-granth*, Ajmer, 1983, pp. 45–8, p. 46.

17. Husain, ibid., p. 411. Husain describes a lecture in Mirzapur (given probably in the autumn of 1879), where a large number of Muslims attended and special arrangements were made for them to sit on chairs, while the Hindu audience sat on the floor.

18. Cf. S.K. Gupta, 'The Anglo-Vedic College Movement (1886–1986)', in *The Punjab Past and Present* 20(1), 1986, pp. 226–41, p. 227.

19. Satyaketu Vidyālaṁkār et al., *Ārya Samāj kā itihās*, VII. vols, Naī Dillī, 1982–8, vol. III, p.131. Satyaketu mentions, amongst others, a certain Raīs Jahāmadār Khan, who donated a full month's salary for the DAV College movement.

20. The following is mainly based on J.T.F. Jordens, *Dayānand Sarasvatī*, pp. 216–26.

21. Cf. also S.B. Freitag, 'Contesting in Public: Colonial Legacies and Contemporary Communalism', in D. Ludden, *Making India Hindu. Religion, Community and the Politics of Democracy in India*, Delhi 1996, pp. 211–34, esp. 215–19.

22. Vidyāvācaspati, *Ārya Samāj ka itihās*, vol. I, p. 190f.

23. Although this self-designation appeared much later (in the Ārya Samāj monthly *Vedic Magazine & Gurukula Samachar*, henceforth *VMGS*, 13(8), March 1923, p. 552), it aptly describes the Ārya Samājīs' self-perception from the 1890s.

24. Cf. S. Lavan, 'Communalism in the Punjab. The Ahmadiyyas versus the

Arya Samaj during the Lifetime of Mirza Ghulam Ahmad', *The Punjab Past and Present* 5(2), 1971, pp. 320–42.

25. The Sanatānī press was trying hard to bias the public (Hindu) opinion against the Ārya Samājīs. Cf. *Sanatana Dharm Gazette*, 15 April 1898 and 16 May 1898, *SNNP* 1898, pp. 319 and 414 respectively.

26. I. Vidyāvācaspati, *Ārya Samāj kā itihās*, vol. II, Dillī, 1957, p. 47f.

27. Of course there had always been the possibility of becoming 'Hindu' but this had been through slow acculturation of whole tribes or clans and not through the single act of conversion by a group or an individual that is typical of the Semitic religions. It has therefore rightly been argued, that the reinterpretation of suddhi is an 'invention of tradition' in the sense Hobsbawm understands the term. Cf. C. Jaffrelot, 'Les Reconversions à l'Hindouisme (1885–1990): Politisation et diffusion d'une invention de tradition', *Archives des Sciences Social des Religions* (87), 1994, pp. 73–98, p. 76.

28. Cf. D.B. Forrester, 'The Depressed Classes and Conversion to Christianity', in G.A. Oddie (ed.), *Religious Conversion and Revival Movements in Medieval and Modern Times*, New Delhi 1977, pp. 35–66.

29. The number of Indian Christians rose from about 900,000 in 1858 to roughly four million at the time of the 1911 census; cf. E.J. Sharpe, 'Christianity in India', in R.D. Baird (ed.), *Religion in Modern India*, 2nd exp. edn, New Delhi, 1989, pp. 221–38, esp. p. 225f.

30. Singh Sahai, 12 April 1895, *SNNP*, 1895, p. 2.

31. For the effect of the Census cf. K.W. Jones, 'Religious Identity and the Indian Census', in N.G. Barrier (ed.), *The Census in British India–New Perspectives*, New Delhi, 1981, pp. 73–101, esp. pp. 84–6.

32. Cf. M. Monier-Williams, *A Sanskrit-English Dictionary* (repr.), Delhi, 1993, p. 1082.

33. Cf. J.T.F. Jordens, 'Reconversion to Hinduism, the Shuddhi of the Arya Samaj', in N.G. Oddie (ed.), *Religious Conversions and Revival Movements* . . ., pp. 145–62, esp. p. 145f.

34. The exact ritual changed several times but it virtually always included the following basic elements: 1. tonsure; 2. *hom* (vedic fire sacrifice), 3. *yajñopavīt* (investiture with the sacred thread); and 4. learning of the *Gāyatrī-Mantra* by the converted. Very often these rituals were followed by the common eating of sweetmeats distributed by the reclaimed. Cf. J.R. Graham, 'The Arya Samaj as a Reformation of Hinduism . . .', p. 465.

35. Cf. e.g. *Akhbar i Am*, 1 April 1895, *SNNP*, 1895, p. 79. Serious clashes with conservative Hindus were reported from Hoshiarpur in 1909, when the Ārya Samājīs were repeatedly beaten up by organized gangs of sanātanī hooligans and prohibited to use the wells in the village. Cf. *Akhbar i Am*, 18 May 1909, *SNNP*, 1909, p. 418f; *Tilak*, 6 May 1909, ibid., p. 471f; and *Hindu Sanatan Dharm Gazette*, ibid., p. 500. In January 1923 a śuddhi worker of the Ārya Samāj died after a severe beating by furious Rajputs in Jammu. Cf. *VMGS*, 18(8), February 1923, p. 552.

36. Cf. M.L. Thakur, 'Factors Leading to the Split of the Arya Samaj in 1893', *Proceedings of the Punjab History Conference* 18 (1983), pp. 225–31.

37. Usually these were clans that had lost their status through defiling work or impure marriages; they hoped to regain prestige and recover their old status through the śuddhi procedure. Between 1896 and 1923, i.e. before the start of the large-scale conversion campaigns, more than 100,000 untouchables were 'purified' by Ārya Samāj preachers—obviously without in fact improving their situation. For details see R.K. Ghai, *The Shuddhi Movement in India. A Study of its Socio-Political Dimensions*, Delhi, 1990, pp. 70–82.

38. Cf. K.W. Jones, 'Ham Hindū Nahin: Arya-Sikh Relations 1877–1905, *JAS* 28(1), 1973, pp. 457–75, p. 46ff.

39. Later śuddhi was also used as an actual method of conversion, initiating to Hinduism individuals from other religions. The first such convert, was a certain Abd'ul Ghaffūr, a Muslim. Although this phenomenon never played a decisive role in terms of numbers, occasional instances of conversions of European and American Christians also occurred. For examples cf. *Hindustan*, 24 December 1909, *SNNP* 1910, p. 296, *Nasim-i-Agra*, 27 June 1911, *Selections from the Native Newspapers Published in the United Provinces* (henceforth *SNNUP*), 1911, p. 571 and *Census of India 1931*, vol. XXIV, Jammu and Kashmir State, *pt I, Report*, p. 294.

40. *Arya Gazette*, 15 July 1899; *SNNP* 1899, p. 408.

41. The response to the appeal for funds must have been positive, since it is reported that the Peshawar Ārya Samāj alone donated Rs 1,000 for the task of 'Madras-pracār'; Cf. Satyadev Vidyālaṁkār, *Svāmī Śraddhānand* (repr.), Haridvar, 1995 ['1933], p. 282f.

42. *Satdharm Pracharak*, 8 September 1899, *SNNP*, 1889, p. 550.

43. *Vakil*, 14 August 1899; ibid., p. 471; *Sanatan Dharm Gazette*, ibid., p. 664. The fierce resistance of the Tamil pandits is also emphasized by Svāmī Śraddhānand in his pamphlet 'Jāti ke dīnō ko mat tyāgo'; in B.Bhāratīya (ed.), *Svāmī Śraddhānand Granthāvalī*, vol. VI, pp. 68–97, p. 93.

44. Not satisfied with the meagre results of the Tinnevelly expedition, the Ārya Samājīs tried four years later to establish a 'Madras Prachar Fund' in order to spread the *Arya dharm* in the Telugu region first. *Arya Patrika*, 12 December 1903, p. 5f.

45. *Arya Gazette*, 30 November 1899, *SNNP*, 1909, p. 722.

46. The only one to mention the Tinnevelly expedition is R.K. Ghai. However, he comes to the conclusion that until 1921 śuddhi 'primarily remained a social movement' and does not recognize the importance of the incident. Cf. Ghai, *The Shuddhi Movement in India . . .*, p. 44. As far as I know, the appeal to the 'parted brothers' is mentioned by no other author.

47. Lajpat Rai, *A History of the Arya Samaj. An Account of its Origin etc.* (2nd edn, revised and expanded by S.R. Sharma, repr.), New Delhi, 1992, p. 120.

48. *Sanatan Dharma Patrika*, June 1909, in *SNNUP*, p. 574. Cf. also Brahman Sarasva, June 1909, ibid., p. 560; *Samrat*, 16 September 1909, ibid., p. 681; and *Brahman Sarasva*, December 1909, *SNNUP*, 1910, p. 173.

49. 'All Hindus [ought to] place the Arya Samajists under social ostracism if they are at all anxious to preserve their purity of blood.' *Shri Yadavendra* (Allahabad), September 1909, *SNNUP*, 1909, p. 681.

50. Cf. e.g. *Prakash*, 6 September 1910, *SNNP*, 1910, p. 820.

51. *Arya Gazette*, 20 May 1909, *SNNP*, 1909, p. 500.

52. Cf. *Hindustan*, 4 November 1910, p. 1018, *Prakash*, 15 November 1910, ibid., p. 1036f.; *Paisa Akhbar*, 25 November 1910, ibid., p. 1071; *The Tribune*, 1 December 1910, ibid., p. 1070f; *The Observer*, 3 December 1910, ibid., p. 1090f.

53. Lajpat Rai states: 'The famous Gait circular proved a good tonic for orthodox Kashi [. . .] it had a quite unexpected effect and galvanized the dying body of orthodox Hinduism', L. Lajpat Rai, *History of the Arya Samaj* . . ., p. 124. An indirect outcome of the uproar about the Gait circular was the founding of the short-lived All-India Shuddhi Sabha, which failed because of the reluctance of the more conservative section of the Hindus towards its radical programme. Cf. *Punjabee*, 10 January 1911, *SNNP*, 1911, p. 36.

54. For the origin and history of the Mappilās see S.F. Dale, *Islamic Society on the South Asian Frontier. The Mappilās of Malabar 1498–1922*, Oxford, 1982. The prehistory of the rebellion is treated exhaustively by K.N. Panikkar, *Against Lord and State. Religion and Peasant Uprisings in Malabar, 1836–1921*, Delhi, 1989.

55. Haṁsraj, 'Bhūmikā', in Satyavrat Śarmā, *Mālābār aur Āryya* [sic] *Samāj*, Agra, ⁴1925, pp. 3–10, p. 6; this and the following translations by the present author.

56. Ibid.; emphasis in the original text.

57. Ibid.

58. Ibid., p. 7.

59. Cf. J. Luett, 'Religion und Politik in Indien. Pandit M.M. Malaviyas Vermittlerrolle im politischen Hinduismus des frühen 20. Jahrhunderts', unpubl. habil. thesis, Heidelberg, 1976, p.144f.

60. Ibid., pp. 149–56.

61. For this concept, see C. Jaffrelot, *Les Nationalistes Hindous. Idéologie, Implantation et Mobilisation des Années 1920 aux Années 1990*, Paris 1993, p. 33ff.

62. The *Devalasmṛti* contains about ninety verses, and probably dates back to about AD 500. For details, see P.V. Kane, *History of the Dharmaśāstra*, vol. I, Poona, ²1968, p. 121; and J.F. Seunarine, *Reconversion to Hinduism through Śuddhi*, Madras, 1977, p. 54.

63. In the Presidential speech to the All-India Shudhhi Sabha Conference 1926 Moonje claimed to have rediscovered the document in a library in Nagpur after learning of the reconversion problems in Malabar. *Hitavada*, 18 April 1926, cited in J. Zavos, '*Sangathan*: The Pursuit of a Hindu Ideal in Colonial India. The Idea of Organization in the Emergence of Hindu Nationalism 1870–1930' (unpublished PhD thesis), Bristol, 1997, p. 192, n. 30.

64. Haṁsraj, 'Bhūmikā', p. 12.

65. Cf. R.L. Hardgrave, 'The Mappila Rebellion 1921: Peasant Revolt in Malabar', *Modern Asian Studies* 11(1) 1977, p. 92. The actual number of the Hindus forcibly converted by the Mappilas is difficult to estimate. According to

J.R. Graham, 'The Arya Samaj as a Reformation of Hinduism . . .', p. 510, n. 2, only 1,766 such conversions were officially registered. For a discussion see also K.N. Panikkar, *Against Lord and State* . . , p. 182, n. 225.

66. The *Vedic Magazine* stated: 'The blessed work of sending relief to the distressed fell to the Arya Samaj, for which this latter body can however claim no credit. *Members of the same community*, it was to the Arya Samajists a sacred duty to go to the help of their suffering Hindu brethren in Malabar. *VMGS* 13(1), July 1922, p. 56 (emphasis mine). It may also be noted that the whole expedition was guided by the moderate wing of the Samaj whereas the Tinnevelly operation had been planned and carried out by the gurukul faction. The moderates had always emphasized their being part of Hinduism.

67. *VMGS* 13(2), August 1922, p. 67.

68. Cf. the protocol of the session, reprinted in H.N. Mitra (ed.), *Indian Annual Register 1922*, vol. II, Calcutta, 1923, p. 943f.

69. Details about the Malkānās may be found in *The Leader*, 17 March 1923, and in Shraddhananda, *Hindu Sangathan. Saviour of the Dying Race*, s.l. 1927, pp. 120ff. For an extensive treatment of the Malkānā campaign, see H. Fischer-Tiné, 'Die Śuddhi-Bewegung des Ārya Samāj und ihre Rolle bei der Konstituierung einer Hindu Identität' (unpublished M.A. thesis), Heidelberg, 1995, pp. 66–87.

70. Cf. S.R. Sharma, *Mahatma Hans Raj. Maker of the Modern Punjab*, Jullundur, ²1965, p. 119.

71. Śraddhānand had borrowed the 'dying race' slogan from the Bengali officer U.N. Mukherjee, whom he had met in Calcutta in 1912. Mukherjee had written a widely read book with the title *Hindus–a Dying Race* in 1909 in which he tried to prove mathematically, that the 'Hindu race' would have completely vanished from the face of the earth after 420 years if the demographic tendencies continued. Cf. K.W. Jones, 'The Negative Component of Hindu Consciousness', *Indo British Review. A Journal of History* 19(1), 1994, pp. 57–72, p. 62f and P.K. Datta, 'Dying Hindus: Production of Hindu Communal Sense in Early Bengal', *Economic and Political Weekly*, 19 June 1993, pp. 1305–19, esp. 1306–10.

72. *VMGS* 13(9), March 1923, p. 616. See also *The Leader*, 17 March 1923, *Hindustan*, 17 March 1923, *Punjab Press Abstracts*, 1923, p. 113, *The Tribune*, 29 March 1923, ibid., p. 186 and *Akash Bani*, 1 April 1923, ibid., p. 198.

73. *Milap*, 23 August 1923, *Punjab Press Abstracts*, 1923, p. 415.

74. Altogether the number of the Malkānās reclaimed between 1923 and 1930 was around 190,000. Cf. H. Fischer-Tiné, 'Die Śuddhi-Bewegung des Ārya Samāj . . ., p. 81f.

75. Cf. *VMGS* 19(2), August 1923, p. 714f.

76. Cf. J.T.F. Jordens, *Swāmī Shraddhānanda*, p. 157f.

77 Śraddhānanda, *Hindu Sangathan*, p. 136f.

78. Among those who wrote a necrologue for the svāmī, praising him as a martyr, were Motilal Nehru, M.M. Mālvīya M.K. Gandhi, Jugalkiśor Birlā and Rabindranath Tagore. Cf. B. Bhāratīya (ed.), *Svāmī Śraddhānand Granthāvalī*, vol. XI, appendix 5, pp. 168–83.

'Duties of Ahmadi Women':[1]
Educative Processes in the Early
Stages of the Ahmadiyya Movement

AVRIL A. POWELL

A NEW PROPHET IN THE PUNJAB

IN THE EARLY 1890s, in the British-ruled province of the Punjab in northwest India, one Mirza Ghulam Ahmad, a hitherto unknown Muslim from the obscure village of Qadiyan, began to proclaim a mission as *masih maw'ud* (promised Messiah), *mujaddid* (restorer) and *mahdi* (guide).[2] If the small, but growing Christian communities of the region were incensed by the first claim, the notion of a 'guide' or 'restorer' during times when Muslims might be deemed to be in danger of straying from the true path, was as familiar among Indian Muslims as elsewhere in the Muslim world. India under British and Christian colonial rule might well be deemed to have been entering just such a crisis, as the recent emergence of other reform movements in the Punjab, Muslim as well as Hindu and Sikh, seemed to indicate. But when a few years later, Ghulam Ahmad re-articulated his mission to endow himself with powers of prophethood, *'ulama* representing the Sunni Muslims of the region, already angered by some of his earlier claims and combative methods, responded with outrage. For the Prophet Muhammad, founder of the religion of Islam, who died in Mecca in AD 632, is believed by all Muslims to have been *khatm al-nabiyyin*, the 'seal' of the prophets, the last of a line of messengers who had possessed the power to transmit Allah's revelations to mankind. This new claim to prophetic powers by an obscure Punjabi was surely heresy.

If proclaimed anywhere else in British India, Ghulam Ahmad's self-ascription as 'prophet' probably would have caused him to be quickly dismissed as *majnun* (demented/possessed). In contrast, in the Punjab province where the bazaars in the urban centres had been resounding since the late 1860s to a cacophony of competing claims to the monopoly of religious truth, the reaction was of a more complex order. Tract warfare and *manazara* (public religious debate) had been adopted by British and American missionaries, and their Indian converts in the 1840s, but had long been practised by Muslim debaters bent on pursuing various internecine theological disputes, who now honed their dialectical skills in retaliation to the Christian attacks on Islam. Finally, declaimers of Hindu revival, followers of the Punjab-based Arya Samaj movement, joined the bazaar disputations in the late 1870s. Tracts attacking rival doctrines and spokesmen proliferated in the 1880s, as each new movement took advantage of the vernacular press to disseminate its own claims and to abuse its rivals. Mirza Ghulam Ahmad had adopted the same techniques to publicize his own mission, but also used his claim to powers of prophecy and miracle to foretell the deaths of his rivals, particular stress being placed on dreams in the course of which he received messages from Allah, and predicted future events, both local and international, ranging from plague in the Punjab to world war. He directed his campaign not only against some well-known Sunni 'ulama of the Deoband and Ahl-i Hadith movements which were increasingly influential among Sunnis in the region, but also against the Christian missionaries and the leaders of the Arya Samaj. He thus drew upon himself the hostility of all the existent religious reform organizations in the Punjab.[3] If it seemed extremely unlikely to many contemporary observers that his movement, whatever his undoubted charismatic qualities, would survive beyond his own life-time, others detected very early on the staying-power of this movement.

For from such unpromising beginnings, the Ahmadiyya movement had proved strong enough after only ten years to be able to claim its followers to be a distinct religious community, the only upholders of 'true Islam', in the face of a Sunni Muslim population of several million it deemed to be *kafir* for not heeding Mirza Ghulam Ahmad's warnings.[4] It soon had sufficient membership, pledged to the founder through *bai'at* (initiation) of a traditional Sufi kind, and centralized through regular fund raising, the publication of journals and the establishment of schools, to justify such a definition. The comments in the decennial censuses carried out by the British show that the Ahmadiyya movement, though never a 'mass movement' was rapidly becoming significant beyond its numerical membership. Following its founder's call for census enumeration separately from the Sunnis, Ahmadis in the Punjab were estimated by the British at approximately 3,450 in 1901, rising in 1911 to 18,695, to 28,851 in 1921, and 55,908 in 1931.[5] Such figures remained only a microscopic minority of the total Muslim population of the Punjab, and were insignificant numerically compared to the growth during the same period of another longer-established Muslim 'return' movement, that of the Ahl-i Hadith, which had emerged from the Tariqa-i Muhammadi (misnamed 'Wahhabi') purification movement of the early nineteenth century.[6] Furthermore, the Ahmadis seemed weakened when, in 1914, disagreements over the succession to the leadership of the movement, following the death of the first *khalifa* (successor), resulted in a split of its membership into a Qadiyan-based organization, which reaffirmed Ghulam Ahmad's prophetic role, and a new, smaller Lahore-based group, which conceived a less controversial 'reformist' and 'restorative' role for the founder. That both branches of a movement which was by then anathema to all other religious movements in the Punjab, nevertheless continued to survive and flourish, was partly a reflection of the divisions and hostilities among its rivals, but also a consequence of Mirza Ghulam Ahmad's early decision to encourage the tacit support of the British colonial state, by urging his followers to acquiesce in the status quo, thereby preaching an interpretation of jihad which urged individual spiritual striving rather than any challenge to the legitimacy of non-Muslim and foreign rule. Furthermore, if the Ahmadis remained numerically insignificant in their homeland of the Punjab, the success of the worldwide overseas missionary movement in Africa, Southeast Asia, North America and Britain, which began during the founder's lifetime, and was continued separately but fervently by both branches, made them unique among the 'new' religious movements of late colonial India. For these reasons the Ahmadiyya movement seems deserving of more study than it has so far received.

SCHOLARSHIP ON THE AHMADIYYA MOVEMENT

Considerable attention has already been paid by its own adherents, and by other scholars, to examining the doctrinal implications of the new movement. From within the Ahmadi community its founder and his khalifas were prolific from the beginning in the publication of Qur'anic commentaries and tracts on particular issues, in expounding the movement's perception of the 'true Islam', in emphasizing the need for spiritual revitalization and redirection to other Muslims, and in justifying the role of Mirza Ghulam Ahmad in that process.[7] From outside the movement, apart from detractors among the other Punjabi religious communities, comment on, and evaluation of the movement, has concentrated on the founder and his message.[8] Wilfred Cantwell Smith's characterization of Ahmadiyya in the 1940s as 'a late Indian sufi version of Islam activated by modern-Western infiltrations' captured the need to consider both the traditional 'spiritual' appeal, and the impact of a changing political environment, upon the emergence and evolution of the movement.[9] More recently the central theological problematic posed by Ghulam Ahmad's claim to prophethood has been examined particularly insightfully in Yohanan Friedmann's placing of prophetology in the historical context of classical and medieval thought on the Qur'an and Hadith, as well as of the Sufi traditions.[10] The movement has fared less well, however, in its socio-political dimensions. Stefan Lavan's *The Ahmadiyah Movement: a History and Perspective* is a useful pioneering study, which (together with the same author's article on sources for study of the movement), has proved the starting-point for most subsequent study.[11] Lavan, admitting that 'issues of a sociological-anthropological nature have not been explored in depth' in his own study, promised a further volume which has not yet appeared.[12] Nor has any other scholar attempted to answer the questions about social origins, composition and mobility which seem so crucial to any understanding of the sudden drawing power exerted, in such unpromising circumstances, by this movement. Indeed Friedmann, while limiting the scope of his own excellent study to 'prophetology and related issues', specifically directed the attention of his readers to the need to examine in the future, not only the influence of 'its Christian missionary rivals' on Ahmadi preaching and organizational structure, but also 'the social nature of the Ahmadiyya'.[13]

While scholars of Ahmadiyya have formulated appropriate questions, but not as yet pursued them, some interesting approaches to the study of the politicization of religious movements in other parts of north India may suggest some theoretical models for any such case study. The Brass/ Robinson exchanges over factors explaining Muslim identity formation amid the increasingly virulent communalism in late-nineteenth-century United Provinces has had positive effects on the examination by others of parallel religious movements in other regions in more rigorous theoretical terms than hitherto.[14] Emphasis has recently been placed on examining the relative significance of the deep-rooted 'primordial' bases of religious identity, *vis-à-vis* new identities constructed in the colonial milieu to further specific political and economic goals. An alternative conceptual framework which to some extent encapsulates both positions is Kenneth Jones's assessment of 'socio-religious reform movements' on a spectrum ranging from 'transitional movements' (originating in the pre-colonial world and from indigenous forms of socio-religious dissent) to 'acculturative movements' (originating within the colonial milieu by leaders who were themselves products of cultural interaction). While Jones, without claiming any firsthand familiarity with the relevant sources, defined the

Ahmadiyya movement, on the basis mainly of Lavan's study, as 'acculturative',[15] Friedmann's simultaneously published study has nevertheless had the significant effect, without denying any more worldly concerns of its late nineteenth-century leaders, of drawing attention back to the 'primordial' roots of this movement within medieval Islam. There is now clearly a need for the recent theoretical insights to be applied to a comprehensive examination of the 'construction' of the Ahmadiyya movement over time, in the way that Harjot Oberoi has recently achieved for the processes through which a uniform Sikh identity was constructed in this same period and place.[16] A number of other scholars, including Harald Fischer-Tiné, are currently at work on some hitherto neglected aspects of the Arya Samaj and Singh Sabha movements, new dimensions of which include the attention now being paid to consideration of the relations between the competing reform movements in the Punjab, and to changing gender identities within and between these movements.[17] Consensus is far from achieved yet, on whether such complex processes of identity construction can be reduced to any common formulae. Ian Talbot, in an overview of the Punjab in the period 1875–1937, has recently re-emphasized the complexity of a situation where

The reformers from all communities acted in the name of 'tradition' but in reality they blended it with modernity in their reinvention of the past and construction of firm identity markers. Janus-faced, they had to defend these against other Punjabis, whilst seeking British recognition and support.[18]

Consideration of the genesis and early growth of the Ahmadiyya movement, apart from addressing the social processes at work within it, may hopefully also assist in refining and qualifying present understandings of some parallel processes of religious identification which were at work more broadly in late-nineteenth- and early-twentieth-century Punjab.

SOCIAL COMPOSITION: CLASS AND LOCATION

In a province that had very few large towns apart from the capital city of Lahore, the missionary and religious reform movements had established their headquarters in a handful of small district towns, such as Amritsar and Sialkot, mainly in central and eastern Punjab, where Christian missionaries of various denominations competed for converts with Arya Samaj, Deobandi and Ahl-i Hadith preachers. Until the mass movements of the last years of the century, affirmation, or change of identity on a religious basis seems to have been a mainly urban phenomenon, involving literate elite, and in spite of the emphasis in the reformers' programmes on eradicating 'popular' accretions to doctrine and practice, leaving the rural masses, some have claimed, relatively unaffected.[19] The Ahmadiyya movement was immediately distinctive from its rivals in overriding and then transforming any such rural–urban distinction. For even if Ghulam Ahmad and his followers subsequently preached and debated in the larger towns, the starting-point and subsequent hub of the movement was a village in the rural Gurdaspur district, which was subsequently raised to urban status only because of the population rise consequent on the movement's success. Ahmadi sources like to stress, in retrospect, the unpropitious environment in which the movement was born, 'a small village, comprising about 2,000 souls, eleven miles from the nearest railway station, where the post arrived about twice a week and the solitary schoolmaster also acted as postmaster, postal clerk and peon'.[20] In contrast to the newly established 'Christian villages' in the Punjab, such as Clarkabad, which remained villages, Qadiyan was transformed through the process of religious revival from a village of small subsistence farmers into a considerable population centre. Sialkot, the second most significant urban focus of Ahmadi conversion and settlement, had linkages, so far unexplored, with Ahmadi families in its satellite village of Daska, as did the city of Amritsar with the nearby village of Jandiala. Clearly, urban–rural dichotomies which have been prominent in many recent studies of colonial Punjab, do not necessarily hold for the foci of Ahmadi activity.

Likewise, the first generation of initiates into the movement defy any easy social categorization. Kenneth Jones, working mainly from Lavan's findings, which scarcely skimmed the surface of these questions, nevertheless made the significant observation that 'the origins of its members produced with the Ahmadis a bipolar pattern'. While, in Jones's view, the appeal was, as with other reform movements, at first 'to middle-class, literate Muslims' (specifically to doctors, attorneys, landowners and small businessmen) from the district towns, its headquarters in a hitherto obscure village, Qadiyan, later attracted 'more members from the less educated, poorer rural classes.'[21] Ahmadi sources are somewhat inconsistent about the social origins of the first generation, in some accounts choosing to stress the poverty of the initial following 'of forty or fifty persons all of whom with the exception of one or two, who were in comparatively easy circumstances, were extremely poor',[22] but in others anxious to affirm the 'respectable' credentials of the converts, and to deny the misapprehension which was adopted in the census of 1901, but subsequently corrected, that Mirza Ghulam Ahmad's appeal was particularly 'to the sweepers'.[23] Inconsistencies in the accounts may partly reflect considerable social mobility in the early Ahmadiyya catchment, founded as the movement was at the precise time, in the early 1890s, when the Punjab governor was introducing positive discrimination for Muslims in the services of the province. Certainly, within two generations, Ahmadis had begun to gain a disproportionate share of service positions, and were earning a reputation as a highly educated, ambitious community. If the social composition of the movement over time remains unclear at present, family and biographical sources, already used for mainly hagiographical purposes, have not as yet been drawn on to answer such questions.

AHMADI WOMEN

The limited objective of this essay is to move only one step into the neglected social history of the Ahmadis by examining some early perceptions within the movement of roles, ideal and real, for its female members, and the preparation and education for those roles deemed appropriate by its male leaders. The focus will be on the family of the founder of the movement, Mirza Ghulam Ahmad, his own khalifas and descendants, and on females directly initiated into the movement by pledging allegiance to the founder or his son. The justification for this emphasis on the socialization of Ahmadi women, apart from their subsequent active roles within the missionary movement, is Wilfred Cantwell Smith's startling statement in the 1940s, that Qadiyan, the focal point of the movement, 'appears to have been much the most literate town in. India, with almost total feminine literacy'.[24] At a time when female literacy figures were very low in the whole subcontinent, and particularly low among Muslim women, the Ahmadiyya achievement is suggestive of a strongly directed educational programme for girls, which deserves some scrutiny. The findings may provide an entry for consideration in the future of some of the wider questions about the social identity of the movement outlined above.

The sources which are drawn on consist of three kinds. First, interpretations by the leaders of the movement of Shari'at norms on women's status, and on appropriate comportment according to Islam. Such publications were often apologetic, addressed to western critics, or to potential converts, rather than to Ahmadi initiates, examples being Mirza Ghulam Ahmad's *Philosophy of the Teachings of Islam* (Lahore 1896) and his son, the second khalifa, Mahmud Ahmad's, *Ahmadiyyat, or the True Islam*.[25] Second are speeches, tracts and letters by the founder Ghulam Ahmad, and sermons by his son, which were addressed to female members of the new community, or to the community in general, on reformist issues affecting women. In this category are Mirza Ghulam Ahmad's *Islah-i khatun* (Women's Reform), 'Advice to women concerning polygamy', 'Teaching on the best manner of treating a wife', and Mahmud Ahmad's *Ahmadi auraton ke fara'iz* (Duties of Ahmadi women), a sermon given in 1920.[26] Third is a small but significant category of biographical material concerning the activities of some Ahmadi women, who were either relatives of the founding family, or wives and daughters of leading members of the first generation of initiates into Ahmadiyya. Notable here is *Hayat-i-javadani, yani: sawanah-Hafsah Qadiyani,* a biography of his recently deceased wife, written by one Mufti Fazl al-Rahman, and published at Qadiyan in 1918.[27] Significantly, Hafsah, the wife in question was the daughter of the first khalifa, Nur ud-Din, and her husband, the author, was a nephew of Nur ud-Din's wife. This couple's proximity to the source of Ahmadi charisma and authority gives the account of their relationship a particular utility for this study. A better known biography is *My Mother,* written by Muhammad Zafrullah Khan in 1938, and republished in English in 1981.[28] Zafrullah Khan also was closely connected with the Ahmadi leadership, his father having given up the legal profession to serve the khalifa. The family's connections with Sialkot also throw light on this secondary centre of Ahmadi growth and activity.

The chronological range of these texts is from the 1890s to the mid-1930s, thus covering the first two generations of initiates. Apart from Mirza Ghulam Ahmad's huge corpus of publications, which are easily available in many reprints, the other sources are found mainly in tract form among the rich collection of Urdu materials in the Oriental and India Office Collections of the British Library. Although such tracts certainly allow some glimpses into the lives of women of the community, they are in all cases refracted through the observations of husbands and sons: so far the voices of female Ahmadis of the first generation, as of women in other contemporary reform movements, such as the Arya Samaj and Singh Sabha, have eluded any direct recovery in their own words. Muted female voices are occasionally to be heard at second hand when the Ahmadi male leaders claim they are themselves responding in their own sermons and tracts to, for example, 'some women who have been criticizing polygamy', or to the request, by letter, of some unidentified women to have sermons addressed specifically to a female audience.

WOMAN'S PLACE IN THE FAMILY

Lavan described the Ahmadiyya community as being 'comparable to an extended family structure',[29] a comparison which will be drawn on in the following discussion to justify perceiving the founder's own family as a microcosm for understanding the mores of the wider community. Mirza

Ghulam Ahmad's teachings on appropriate behaviour for women were, in many respects, at least as conservative as those of any Sunni 'reformer' at this date. Sir Sayyid Ahmad Khan, progressive in most other matters, was, after all, conservative in his attitude to female education and roles, and discouraged initiatives for the encouragement of public schooling for girls.[30] Only in the last years of the nineteenth century did a handful of male Muslim writers begin to advocate education for women, to be embarked on very circumspectly, and, as Gail Minault's studies have shown, almost always from within the seclusion of the home, or in classes held in private houses, where purdah was very strictly upheld.[31] In such an environment, the hostility with which the Ahmadiyya movement was regarded in Sunni circles necessitated, its leaders considered, more than usual adherence to Shari'at stipulations, especially regarding seclusion, in order not to give any pretext for accusations of moral laxity against the movement generally. Women in this movement, as in other reformist movements, were held to be responsible for both the 'honour' and the 'shame' which others, based on their behaviour, would associate with their menfolk and family.

This theme is reiterated in many of Ghulam Ahmad's tracts, examples of his admonitions being, 'their [husbands'], honour is in your hands', and 'the first test of man's morality is his wife'.[32] Mirza Ghulam Ahmad's own family in particular, and those of his closest followers, were projected as exemplars of right comportment, and of appropriate relationships between family members. Until his death in 1908, he personally initiated women as well as men into the movement (including the two women, Hafsah, daughter of Nur ud-Din, the first khalifa, and Husain Bibi, wife of the secretary of the second khalifa, and mother of Zafrullah Khan, whose biographies are drawn on here). In addition, he played a decisive role in the arrangement of suitable marriages for other daughters of this expanding inner circle.[33] For apart from overseeing betrothal arrangements between those already initiated into the movement, marriage was regarded as an important means to extend the new community of 'true Muslims'. Thus the founder and his khalifas also exercised influence over the choice of brides from 'outside', who, after marriage then required appropriate education according to the doctrinal and social teachings of the Ahmadis. In contrast, after 1915, it was 'prohibited that Ahmadis should give their daughters in marriage to non-Ahmadis, for wives are generally influenced by their husbands'.[34] Marriage was thus a key means to facilitate both the expansion and the desired control of the membership. Other opportunities to demonstrate the authority of the head of the movement over women occurred during meetings arranged, usually on the occasion of the annual *jalsa* at Qadiyan, but also at other times in towns such as Sialkot, and other centres of conversion and settlement, when the khalifa would deliver sermons to assemblies of women on particular points of doctrine and behaviour. One such sermon, given at Sialkot in 1920 by the second khalifa will be drawn on extensively in this paper.[35]

The particular Ahmadi nuances on 'woman's place in the family' will be identified by examining the ways in which the sources identified above comment on the life-cycle roles of women in the successive stages of daughter, wife, mother and 'elder' of the community.

The Forming of a Pious Daughter

Ahmadi girls were initially encouraged, as were the daughters of many other reformist groups, to study the injunctions of Islam within the confines of their father's home. The emphasis was on correct understanding of the Shari'at particularly the Qur'an, and to this end the learning of Arabic was positively advocated. As pointed out in one of khalifa Mahmud Ahmad's sermons for women, it was possible to ask male relatives to read the Qur'an to their womenfolk, but 'between reading yourself and listening to someone else, there's a great difference. In listening only the ears are occupied, but in reading for yourself the eyes too are occupied, and this way there is more reward (*sawab*)'.[36] He reminded his listeners that a reading book was available for sale in Qadiyan which had been prepared to help women read the Qur'an. In addition, advertisements appended to tracts, or inserted in Ahmadi journals, indicate that from an early stage literate women could have recourse to Urdu tracts prepared especially for them. One such was a commentary on Surah 'Nur', which among other stipulations about appropriate behaviour between the sexes, contains the verses on which the necessity for the observance of purdah is usually based.[37]

Apart from overtly religious literature of this kind, there was also a growing body of didactic literature specifically for Ahmadi women which used role models to point moral lessons. While the models used in the religious tracts were usually the wives of the Prophet, drawn from the Qur'an and the Hadith, the second generation of Ahmadi women were increasingly enjoined to follow role models from within the movement itself. Some of these were anonymous, possibly fictional exemplars of virtuous conduct, such as those eulogized in the series, 'Stories of Ahmadiyya Women', in one of which, *Sabar ka ajar* (Patience and its fruit), a husband at first dislikes his wife, but because she is of a very religious bent, she 'at last gained his love'.[38] The second generation could also benefit from biographical accounts of wives and mothers written by males belonging to prominent families within the movement, who often had close relationships, through marriage and service, with the founder's family.

While these biographies will be drawn on extensively in the subsequent discussion to illustrate 'wifely' virtues, they also afford some glimpses of childhood routines and expectations. Thus Zafrullah Khan's biography of his mother, Husain Bibi, born in 1863, and initiated into the movement in 1904 by Mirza Ghulam Ahmad, is a eulogy of a woman of the first generation, who prided herself that 'I have no book learning', but who nevertheless later exerted unusually strong influence within the movement.[39] In contrast, the subject of *Hayat-i-javadani*, Hafsah, the daughter of the first khalifa Nur ud-Din, who was born a decade later in 1874, received an intensive, book-based education, in which she excelled. She is portrayed as an avid scholar, who benefited from her father's wish to initiate her himself into the study of the Qur'an and Hadith, but also into his own medical practice of Yunani *tib*. In addition he employed a maulvi to teach his daughters at home. When she married, a trunk of books, on *tafsir* (Qur'anic commentary), *hadith*, (traditions) and 'other religious matters' accompanied her in the dowry, together with a letter from her father, reminding her of her religious duties, which she continued to re-read every day of her married life.[40] Among the secular books her father advised her to continue to read was the *Mirat al-'arus* (The Bride's Mirror), a popular didactic novel, published by Deputy Nazir Ahmad in 1869.[41]

While her husband was clearly at pains to eulogize both her scholarly leanings and her charitable works, this account is nuanced by Hafsah's portrayal as a hot-tempered, even wilful, girl who was unlikely to subordinate herself easily to the role of wife. Mirza Ghulam Ahmad, who knew both families well, and gave approval to the betrothal (following a dream in which the groom appeared to him as suitably pious), noticed the imminent clash of temperaments, and expressed his fears of the outcome unless the pair received God's special blessing.[42] Thus this scholarly girl, virtuous in many ways, and unusually well educated in Islam, was perceived in her childhood as a force for danger unless successfully subdued in the marriage home. In contrast to the stereotypical 'good' and 'bad' girls of Deputy Nazir Ahmad's *Mirat al-'arus*, who had been the subjects of her own girlhood reading, the real-life Hafsah is presented as a mixture of admirable housewifely qualities, which other girls should emulate, combined with potentially socially disruptive faults, which, uncurbed, would reflect adversely on the honour of her husband and family. The rest of the biography recounts how, under the management of her new husband she is appropriately subdued, although, as will become apparent, he seems to take pleasure in showing, in ways which might normally be expected to reflect badly on his 'honour', that his wife had actually subtly subordinated him to her own will in certain significant dimensions of their relationship.

The Virtuous Wife

It was particularly important to emphasize Ahmadi values to new brides because of the influx of girls from outside the movement. Whereas the biographical sources which are drawn on here inform only on 'insider' wives, the apologetic works of the founder and the second khalifa provide indications of Ahmadi emphases on Shari'at norms concerning 'right conduct' within the marriage relationship. The necessity for Ahmadis to be seen to be upholding the Shari'at even more strictly than most other Muslims has already been stressed. The result was marked social conservatism concerning women's status and conduct which appears at first sight contradictory to the strong emphasis on female literacy within the movement. Strictures on polygamy, divorce and seclusion in the founder's voluminous publications set the tone for subsequent discourse.

Ghulam Ahmad's 'Advice to women concerning polygamy' was originally written in response to criticism of polygamous marriages voiced by 'some women', an action on their part which he described as 'innovatory'.[43] He therefore undertook to defend the institution, basing his argument on the Qur'anic verse, 'marry such women as seem good to you, two, three, or four', and supporting it with a rationale, very familiar in Muslim patriarchal discourse, that a husband must be able to satisfy his natural urges, specifying the incurable illness or insanity of the first wife as obstacles to his need. Although the argument is familiar, he employed a striking bazaari simile to emphasize his point, explaining that the Shari'at is like a chemist's stall, which would not fulfil its function if the chemist failed to supply appropriate cures. Thus, polygamy should be seen as the appropriate functional cure for the husband's physical needs.[44] There is no question of women having reciprocal rights, and he responds rhetorically to any objections, such as those put forward by his anonymous female critics, by stressing the wifely virtue of patience under apparent adversity, for a husband who does not deal justly with two or more wives can only be influenced for the better by the acquiescence and piety of his wives,[45] a theme which is later reiterated in some of the imaginative and biographical writings by Ahmadi males, notably in *Sabr ka ajar* and *Hayat-i javadani*.

In the same tract Ghulam Ahmad made an important reference to divorce, in which, while reiterating the virtue of 'patience', he nevertheless reminded women that wives might have recourse to the courts to initiate divorce if a husband became incurably ill, or the conditions of a polygamous marriage could be proved to contravene the Shari'at.[46] In reality, however, Ahmadi women probably found it just as difficult as women in other Muslim communities to initiate court proceedings to free them from the marriage bond, and the emphasis overall in such tracts is on the upholding of patriarchal control over marriage arrangements, of which, as has been shown, Ghulam Ahmad himself was usually the enabler, at least for marriages among the inner circle of Ahmadi families.

His stance on seclusion, and that of his, khalifas was also conservative, and closely linked to his defence of polygamy. For although both sexes are enjoined in the Qur'an to 'restrain their sexual passions', he reiterates that the male has a 'natural propensity' to fulfil his sexual appetite, unless temptation is removed from his vicinity. Thus, in his early apologetic work, *Philosophy of the Teachings of Islam*, Ghulam Ahmad explained:

The Word of God restrains the carnal desires of man even from smouldering in secret and enjoins upon him to avoid the very occasions where there is danger of excitement of evil passions. This is the secret underlying the principle of the seclusion of women in Islam.[47]

He insisted, moreover, that female seclusion, far from 'shutting up women like prisoners in gaol', served a positive good in helping to ensure the virtue of the whole society, for 'this excellent rule is conducive to the good of both sexes'. His successor, Nur ud-Din, also preached the 'necessity' of purdah.[48]

The insistence by the movement's leaders on the upholding of seclusion can be evaluated within their own extended family and close circle, for the biographical sources informative in suggesting gradations in the observation of purdah among Ahmadi women through the various stages of the life-cycle. Thus, whereas the 'wilful' young Hafsah had been allowed, until her betrothal at the age of fourteen, to be careless about purdah, at the time of engagement her father, Nur ud-Din, the first, khalifa, reminded his new son-in-law to insist that his daughter should now keep strict purdah. Hafsah immediately acquiesced, insisting that she fully seclude herself even before a very elderly and deaf uncle before whom she had in childhood been entirely free to come and go. This decision exemplified, in the eyes of her husband-biographer, one of the several ways he successfully subordinated her to his will.[49] She then continued to keep strict purdah for the rest of her relatively short life, dying before him in 1917, at the age of about forty-three. The biography of Husain Bibi, Zafrullah Khan's mother, also confirms, the strictness with which the first generation of Ahmadis observed purdah, but shows that in old age a strong-minded woman, no longer a 'temptation' to males in the sense stressed by Ghulam Ahmad, might discard purdah either permanently, or temporarily in particular situations. Husain Bibi, for example, justified the abandonment of strict purdah when anxious to confront the Viceroy and his wife concerning Ahrar victimization of the Ahmadis in the 1930s. She justified her decision to her son by saying, 'I am an old woman and am permitted a certain degree of freedom in the social sphere.'[50] Biographies such as these also allow some insights into the dynamics of husband-wife relationships in the spaces beyond the formal injunctions of the Shari'at, where relationships were beginning to be negotiated under some new and un-Islamic influences consequent on colonial rule. Adjustments to the norms and relationships among the *ashraf,* urban and middle-class Ahmadis, which they reflect, might be compared with the strict admonishments on 'duties' delivered in sermons to audiences which were likely to have consisted of illiterate and poorer village women, as one means to test the validity of Kenneth Jones's suggestion of a 'bipolar' social division of the Ahmadi community. Sources bearing on the literate females, close to the heart of the movement, will be considered first.

It has already been suggested that Hafsah's husband did not get his own way entirely, and he even seemed to feel an inverted kind of pride, rather than suffering a sense of damaged honour, when his pious and gifted, but allegedly 'wilful' wife occasionally bested him. While there is no doubt that this household remained essentially patriarchal, both he and Ghulam Ahmad before him seemed concerned to project the 'companionate' ideal of marriage in some dimensions of Ahmadi husband-wife relationships. It has been suggested in other studies on gender issues in late-nineteenth-century India that the Victorian 'helpmeet' concept of the relationship of a wife to her husband began to affect the way some Indian elite perceived marriage. Whether or not there was any conscious influence, possibly in response to late-nineteenth-century British criticisms of Muslim family life,[51] these Ahmadi writers certainly interspersed the language of the companionate ideal in an otherwise markedly patriarchal discourse. Thus Ghulam Ahmad's letter on 'Teaching on the best manner of treating a wife', initially written to a friend, and then published in journals and tracts in 1905 and 1922, reaffirmed, in a very patriarchal fashion, the necessity for the man, who is by nature 'strong', to have authority over the 'weak' woman, but urged at the same time that husbands 'should treat them [wives] as your bosom companions in this transitory state.[52] He illustrated the ideal relationship with the image of a host (the husband), who should treat the respected guest (his wife), for whom he is responsible, with great kindness. If this remains a very patronizing ideal, which was, in any case, probably being preached merely to wean some husbands from their habit of physical violence against their wives, the companionate/helpmeet model was, according to her own husband's account, realized in at least some of its aspects in Hafsah's household.

As the *Hayat-i javadani* was dedicated to 'the benefit of Muslim women', Hafsah's husband clearly intended the convolutions of his own marriage relationship to have positive lessons for others. Certainly, it is suffused with evidence of the husband's devotion to his recently deceased wife, its compilation having served a cathartic purpose for the author as he struggled to cope with his deep sense of loss: 'Twenty-six years of companionship (*rafaqat*) which is a quarter of a century, and such that it was a matter of two hearts in one life'.[53] Zafrullah Khan, too, recalled the relationship between his mother and father as 'a faithful and loving companionship, extending over close upon half a century'.[54] Hafsah's husband extolled 'the marriage relationship as the most important of all human relationships, and constantly praised those qualities in his wife which had strengthened and sustained their close relationship, notably her deep faith, compared to his own tendency to falter, her patience in adversity, compared to his own pessimistic temperament, and also her prudent running of the household. The most telling hint of the vicissitudes within a very intimate relationship is his recalling of her insistence that they should have 'time' reserved for each other each evening, and that they should always make up petty quarrels before retiring to bed, lest one of them should die during the night without any chance to restore harmony between them.[55]

That the subordination of the wife to the husband was assumed even in a 'companionate' relationship is implicit in the comment that Hafsah, not her husband, was always the one to apologize after a quarrel, regardless of whether the initial fault had been hers. He had been surprised and gratified to find that her girlish wilfulness and independence seemed to disappear almost immediately after the marriage.[56] As noted above, she accepted his stipulations about observing strict purdah, and in most situations appeared to fulfil the traditional expectations of a young bride living in her husband's household, taking care of all domestic matters, observing his food preferences, and ministering to his every physical and mental need. The harsher aspects of female subordination are also evident when Fazl al-Rahman refers, almost in passing, to the occasional need to chastise her physically for perceived misdemeanours, aberrations which reflected, perhaps, the resurgence of her girlish high spirits and 'wilfulness'.

Such beatings she bore, he noted, with due humility and fortitude, on one occasion taking great care not to admit to her mother that he had beaten her.[57]

If the impression is emerging, in spite of lip-service to notions of a companionate marriage, of a thoroughly patriarchal husband-wife relationship, it should be qualified by some indications of Hafsah's subtle management of her husband from this position of seeming subordination. At one level he seems anxious to explain, for other women's benefit, how the tables were turned, quoting her as saying,

It's an easy thing to fashion a husband as we wish. Those women are very stupid who want to make their husbands subordinate by defying their wishes. If a woman is obedient to her husband then the husband himself becomes agreeable to her.[58]

That such a strategy of outward compliance in order to gain long-term influence was probably a commonplace in male discourse on appropriate female behaviour within marriage is suggested by its closeness to Ghulam Ahmad's own advice to wives in his tract on polygamy in which he had urged obedience and patience as the appropriate means to turn the husband's behaviour in the desired direction. That it nevertheless took some unusual turns in the case of the highly educated, strong-willed Hafsah seems to be borne out in her husband's account. This reflected her strong spiritual power, based partly on the piety and learning inculcated in her childhood, but also on the understanding that she shared in the 'dream power' which, as has been indicated, was a distinctive claim underlying the magnetism of the founder of the Ahmadiyya movement, and was also claimed from time to time by others in his inner circle, including women.

The most striking situation in which she drew on such power was when in 1892, soon after their marriage, they went together to Qadiyan where, after becoming one of the first to be initiated into the movement by Ghulam Ahmad, she expressed a wish to settle permanently. This produced a conflict because Fazl al-Rahman, her husband, was in service elsewhere. While admitting to him, submissively, that 'I cannot disobey your order', she nevertheless achieved a compromise by securing his reluctant agreement that she should stay in Qadiyan, while he returned to his post. So matters continued until, in 1898, Fazl al-Rahman fell ill. Hafsah then recounted a dream in which, when she appeared before her father unveiled, she replied to his question concerning the absence of her *dupatta* (head scarf) that it had blown away in a storm. She interpreted the dream to signify the absence, even imminent death, of her husband.

After much prayer on her part, a subsequent dream in which the dupatta was miraculously restored signified to her the necessity for a reunion of husband and wife in Qadiyan to prevent him suffering a lonely death, uncared for by his wife. Overwhelmed by the portent of these dreams Fazl al-Rahman then succumbed to her plea that he should resign his post and settle in Qadiyan.[59] That other female initiates were attributed with 'dream power' is supported by the many instances in Zafrullah Khan's biography of his mother when Husain Bibi received premonitions through dreams, which included the foretelling of births and deaths in her own, and the British royal family, the promotion of her son, and the onset of the plague in the Punjab.[60] That Hafsah and Fazl al-Rahman did finally settle together in Qadiyan as a result of her dreams also reflects the strong influence exerted by the inner circle of the movement on the daily lives of many of those who had pledged spiritual allegiance, which soon resulted in the expansion and strengthening of the community in that hitherto 'obscure' village.

A more mundane example of Hafsah's management of her husband reflected her concern, noted above, to be able to share time with him in conjugal harmony. To this end she succeeded in prohibiting him from leaving the house in the evenings, whether to attend musical performances or to visit friends, saying, 'see I'm not stopping you, but God has made the daytime for men's business affairs, when you can do as you wish. At night your duty is that you should stay with us.'[61] His reply, 'thus I stopped' indicates another aspect of their life about which he was proud to inform other women he had submitted to his wife's wishes.

In terms of the 'bipolar pattern' characteristic of the social origins of the Ahmadis, noted by Kenneth Jones, the 'other Muslim women' Fazl al-Rahman believed would benefit by reading of his wife's example, were probably the literate wives of the 'doctors, attorneys, landowners and businessmen' of the central and eastern Punjab's district towns. In contrast, teachings about behaviour appropriate for the wives of the 'rural and less affluent', and initially illiterate, members who made up the other 'pole', can be evaluated through the admonitions in a sermon addressed by the second khalifa, Mahmud Ahmad, to a gathering of Ahmadi women in Sialkot in 1920. While there is no evidence for the actual composition of this crowd, there are some clues both in the content and the language of the sermon that many of the women had come in from the surrounding villages for the chance of seeing and hearing the second khalifa. That it was a mere whistle-stop speaking engagement in a busy schedule is suggested by Mahmud Ahmad's need to make a quick departure by train as soon as an abbreviated version of his sermon had been delivered. He spoke in Punjabi, but the full text was later translated and published in Urdu.[62]

Much of the positive content of his sermon might have been pronounced by any Sunni *'alim* of a reforming disposition, as the emphasis was first on understanding the meaning of 'true Islam', then on putting into practice each of the 'duties' required by the Shari'at. Negatively, the need to put aside 'custom-laden' Islam, as currently practised in the Punjab, under the influence both of Hindu custom, and fear of 'what the [Muslim] neighbours might say', was strongly stressed. What, then, if anything, was particularly 'Ahmadi' about this address, and what can be gleaned about the particular audience of women to whom it was addressed?

Early in the sermon the priority of the relationship with God above all other relationships was stressed, and at a later stage the audience was reminded that Muhammad was the greatest of all prophets, before whom no other should be given precedence. Two warnings given at this point reflect recent and ongoing religious conflicts in the Punjab. The first, reflecting the activity of Protestant missionaries in the Sialkot region, was addressed to the danger of elevating Christ above Muhammad, for Mahmud Ahmad lamented, 'in our country, out of ignorance, Muslims have given great status to Hazrat 'Isa' (Jesus).[63] The second was an explanation of Mirza Ghulam Ahmad's relationship with God, Muhammad and the rest of humanity, the inclusion of which reflected the recent split in the Ahmadi movement over the status and powers of the founder. Referring to the religious turmoil of 'the present age', the speaker, the son of the founder, declared his father, Mirza Ghulam Ahmad to have been a 'prophet' (*nabi*), but denied that he was a 'separate prophet' ('*alihadah nabi*), describing him rather as a 'servant' (*ghulam*) to his 'master' (*aqa*), the Prophet Muhammad.[64] In criticizing the tendency of women to use spells and amulets, customary practices at variance with the Shari'at, he warned them to prostrate themselves to God alone, but neither to Prophet Muhammad, nor to Hazrat Masih (Mirza Ghulam Ahmad), who is defined here as 'the restorer/reformer (muslah) of this age'.[65] These are the only two references in the sermon to the explicit role of the founder of the movement. Significantly, the negative danger to all Muslims represented by Christianity seemed to receive greater emphasis on this occasion than did the person of Mirza Ghulam Ahmad, probably reflecting Sialkot's prominence during recent years as a centre of mass conversions to Christianity. Women are addressed specifically on this issue, it seems, only because he deems they are even more prone than men to misunderstand or neglect the priority to be attributed to

God and to Muhammad, and are more likely to encourage *bid'at* (innovation), such as the un-Islamic worship of merely human religious leaders, and are, thereby, perceived as more likely to fall into missionary hands.

Much can be learned from the language and tone of this particular sermon about the second khalifa's perception of the spiritual and behavioural shortcomings of small-town and village women in the Punjab. This is the voice of patriarchy, chastising women for their shortcomings, comparing them to children in regarding religious gatherings as spectacles (*tamashas*), and to school pupils who cannot take in a second lesson until they have thoroughly digested the first. While men also resort to many customary practices which are opposed to the Shari'at, women are the worse offenders, 'so their situation is deserving of much pity'.[66] When he turns to observance of the 'five pillars', his criticisms are directed to what he regards as specifically 'female' excuses, such as lack of time to say *namaz* because of caring for the children, and avoidance of the *zakat* tax due on jewellery.[67] In a section on the need for women to study appropriate manners and etiquette, Mahmud Ahmad upbraids them particularly for 'backbiting', for 'the disease of tale-telling and slander is very much to be found among women'.[68] He points to the women's *majlises*, set up by the Ahmadis, as breeding-grounds of gossip and quarrel, comparing their behaviour to that of animals rather than human beings. The atmosphere of such meetings should be reformed, he urged, so that the members converse together affectionately and in a seemly fashion. Significantly, some of these points had also been made by khalifa Nur ud-Din in his letter of advice to his daughter, Hafsah, at the time of her marriage, and her husband later expressed his pride that she did not indulge in gossip, and always spoke frankly to him about his faults, rather than complaining about him behind his back in the manner of uneducated women.

By the date of this sermon (1920) both branches of the Ahmadiyya movement provided facilities for women to meet in religious discussion groups, and encouragement was given to the acquisition of basic literacy. That such a goal had not yet been attained, except perhaps in Qadiyan itself, was implicit in Mahmud Ahmad's statement that 'usually women are not literate'.[69] Outstanding therefore, in a sermon which seemed to place a low value on women's current worth and abilities, was the urgency with which he encouraged the learning of Arabic, as well as Urdu, for the purpose of reading the Qur'an.[70]

Although the advice being disseminated here might seem little different from that given by Sunni reformers throughout north India, there are some suggestions that the audience reflected the stage when the Qadiyani branch was penetrating into the rural *mufassil* surrounding small towns such as Sialkot. The cursory treatment of *hajj*, in the part of the sermon devoted to quite detailed reminders about the other four pillars of Islam, would seem to take account that women in this particular location and social setting would have little opportunity to fulfil the religious obligation of pilgrimage to Mecca, even if they had wished to do so.[71] If the patronizing and admonitory tone adopted to voice some of the criticisms of behaviour and practice cited above proves little in itself, some of the imagery employed to convey the message is certainly suggestive of a rural, rather than a more sophisticated urban audience. Mahmud Ahmad referred, for instance, to the mother's relationship with the child she has carried in her womb as like that of a traveller with a tree against which he takes a short rest, compared to the infinitely deeper relationship of the human being with God.[72] A person who has not yet digested one *roti* (implying 'religious lesson') should not, he said, be given a second.[73] Lazy women who do namaz in a perfunctory manner are like birds pecking at seed in the courtyard.[74] A woman should say the required namaz, even if her clothes are covered in her child's urine: in such an emergency you should say namaz just as you are: just rinse your clothes and squeeze them out, and they will be considered as clean.[75] Women who hold back jewellery on which zakat should be paid, should be made to pay up until the last string tethering the camel has been given up. While such choice of metaphor and example may, of course, reveal more about the speaker's own origins and education than it does about his audience's social status, there nevertheless seem to be sufficient indications here to suggest that this sermon formed part of a Qadiyani programme initiated about this time to encourage explicit religious and moral teaching for females from poorer rural backgrounds who were by then being initiated in growing numbers into the movement.

Motherly Roles

The biographical sources which present role-models for the 'perfect wife' also provide didactic messages about the stages in the female life-cycle of mother, and then 'elder' of the community. Hafsah's husband, desolate after her lingering death, declared that apart from the husband-wife relationship, the parent-child bond was the one other supremely significant relationship between human beings. Certainly all the sources being drawn on, whether sermonizing or biographical, eulogize women who fulfilled their duties as mothers to perfection, the emphasis being, once again, on the transmission to their children of the teachings of 'true Islam'. Fazl al-Rahman, for instance, devoted a chapter of his biography to Hafzah's relationship with her children.[76] Her father, the khalifa, Nur ud-Din, had reminded her of her duty to teach her daughters the Qur'an in his wedding-day letter to her which she re-read every day of her married life. She certainly fulfilled all the required duties towards her children, both spiritual and physical. But the source, *par excellence*, for understanding the idealization of the mother-child bond is Zafrullah Khan's *My Mother*. Read in isolation, his eulogy of his mother, Husain Bibi, and indeed of his own role as loving son, might seem a merely doting panegyric, but external evidence of the closeness of their relationship supports his own subjective account of her influence over him. The biography provides, at the same time, much important evidence of his mother's role in the wider Ahmadiyya movement.

Zafrullah Khan's account is suffused with evidence of the unusually 'strong bond between us', even to the extent of his describing his mother and himself as 'sweethearts'.[77] This self-avowed 'mother's boy', who accepted Husain Bibi's advice and interference on many matters concerning his career, had already reached high official positions in the Punjab government during her lifetime, and was later to become Foreign Minister of Pakistan and President of the General Assembly of the United Nations, an Ahmadi 'achiever' *par excellence*. The extent of her influence ranged from the trivial to the politically highly significant. When he was already a barrister, but still relatively young, she made him apologize to a friend for taking offence over a minor incident. In true reforming spirit, she later forbade him to attend ostentatious wedding celebrations which she regarded as a 'silly, superstitious farce'.[78] In these matters he was happy to be guided, but the extreme of interference was reached in 1934, for when he was offered a post in the Punjab government, he recorded her as having advised him, 'no darling, 1 do not think we should officiate for Sir Sikandar'.[79] 'They were both very self-conscious of their 'special relationship', which marked them off in their own eyes from her other offspring, his siblings and the extended family. When a friend's mother behaved ungraciously to her son, Husain Bibi reminded her own son that, 'Darling, the relationship between you and me demands not only that the son should be like you, but also that the mother should be like me!', thus setting themselves apart as a unique mother-son phenomenon, but in the eyes of the sponsor of the biography, clearly a 'model' for other women's behaviour towards their children.[80]

This biography is a revealing source too, for understanding the changes in comportment which were acceptable in the later stages of the female life-cycle, when mothers became grandmothers, and 'elders' within the family, neighbourhood and wider community. Zafrullah thus explained his mother's astounding temerity in seeking an audience with the Viceroy, on the occasion of Ahrar attacks on Ahmadis, as a reflection of her own sense that she was 'seventy-two and permitted some relaxation in respect of the observation of the regulations relating to purdah'.[81] For this specific purpose, perceived as crucial to the movement's security, she therefore allowed herself to break purdah. Yet, later, when some Punjabi women who 'considered themselves "advanced", had discarded the veil', Husain Bibi rejected their pleas that she should encourage her son's wife to do the same, placing Qur'anic teaching at the centre of her argument, for, she said, 'it would be contrary to the commandments of our God and his Messenger' to do so.[82] From her position of respected 'elder of the community' she continued to influence not only her own family, but neighbours and other Muslim women on her own perceptions of 'right conduct' within Islam.

CONCLUSION: AHMADI WOMEN IN THE PUBLIC SPHERE

The key to Husain Bibi's influence both over her highly placed son, and over the Muslim women she encountered, lies in the status she had early acquired within the Ahmadiyya movement. This was achieved, in spite of her lack of 'book learning', because of the efficacy of her 'dream power' in influencing those around her to esteem her as one possessing special spiritual attributes. The significance attached to dreams and their interpretation in ensuring the success of Ghulam Ahmad's mission has already been stressed, as has the claim to such power in the successful managing of her husband by Hafsah Qadiyani. Thus Zafrullah Khan structured his biography of his pious mother around the dreams which had served at key stages of her spiritual life, either as indicators of the right course to take in the future, or as presagers of events significant for the family or the movement. The most influential of Husain Bibi's dreams, which ensured she would be taken notice of in the future, was a vision in 1904 which led to her decision that she must seek initiation into the Ahmadiyya movement. On this occasion, she dreamt that she was persuading her husband to attend a religious gathering held on a wide plain. A bright light shining from a covered cradle, which seemed to be suspended 'from ropes that reached into heaven', and which swung from side to side across the crowded audience 'presaged a multiplicity of events that were all manifested in due course'. Her father, already an Ahmadi, interpreted this dream, and others which followed soon afterwards, to indicate that she must pledge her allegiance to Mirza Ghulam Ahmad. Against her husband's express command, she went alone to take the pledge, an action which he first reprimanded, but which he very soon afterwards emulated by also seeking initiation into the Ahmadiyya movement.[83]

Her initiation, at the hands of Mirza Ghulam Ahmad, marked the beginning of a close relationship which Husain Bibi established, in her own right, with the founder of the movement and his successors. When she died in 1938, the second khalifa, Mahmud Ahmad, acknowledged her role for more than thirty active years in expanding and consolidating the Ahmadiyya movement in the Punjab, particularly in her ancestral home of Daska village, and in nearby Sialkot. His emphasis on her initiative and her missionary work is instructive:

Despite the fact that the relationship of most women with the Movement is vicarious, that is to say, through father, son or brother, she was one of those exceptional women who have a direct relationship of their own. She joined the Movement before her husband did, and on the occasion of the split swore allegiance to the Khalifa before he did. She always gave proof of her intense devotion to and jealousy for the faith.[84]

Her son provided 'proof' also of the 'direct relationship' claimed for her within the movement, for 'it was mainly through her efforts that an Ahmadiyya Community was established at Daska', where 'my mother's example and her benevolence towards everyone helped to rouse interest in the Movement'.[85] An example of the way she won over Sunni opponents was the making of clothes for the grandchildren of a local maulvi who was misrepresenting the movement, thereby demonstrating that Ahmadis would continue to behave in a neighbourly way with those who opposed them.[86] When she finally moved from Daska to Qadiyan in her old age she insisted on choosing a suite of rooms in her son's house which would give access to enquirers from all classes, and led by example in refusing the use of a car, lest it should spray dust on other pious people.[87]

Khalifa Mahmud Ahmad's funeral tribute, on her death in 1938, is certainly informative in putting Husain Bibi's role in the movement in a wider perspective. She was no doubt an exceptional case, and sources do not at present permit the charting of the merely 'vicarious' roles attributed by the khalifa to 'most women' during the early years of the missionary programme in the Punjab. However, those drawn on here, particularly the biography of Hafsah, and the sermon to Ahmadi women in Sialkot, confirm that by about 1920, it was both the enjoined duty, and the practice of female initiates to induct first their children, then their wider kin and neighbourhood groups into 'true Islam' by a mixture of precept and example. Around this time too, the movement began to place a stronger emphasis on formal schooling for girls as well as boys, with the result remarked on by Wilfred Cantwell Smith that within two decades the girls of Qadiyan were exceptionally literate.[88] How far the Ahmadi girls of other towns and villages followed suit, and how far such literacy was actually achieved, given the emphasis on maintenance of purdah, by a continuation of home tuition at the hands of parents and maulvis, rather than by formal schooling in a semi-public sphere, is probably impossible to quantify. Yet for at least a decade there had been an emphasis on opening Ahmadi primary schools in many small towns and villages where the movement was expanding. In 1919 these numbered about forty, together with five middle schools.[89] Not surprisingly, boys were better catered for than girls, but in 1918 a British visitor to Qadiyan had reported 'that a beginning has been made in the education of women' in a community which he deemed to hold women in higher status than 'the standard obtaining in Islam generally'.[90] In 1922 the Majlis-i-shura, at its annual meeting in Qadiyan, decided to strengthen its efforts for girls' formal education. It was indeed a pioneer organization in India in deciding to make girls' education compulsory, ruling that

female education should be made compulsory for the Community and wherever there did not already exist Ahmadia schools for girls new Ahmadia schools might be started and where the starting of the school was not practicable, Ahmadi girls might be educated in the Government Girls' Schools up to the 3rd standard of the primary schools compulsorily and that after this stage had been reached choice might be given to the individuals to pursue any course that they thought best to follow according to their peculiar circumstances and that where there were no Government Girls' Schools, girls be educated at home.[91]

This initiative seems sufficient explanation for the phenomenon of 'educated daughters' so often remarked on by observers of the movement by the 1930s. In suggesting that girls also shared in the social mobility which was certainly a hallmark of male Ahmadis by the 1930s, Lavan would go further, claiming that 'anyone who wished to see his son or daughter live a more meaningful life knew that the community provided education that could lead to a career of significance'.[92]

If such 'careers of significance', often in the civil service, armed services, and legal and business professions, remained the prerogative of the husband, it seems that a number of Ahmadi women, apart from the exceptional Husain Bibi, also played important roles in the missionary movement. The sister of Hafsah Qadiyani, for example, after marrying the second khalifa, not only became 'a pillar of female education among the members of the Ahmadiyya community', but used her influence to persuade him to establish at Qadiyan, the Lajnat ul-Amaillah (Women's Society of the Servants of Allah).[93] In 1922 the Majlis-i-Shura then decreed that similar women's clubs should be established at other centres of Ahmadi settlement, such as Lahore, Ferozpur, Delhi and Sialkot, 'the duty of these clubs' being, among other charitable purposes, 'to teach women to make use of the education they have received so far'.[94] Thus the gossiping, illiterate women, whom the second khalifa had reprimanded like naughty children in his 1920 sermon, seemed well set by 1930 to play roles as foci of serious educational, missionary and charitable activity by leading women of the community who were literate in Urdu and Arabic, read the Qur'an for themselves, and many of whom had gained several years primary schooling in the villages as well as the district towns of the Punjab.

Ahmadi teaching in the movement's girls' schools initially differed little in content and mode of instruction, it would seem, from the programmes of other reformist organizations at that date. It seems probable too, that the paradox noted by Gail Minault, that schooling for Sunni girls in the Punjab and the United Provinces served to reinforce conservative norms, and to strengthen the practice of purdah, was true also of the Ahmadi schools.[95] The messages being conveyed in the didactic literature prepared by Ahmadi men for their womenfolk, as surveyed above, differed little in tone and emphasis from handbooks for women, such as the *Bihishti zewar*, which were written by Sunni reformers.[96] What was different, however, was the widespread availability of Ahmadi schools at village level as well as in the towns of the Punjab, with the result that education for girls seems to have acted as one of the factors which, during its early decades, began to reduce the distance between the urban and rural poles of recruitment to this new religious movement. If the 'social nature of the Ahmadiyya'[97] in its Punjab homeland remains elusive, further examination of formal and informal educative processes, and of marriage and initiation patterns within and outside the region, may substantiate or qualify in the future, the indications in the homiletic and biographical sources presented here, of the significant part played in the movement's early success by 'dutiful' daughters, wives and mothers.

NOTES

1. Translation of the title of a sermon for women, *Ahmadi 'auraton ke fara'iz*, delivered at Sialkot in 1920, which is central to the following discussion.

2. Mirza Ghulam Ahmad described himself as 'an unknown person', living in 'anonymity' before his mission commenced. *Haqiqat al-wahy*, p. 211, quoted

in S. Abul Hasan Nadwi, *Qadianism: a Critical Study*, Jeddah, 1975, p. 20. For the stages in the proclamation of his mission, see W. Cantwell Smith, 'Ahmadiyya', in *Encyclopaedia of Islam*, 2nd edn, vol. 1, p. 301.

3. For discussion of religious disputation in the Punjab and the United Provinces in the nineteenth century, see K.W. Jones, *Socio-Religious Reform Movements in British India*, Cambridge, 1989, pp. 48–121; B.D. Metcalf, *Islamic Revival in British India: Deoband, 1860–1900*, Princeton, 1982, pp. 215–34; A.A. Powell, *Muslims and Missionaries in Pre-Mutiny India*, London, 1993.

4. S. Lavan, *The Ahmadiyah Movement: A History and Perspective*, New Delhi, 1974, p. 58.

5. *Census of India*, 1901, vol. 17 (Punjab), pt 1, p. 143; 1911, vol. 14 (Punjab), pt 1, pp. 168–70; 1921, vol. 15 (Punjab), pt 1, p. 176; 1931, vol. 17 (Punjab), pt 1, p. 313.

6. Ibid.

7. For the more than seventy separate publications by Ghulam Ahmad, see 'Works in Urdu by Mirza Ghulam Ahmad', in S. Lavan, *The Ahmadiyah Movement*, pp. 210–11, and 'Works by Ghulam Ahmad', in Y. Friedmann, *Prophecy Continuous: Aspects of Ahmadi Religious Thought and its Medieval Background*, Berkeley, 1989, pp. 201–30. His son, the second khalifa, Mirza Bashir ud-din Mahmud Ahmad's many publications are also listed in these bibliographies.

8. H.A. Walter, *The Ahmadiya Movement*, Calcutta, 1918.

9. W. Cantwell Smith, 'Ahmadiyya', p. 301.

10. Y. Friedmann, *Prophecy Continuous* . . . .

11. S. Lavan, *The Ahmadiyah Movement* . . .; 'Sources for Ahmadiyah History: a Muslim Reform Tradition in the Punjab', in W.E. Gustafson and K.W. Jones (eds), *Sources on Punjab History*, New Delhi, 1975, pp. 87–129.

12. Lavan, ibid., p. 18, n. 2.

13. Friedmann, *Prophecy Continuous* . . ., p. xii.

14. P.R. Brass, 'Elite Groups, Symbol Manipulation and Ethnic Identity among the Muslims of South Asia'; F. Robinson, 'Islam and Muslim Separatism', in D. Taylor and M. Yapp (eds), *Political Identity in South Asia*, London, 1979, pp. 35–77, 78–112.

15. K.W. Jones, *Socio-Religious Reform Movements* . . . . See, esp., 'An Acculturative Movement among Punjabi Muslims: the Ahmadiyahs', pp. 115–19.

16. H. Oberoi, *The Construction of Religious Boundaries: Culture, Identity and Diversity in the Sikh Tradition*, New Delhi, 1994.

17. For example, H. Fischer-Tiné in this volume; Anshu Malhotra, ' Pativratas and Kupattis: Gender, Caste and Identity in Punjab, 1870s–1920s', unpublished PhD thesis, University of London, 1998.

18. I. Talbot, 'State, Society and Identity: the British Punjab 1875–1937', in G. Singh and I. Talbot (eds), *Punjabi Identity: Continuity and Change*, New Delhi, 1996.

19. 'To a large extent, political and religious activism remained confined to

urban areas.' I. H. Malik, 'Identity Formation and Muslim Party Politics in the Punjab, 1897–1936: a Retrospective Analysis', *Modern Asian Studies* 29(2), 1995, p. 298.

20. Mirza Bashir-ud-Din Mahmud Ahmad, *Ahmadiyyat or the True Islam*, Qadian, 1924, p. 137.

21. K.W. Jones, *Socio-Religious Reform Movements . . .*, p. 119.

22. Mirza Bashir-ud-Din Ahmad, *Ahmadiyyat or the True Islam*, p. 137.

23. Punjab Census Report, 1901, p. 143. For correction to the 'sweeper' claim, see *Punjab District Gazetteers, vol. 21A: Gurdaspur District*, Lahore, 1915, p. 57.

24. W. Cantwell Smith, 'Ahmadiyya,' p. 302, col. 1. In 'A Note on the Ahmadiyah Movement', also written in the 1940s, Cantwell Smith reported that the movement 'claims 100% male literacy, 75% female (in *pardah* schools).' *Modern Islam in India: a Social Analysis* (revd edn, London, 1946, reprinted Lahore, 1969), p. 370.

25. Mirza Ghulam Ahmad, *Philosophy of the Teachings of Islam*, Lahore, 1896; Mirza Bashir-ud-Din Ahmad, *Ahmadiyyat, or the True Islam; Hazrat Mohammad (S.A.W.): le liberateur de la Femme*, trans. S. Sookia, Mauritius, n.d.

26. Mirza Ghulam Ahmad, *Islah-i khatun* (Women's Reform), part 2 of *Rahnuma-i khatun* (Guidance for women), Qadiyan, n.d.; *'Masturat ko Hazrat Masih maw'ud ki nasihat ta'addud izdiwaj ke muta'alliq'* (Hazrat Masih's advice to women concerning polygamy), in Mirza Bashir ud-Din Mahmud Ahmad, *Ahmadi 'auraton ke fara'iz* (Duties of Ahmadi women), Qadiyan, 1922, pp. 17–18; *'Bivi se husn ma'asharat ki ta'lim* (Teaching on the best means of treating a wife), *al-Badr* 4(2) (April 1905), repub. 1922 in Mahmud Ahmad, *Ahmadi 'auraton ke fara'iz*, p. 16.

27. Mufti Fazl al-Rahman, *Hayat-i javadani, yani: sawanah-Hafsah Qadiyani*, Qadiyan 1918. A biography of his deceased wife, Hafsah, published 'for the benefit of Muslim women'.

28. Muhammad Zafrullah Khan, *My Mother*, London, 1981 (Urdu 1938).

29. S. Lavan, *The Ahmadiyah Movement . . .*, p. 194.

30. G. Minault, 'Purdah's progress: the beginnings of school education for Indian Muslim women', in J.P. Sharma, *Individuals and Ideas in Modern India*, Calcutta, 1982, pp. 80–1.

31. Ibid., p. 91.

32. *'Masturat ko Hazrat Masih maw'ud ki nisat . . .'* p.18; *'Bivi se husn ma'asharat ki ta'lim'*, p. 16.

33. There are many references to Ghulam Ahmad's role in making suitable marriage alliances for young Ahmadis; e.g. the father of Hafsah's husband was advised to marry his son to the daughter of the first khalifa, Nur ud-Din, and subsequently did so. *Hayat-i Javadani*, p. 4.

34. 'Conditions of Bai'at', *Review of Religions* 14 (May 1915), p. 99, quoted in S. Lavan, *The Ahmadiyah Movement*, p. 114.

35. *Ahmadi 'auraton ke fara'iz*.

36. Ibid., pp. 10–11.

37. See advertisement, 'auraton ke lie zaruri kitab' (a necessary book for women), frontispiece to *Ahmadi 'auraton ke fara'iz.*

38. Ahmad Husain Ahmadi Faridabadi, *Sabar ka ajar*, part 1, no. 4, Qadiyan/ Amritsar, 1919.

39. *My Mother*, p. 20.

40. *Hayat-i Javadani*, pp. 3–13.

41. Ibid., p. 13. For discussion of Nazir Ahmad's literary works, see C.M. Naim, 'Prize-winning adab', in B.D. Metcalf (ed.), *Moral Conduct and Authority:The place of Adab in South Asian Islam*, Berkeley, 1984, esp. pp. 300–14.

42. *Hayat-i Javadani*, pp. 13–14. Urdu terms for Hafsah's temperament include, *mizaj garm; mizaj bohat tez aur ghazab wali hai.*

43. *'Masturat ko Hazrat Masih maw'ud ki nasihat . . .'*, p. 17.

44. Ibid.

45. Ibid., p. 18.

46. Ibid., p. 17; Fyzee points out that although Indian Muslim women could initiate both *talaq-i tafwid* (delegated) and *khula'* divorce, in practice Hanafi law was among the least favourable of the law schools to wives wishing to initiate dissolution of marriage, a situation which was not remedied until the Dissolution of Muslim Marriages Act, VIII, of 1939, which restored in British India the Shari'at-based right of dissolution. Asaf A.A. Fyzee, *Outlines of Muhammadan Law*, 4th edn, Delhi, 1974, ch. 4, 'Dissolution of Marriage'.

47. Speech by Mirza Ghulam Ahmad, read at a religious conference at Lahore, December 1896, trans. Maulana Muhammad Ali as *Teachings of Islam*, 1910 (7th edn, 1983), section on 'chastity', pp. 61–6.

48. *Hayat-i javadani*, p. 13.

49. Ibid., pp. 13–14.

50. Zafrullah Khan, *My Mother*, p. 77.

51. Among British officials in northern India writing critically on the treatment of Muslim wives was Sir William Muir, Lieutenant-Governor of the North-Western Provinces (1860–74), who, the year the Ahmadiyya movement was founded, expressed the view in a widely circulated book that purdah and 'the domestic injunctions of the Coran' excluded 'woman from her legitimate place and function in social life'. *The Caliphate: its Rise, Decline, and Fall*, London, 1891. Sayyid Amir Ali rebutted Muir's criticisms in an apologetic defence of 'the status of women in Islam' in his simultaneously published *Life and Teachings of Mohammed: The Spirit of Islam*, Calcutta, 1891.

52. *Bivi se husn ma'asharat ki ta'lim*, p. 16.

53. *Hayat-i Javadani*, p. 38.

54. Zafrullah Khan, *My Mother*, p. 38.

55. *Hayat-i javadani*, p. 17.

56. Ibid., p. 14.

57. Ibid., p. 20.

58. Ibid., p. 14.

59. Ibid., pp. 15–16.
60. Zafrullah Khan, *My Mother, passim.*
61. *Hayat-i Javadani*, p. 18.
62. Hazrat Mirza Bashir ud-din Mahmud Ahmad, *Ahmadi 'auraton ke fara'iz* (ed. Ghulam Nabi), a sermon delivered in Punjabi to Ahmadi women at Sialkot, 12 April 1920, Urdu trans. published by Mazhar Press, Qadiyan, 1922.
63. Ibid., p. 11.
64. Ibid., p. 12.
65. Ibid., p. 10.
66. Ibid., p. 7.
67. Ibid., pp. 12–13.
68. Ibid., pp. 14–15.
69. Ibid., p. 10.
70. Ibid., pp. 10–11.
71. Ibid., p. 14.
72. Ibid., p. 4.
73. Ibid., p. 2.
74. Ibid., p. 12.
75. Ibid., 12–13.
76. *Hayat-i Javadani*, pp. 23–6.
77. Zafrullah Khan, *My Mother*, p. 102.
78. Ibid., p. 86.
79. Ibid., p. 89.
80. Ibid., pp. 90–91. An Afghan Sunni, who sponsored a reprint of the Urdu edition of *My Mother*, wrote: 'this booklet is throughout a lesson, an instruction, an exhortation. . . . It has a message for every Muslim woman' (p. ix).
81. Ibid., p. 76
82. Ibid., p. 89.
83. Ibid., p. 16–23.
84. Ibid., p. 104.
85. Ibid., p. 31.
86. Ibid.
87. Ibid., p. 91.
88. W. Cantwell Smith, *Modern Islam in India*, p. 370.
89. *Review of Religions* 19 (1920), p. 63.
90. H.A. Walter, *The Ahmadiya Movement*, p. 117.
91. *Review of Religions* 22: 1–3 (January–March 1923), p. 23.
92. S. Lavan, *The Ahmadiyah Movement*, p. 194.
93. *Review of Religions* 27: 12 (December 1924), p. 415.
94. *Review of Religions* 22: 1–3 (January-March 1923), p. 23.
95. G. Minault, 'Purdah's progress', pp. 92–3.
96. B.D. Metcalf, *Perfecting Women* (translation and commentary of Maulana Ashraf 'Ali Thanawi's *Bihishti zewar*), Delhi, 1992.
97. Y. Friedmann, *Prophecy Continuous . . .*, p. xii.

The Theosophical Movement

Theosophy as a Political Movement[1]

MARK BEVIR

OFFICIALLY THE THEOSOPHICAL SOCIETY is 'unconcerned about politics', a fact made clear in the first issue of *The Theosophist*.[2] The apolitical nature of theosophy was symbolized dramatically at the Society's annual convention in 1884. Several Indian theosophists wanted to meet to discuss the formation of a national political movement, and they planned to do so at that convention, which was to be held at the Society's headquarters in Adyar, just outside Madras. Yet the Society emphatically refused to become embroiled in politics. Helena Blavatsky, its inspirational prophet, and Henry Olcott, its president, earlier had assured the colonial authorities they would restrict themselves to philosophical and scientific studies and avoid all political matters.[3] The would-be nationalists had to meet, therefore, not in the Society's headquarters under the auspices of its annual convention, but rather across the road as a clearly distinct group. It is significant, however, that an important attempt to form a national political movement had such close ties to the Society. It is also significant that the colonial authorities kept Blavatsky and Olcott under police surveillance because they feared that their embroilment with native religions and cultures would have a destabilizing effect on British rule. Whatever the official position of the Theosophical Society, and whatever Blavatsky and Olcott might have said or intended, it quite clearly played a political role within India.

The paradox of a movement both officially divorced from politics and yet clearly entangled with the nationalist struggle becomes even more apparent if we jump forward to the early years of the twentieth century. Annie Besant, who succeeded Olcott as president of the Society, clearly identified its role as a religious and cultural one to the exclusion of politics.[4] At first she even said that the genius of India 'is for religion and not for politics, and her most gifted children are needed as spiritual teachers, not as competing candidates in the political arena.'[5] By 1915, however, she had founded the All-India Home Rule League in a clear attempt to foist a more radical political programme on to the Indian National Congress. Her success in doing so climaxed with her being elected president of the Congress in 1917. Although the League remained independent of the Society, and although Besant generally continued to deny that the Society was in any way political, the League relied heavily on people and networks brought together by the Society. Once again, therefore, whatever its official position and whatever Besant might have said or intended, the Society quite clearly played a political role in India. The significance of the Theosophical Society's political role came primarily from its religious ideas. In India, theosophy became an integral part of a wider movement of neo-Hinduism, which helped provide Indian nationalists with a legitimating ideology, a new-found confidence, and experience of organization. In thus unpacking the general pressures that pushed a political role on to theosophy, we shall have to abstract somewhat from the particular role of individuals with their peculiar gifts and quirks, and of theosophical lodges with their intricate personal and social networks, but at least we shall do so for a good cause: to say something more general about the relationship between religious reform movements and political nationalism in late colonial India.

THEOSOPHY AND NEO-HINDUISM

The Theosophical Society was formed in the United States in 1875.[6] It had three explicit aims: to explore the psychic powers latent within man, to promote the study of comparative religion, and to defend human brotherhood. Beyond these explicit aims, it stood for Blavatsky's modern occultism, according to which the ancient wisdom, or the universal religion, derived from the East. Theosophy arose as part of an upsurge of occult movements throughout the West in the late nineteenth century. Indeed, its specific roots were in the spiritualist movements, with Blavatsky and Olcott meeting when both of them went to investigate spirit-raps in Vermont.[7]

Blavatsky transformed the occult tradition in two significant ways.[8] The first of these appears in the way she rewrote ancient wisdom in response to the scientific and moral doctrines that were then producing a widespread crisis of faith. She incorporated a modern geological time-scale, a theory of evolution, and a concern with duty and service in her theosophical teachings. The universe, she argued, emanates from an infinite being that infuses all things, and thereafter it evolves through a plethora of cycles, moving out from the infinite and becoming increasingly physical, until, at last, it reaches a turning-point, after which it retraces its route, finally being reabsorbed into the divine whence it first arose. The driving force behind the evolutionary process, therefore, is not a blind mechanical law, but the purposive movement of divine spirit. All people, all things, all matter contain a divine spirit, which is the 'source of all forces, alone and indestructible'.[9] Moreover, we come in contact with the divine spark within us by adopting an appropriate set of ascetic practices: mystics purify themselves in order to have an unmediated experience of their true unity with God. Although the most advanced portion of humanity already have become highly spiritual beings, some of them have chosen to watch over our progress, and, when necessary, to aid us by suitable interventions in the physical and spiritual realms. Blavatsky claimed that these Masters constituted a Great White Brotherhood of Mahatmas who lived in the Himalayas and who gave her her orders.[10] It was they who instructed her to establish the Theosophical Society, and it was they who told her what to write in her works.

The second significant way in which Blavatsky transformed the occult tradition was to identify India as the source of ancient wisdom. Whereas earlier occultists typically traced their doctrines back to ancient Egypt, she argued that the 'very same ideas expressed in almost identical language, may be read in Buddhistic and Brahmanical literature.'[11] Impressed by the work of orientalists, such as Jacolliot and Jones on the antiquity of Indian religions and their influence on western culture, she asserted that Judaism, Christianity, and indeed all faiths, had their roots in a universal religion she equated with the teachings of the Vedas. No doubt Indian religions really did embrace some doctrines resembling those Blavatsky arrived at whilst reworking the occult tradition to meet a widespread crisis of faith in the West. None the less, certain features of contemporary Hinduism, such as child marriage and sati clearly did not fit with her idea that India embodied ancient wisdom. Blavatsky resolved this difficulty by distinguishing the corrupted, exoteric teachings and practices found in modern Hinduism from the true, esoteric ones of ancient Brahmanism. Modern India needed reform; its people needed to return to the pure ways of the Vedas.

Blavatsky and Olcott landed at Bombay in January 1879 and soon attracted interest, even some support, from the British community. Westerners living in India were not immune from the crisis of faith that had led various people in Europe and America—including powerful and respected families such as the Balfours, Gladstones and Sidgwicks—to dabble in spiritualism. In India, too, an interest in spiritualism easily could develop into one in theosophy. Blavatsky and Olcott obtained their entry into Imperial Society, for example, largely through the good offices of A.P. Sinnett, whose theosophical convictions developed out of his earlier fascination with spiritualism.[12] Similarly, Allan Octavian Hume met Blavatsky at Allahabad, and after spending some time with her, he concluded that many of the spiritualist phenomena associated with her—about which Sinnett wrote—were genuine.[13] Hume joined the Theosophical Society in 1880, became president of its Simla Lodge in 1881, and he seems also to have provided much of the financial support for the launch of *The Theosophist*. Although he broke with Blavatsky and resigned his post in the Simla Lodge in 1883, he still continued to believe in her teachings—including the existence of the Mahatmas and their special mission to aid the spiritual evolution of humanity.

If the appeal of theosophy to some westerners in India should not surprise us, the same might not appear to be true of its appeal to Indians. After all, men such as Subramanian Aiyar, B.M. Malabari, Ranganath Rao, Nurendranath Sen, and Kashinath Telang can scarcely be said to have responded to a crisis in Christianity by turning to spiritualism. In their case, not only did Blavatsky assure them of the worth of their cultural heritage, she also unpacked this cultural heritage in a way that soothed fears and concerns raised in them by their contact with contemporary western ideas and practices. Western-educated Hindus were almost bound to experience some sort of cultural dislocation—tension between the religious tradition in which they had been raised and the apparent scientific and ethical rationalism of the West. Theosophy offered a way to deal with this dislocation.[14]

The suitability of theosophy as a belief system for Hindus struggling to come to terms with the impact of the West on their cultural heritage appears in the extent to which it incorporates doctrines characteristic of Hindu reform movements of the time. Blavatsky, like Swami Vivekananda and Sri Aurobindo, and, perhaps slightly more awkwardly like Dayananda Sarasvati, eulogized the Hindu tradition whilst also calling for reform of corruptions found in its expressions. She, like them, evoked a true Hinduism that incorporated a monotheistic and evolutionary cosmology according to which the divine could be found at work within all things. She, like them, evoked an idealized past in which Indian society had been a pure and harmonious expression of this true, spiritual Hinduism. And she, like them, wanted modern Indians to return to this true Hinduism by purging their society of corruptions such as child-marriage. Hinduism, they all concluded, incorporated the central insights of modern science, such as a geological time-scale and a theory of evolution, and also a rational, even liberal, ethic emphasizing things such as social service.

The powerful resemblance between the teachings of the Theosophical Society, the Ramakrishna movement, Aurobindo, and, perhaps a little awkwardly the Arya Samaj, enables us to refer to them collectively as a distinct neo-Hinduism.[15] In speaking of these reform movements together, we imply that they can be treated collectively as responses to the stress of phenomena such as modernization and foreign belief systems. They constitute a coherent and related set of religious ideas and movements constructed in a particular social and cultural context, a set of attempts to fashion a new spirituality to resolve the dilemmas posed by colonial rule and contemporary scientific discoveries. Thus locating them in their specific historical context seems to be more or less indispensable if we are to explain theosophy's place among them. How else can we bring a product of western occultism that exhibited a fascination with spiritualism and natural magic in line with Hinduism as it developed in the late colonial era? To emphasize the historical specificity of such movements, however, need not be to deny that many of them had points of contact with traditional forms of Hinduism. It would be a mistake to suppose that we must see these movements as either conforming to the Hindu tradition or as breaking completely with it. All religious thinkers necessarily innovate against an inherited background, retaining aspects of their inheritance at the same time as they modify it. The question is: does neo-Hinduism exhibit sufficient novelty for us to regard it as a fairly decisive break within the Hindu tradition? The answer surely must be yes, if only because Blavatsky, Vivekananda, Aurobindo and others used concepts taken from modern western thought, notably evolution, and crucially, to accommodate all these alien concepts they had to modify Hinduism considerably.

To emphasize that neo-Hindu thinkers and movements exhibit common features explicable in terms of their shared historical setting is not to deny that they also differ from each other, with the differences often reflecting more specific features of their respective historical settings. A more detailed study might look at Vivekananda's Bengali heritage, the Punjabi setting of so much of the Arya Samaj's activities, or the castes from which Indian theosophists came, and it might then trace these regional or social influences through to the political impact these various movements had. But even such detailed study would occur within the context of the sort of general study we are undertaking here.

THEOSOPHY AND NATIONALIST IDEOLOGY

To some extent the place of theosophy within a broader neo-Hinduism means that in examining its political role we are looking at a particular instance of the more general relationship of neo-Hinduism to political nationalism. There are many interesting parallels between the way in which the theosophy of people such as Besant supported their nationalist thought and the way in which neo-Hinduism did so both for people vaguely influenced by theosophy, such as Gandhi, and also others, such as Aurobindo. Despite these interesting parallels, we shall focus here on the particular case of theosophy.

To appreciate how theosophy fed into nationalist ideology, we have to contrast it with the official discourse of the Raj. Although Christianity clearly played very different roles in the lives of different individuals in British India, the colonial authorities equally clearly relied on a particular Christian discourse to define and to legitimize their role. The key idea was that only in a Christian society can individuals develop as properly rational beings in accord with the will of God. The Raj, in other words, was needed to secure the conditions under which Indians could realize their God-given capacities.[16] Hindu society, in contrast, was denounced, first, for obscuring the worth of the individual behind a fatalistic pantheism, and second, for preventing a rational concern with the facts by representing the world as maya, that is, an evil illusion to be overcome by ascetic withdrawal.[17]

Theosophy turned upside down the official denunciation of Hinduism. Whereas the ruling discourse of the Raj complained of Hinduism reducing the individual to a mere part of a greater whole, many theosophists complained of Christianity fostering an unhealthy individualism. Blavatsky taught, allegedly following traditional Hinduism, that all beings are manifestations of the one divine form and so interlinked with one another. As Besant explained, this had as its 'inevitable corollary' acceptance of a 'solidarity' based on 'universal brotherhood.'[18] Hinduism, she argued, put the individual in a proper relationship to the social whole; it recognized that the good of the individual was bound inextricably to that of society; it taught that 'the primary truth of Morality, as of Religion and of Science, is the Unity of Life.'[19] The unity of life did not imply a lack of respect for individual differences, nor did it imply a flat, western-style equality, defined in terms of the rights of man. Rather, it implied that individuals should use their diverse talents and abilities for the good of the whole. Hinduism, therefore, incorporated an admirable social morality. It taught that 'we live not to assert our rights but to do our duties, and so to make one mighty unit where each shall discharge his functions for the common good of all.'[20] It taught the importance of performing dharma. The introduction of Christianity into India, however, undermined this traditional, Hindu focus on brotherhood, service, and duty. Christianity emphasized the salvation of the individual in a way that prevented people seeing themselves correctly as part of a social whole: it encouraged the illusory idea, so popular in the West, that the individual is an independent entity with private ends; it led people to think in terms of individual rights rather than social duties.

Moreover, whereas the ruling discourse of the Raj complained of Hinduism encouraging an ascetic withdrawal from the world conceived as an evil illusion, many theosophists complained of western thought failing to provide an adequate basis for moral action. They argued that Hinduism offered a purely natural account of ethics based on the doctrine of reincarnation and the law of karma. Because the evils afflicting people were necessary consequences of their past actions, people had reason to behave morally—they knew that they later would reap the harvest of what they now sowed. In the theosophical writings, the concept of karma generally acted as a call to action; it required one to strive to make life better for others and so for oneself. Although Hinduism taught that one could escape from a cycle of rebirths only by ridding oneself of desire, one needed to take this teaching as an injunction to renounce only selfish desires, and not the desire to do good to others. Besant told her fellow theosophists, 'the word of freedom' is 'Sacrifice—that which is done for the sake of carrying out the Divine Will in the world'; she said, 'that which you do as living in God and doing God's work—that action alone does not bind the man, for it is an action that is sacrifice, and has no binding power.'[21]

The law of karma did not mean that one had a fate to be endured. It meant that one was called upon to act selflessly for the good of others. Hinduism, and its concept of karma, therefore, provided an impetus to rational, moral behaviour in a way neither western science nor Christianity did. On the one hand, the materialist premises of western science seemed to rule out belief in a divine or ethical order, so science undermined supernaturalism—faith in the Bible as revealed truth—without providing an alternative, naturalist account of ethics. On the other hand, Christianity, with its doctrine of vicarious atonement, suggested that one could commit sins with impunity provided only that one later repented in faith. As Blavatsky explained to her aunt:

A Buddhist, Brahmanist, Lamaist, and Mahomedan does not take alcohol, does not steal, does not lie while he holds fast to the principles of his own heathen religion. But as soon as the Christian missionaries appear, as soon as they enlighten the heathen with Christ's faith, he becomes a drunkard, a thief, a liar, a hypocrite. While they are heathen, every one of them knows that each sin of his will return to him according to the law of justice and readjustment. A Christian ceases to rely on himself, he loses self-respect. 'I shall meet a priest, he will forgive me,' as answered a newly initiated to Father Kiriak.[22]

Western thought undermined the traditional Hindu basis for moral behaviour.

The theosophists' defence of Hinduism fed readily into an idealization of a golden age in Indian history. Whereas the official discourse of the Raj portrayed India as an unchanging land in which individual liberty lay crushed beneath religious superstition and traditional custom, theosophy implied that traditional Indian society embodied an ideal religion and ethic. The Indian nation, in essence, was an organic community of individuals bound together to pursue spiritual enlightenment through a recognition of personal duty. The Aryan polity, with its caste system, was designed to serve the religious purpose of advancing the universal process of spiritual evolution. For a start, Aryan society aided the growth of the soul by subordinating man's lower nature to his higher one. The hierarchy of castes showed that the Aryans prized spiritual life over material luxury, for, as Besant explained, 'the highest caste in the olden days, the Brahmans, were a poor class, and the wealth of the Brahman lay in his wisdom, not in his money-bags.'[23] The Aryans lived pure, simple lives dedicated to the conquest of their lower selves as a means of contact with the divine. In addition, Aryan society promoted spiritual advancement by defining, and so encouraging performance of, one's dharma. The location of individuals within a caste indicated that they were part of a greater whole. Each individual occupied a specific place within a social whole, and had a duty to act in accord with that place. Caste indicated the nature of people's dharma. It encouraged them to do their duty and thereby facilitated their spiritual development. Finally, the emphasis the Aryans placed on simple living and social duty produced an organic community in which religion ruled social conduct and each individual cared for his neighbours. Aryan society was an association of individuals bound together in pursuit of shared spiritual goals, not a neutral arena in which atomistic individuals fought for competing, private goods.

According to Besant, the self-governing village stood as the institutional embodiment of the organic nature of Aryan society. The village had been the fundamental, enduring feature of Indian society through the ages: emperors came and went, but the village remained a self-sufficient community providing stability and continuity in the lives of ordinary people. Each village was composed of a core area of buildings for living, working, and resting, surrounded by arable land, then pasture land, and finally a natural or planted forest. The village owned the land on which it was situated, and the villagers treated each piece of land as a common possession on loan to the family cultivating it. Everyone had a common right to both the pasture land, where they grazed animals under the watchful eye of a shepherd, and the forest, where they gathered wood for fuel and building. Each village supported craftsmen, such as carpenters and potters, and professionals, such as astrologers and priests, by granting them a share in village lands, or, more usually, village crops, and by making gifts to them during religious festivals. The life of the community always revolved around the temple, which fostered religion and moral culture. Everybody willingly devoted time and effort to work on community projects such as digging wells.

A view of Indian society as organic and spiritual left theosophists needing a very different historiography from that incorporated in the official discourse of the Raj. They could not accept that India was a land of unchanging superstitions being liberated and made rational by the British. Instead, they needed to explain how Indian society had fallen away from the Aryan ideal. Typically they did so by pointing to the disruptive effects of foreign, and especially British, rule. Earlier invaders rarely touched the soul of India. Indeed, India typically captured the invaders by turning them into Aryans whilst also being enriched by their culture. The British, in contrast, had destroyed the great religious basis of India by pushing western ideas and habits on to her people. The crucial difference, at least according to Besant, was that the British had been the first foreigners to come to India exclusively for profit with no intention of learning from her culture. They had invaded India not to spread Christianity, nor to free a subject people, nor to find adventure, but rather to trade, and, in particular, to find new markets for the products that they produced in such vast quantities after the industrial revolution. They had even conquered India by the dishonest means of the merchant class. The East India Company paid scant heed to treaties and also initiated quarrels among Indians. It played rulers off against one another by, say, hiring troops to one until he became powerful enough, when it would help his rival. Almost every quarrel in eighteenth-century India was encouraged, or actively started, by Europeans fighting over trade. 'England', Besant concluded, 'did not "conquer her [India] by the sword" but by the help of her own swords, by bribery, intrigue, and most quiet diplomacy, fomenting of divisions, and playing of one party against another.'[24]

Having conquered India, the British systematically discredited Hinduism by teaching not the indigenous literature and religion, but rather subjects designed to produce the clerks needed first by the East India Company and then by imperial rule. Worse still, the British instilled in India a European concern with rights. Thus, Indians now regarded caste as a mark of privilege and status indicating how much respect an individual should be shown. Caste now stood for social distinction, not social duty, so that the lower castes had naturally become angry and jealous of the higher ones. The resulting conflicts ruined Indian society, for 'out of the base marriage of Caste to Separateness, instead of the true wedlock of Caste with Service, there sprang a huge and monstrous progeny of social evils, which preyed, and are still preying, on the life of India.'[25] As well as corrupting the great religious culture of India, British rule had destroyed her economy and denied her people the right to self-government. Besant complained of the drain on Indian wealth that was needed to pay for the India Office, pensions to retired civil servants, and an army only allegedly needed to defend India's frontiers. British rule had led to increased taxation of the Indian peasant, and so, in turn, to recurring famines and a neglect of the public works, such as irrigation, that were needed to promote economic development. In addition, the British had ruined the self-governing village of the Aryans by introducing peasant proprietors instead of common ownership of the land, and also by replacing elected officers responsible to the village itself with appointed officials responsible to the higher echelons of government. The British had failed to recognize, let alone use, the genius of the Indian people for democratically managing their own affairs. They ruled India through an administrative bureaucracy that paid no attention to the voices of Indians, but relied instead on executive fiat reinforced by large doses of repressive legislation. Theosophists denied, therefore, that the British were creating the basis for a liberal and rational form of government in India. On the contrary, the British had brought to India a corrupt individualism and decadent materialism which had done much to destroy the glories of the Aryan polity. The key political question was not how long it would take the Indians to adopt the Christian values needed for self-rule. It was, rather, how best to return India to its true self.

The whole tenor of theosophy led, therefore, to a view of India's nature, its past and its current situation, very different from the one that informed the Raj. But theosophy did not just question the self-justification of British rule, it also promoted, with respect to India, those doctrines we regard as characteristic of nationalist movements wherever they arise— the glories of the native culture, a golden age some time in the past, and, of course, a bewailing of the disruptive effects of foreign rule. In promoting nationalist doctrines, theosophy encouraged Indians to ask themselves not 'how can we adopt for ourselves the British system of governance?' but rather 'how can we recapture our former glories?' There were, of course, all sorts of answers they might give to the latter question, not all of which entailed independence but then not all nationalists demanded independence.

What theosophy certainly did do, particularly when placed alongside other forms of neo-Hinduism, was to provide a clear basis for a nationalist ideology. The British often argued that India could not be united and independent because the Indian people did not constitute a nation—the Indian people belonged to diverse regions, faiths, and castes, each of which had its own special identity. Neo-Hinduism, including theosophy, gave nationalists a clear response to this argument. Nationalists could say not only that India had been a nation in a past golden age, but also that she was becoming one again. Nationalists could point to objective factors promoting a sense of national identity—British rule over the whole subcontinent and a growth of economic links between the regions—to the emergence of a subjective awareness of a national identity—a growing sense of a common past and a shared predicament—and to the emergence of all-India organizations for religious reform. The Indian nation, they could say, was at last waking up from its long slumber.

Theosophy and neo-Hinduism helped provide Indian nationalists with an ideology. They encouraged nationalists to describe India as a unified entity that had a common heritage and that faced a common set of problems requiring an all-India solution. They popularized a belief in a golden age when India had been a paradise free from the spiritual and social problems of modernity. Even in the present times, India has a valuable understanding of matters of the spirit that was absent in the West, and without which the West could not for long avert disaster.[26] Unfortunately, however, a number of corruptions had crept into Indian spirituality and thereby undermined this golden age, corruptions that Blavatsky characteristically equated with passages she thought the Brahmins had added to the sacred texts so as to justify a distasteful version of the caste system. These corruptions had left India vulnerable to British rule, arguably even in need of British rule to provide the necessary impetus to reform. A suitable scheme of reform, however, would enable India to attain independence and to recover her lost greatness.

THEOSOPHY AND NATIONALIST POLITICS

When Olcott disembarked at Bombay in 1879, the first thing he did was to 'stoop down and kiss the granite step' in an 'instinctive act of pooja'.[27] Olcott and Blavatsky then went to live in the Indian quarters of the city, not among the Europeans. From then on, they constantly lauded Indian religions and cultures, arguing that the true source of all religion lay in the Vedas. The theosophists thought of India as a sacred land, so they showed it, its people, and their practices, a respect verging at times on worship. Theosophy helped provide Indians not only with a nationalist ideology but also with a new confidence in the worth of their culture. It suggested that their past, their customs, their religion, and their way of life, were as good as, and even better than, those of their imperial rulers.

If such confidence was in some ways an inevitable corollary of Indians adopting theosophical beliefs, the same cannot be said of the other great contribution theosophy made to the nationalist movement. The Theosophical Society, and neo-Hindu groups in general, provided nationalists with experience of organization—of coming together and acting in concert—and with contacts and networks which they then could draw upon for political purposes.

Nineteenth-century Indians had little experience of modern politics with its emphasis on popular participation and agitation. Indeed, India as a whole remained, in many ways, a divided society with few cooperative lines of communication running between its different regions, castes and classes.[28] Neo-Hinduism did much to change this. Even Dayananda, although he initially set out to reform Hinduism by converting his fellow Brahmins alone—conveyed his message through Sanskrit and retained the dress and traditions of the sannyasi—later used the Arya Samaj to appeal to the Hindu faithful as a whole, adopting Hindi and dropping most of the practices of the sannyasi.[29]

Theosophy was especially important here because of the very diversity of those it brought together. Whereas the Arya Samaj had little impact except on Punjabi Hindus, and the Brahmo Sabha on Bengali Hindus, the Theosophical Society was more of an all-India organization. Its members came from all over the subcontinent. Besides Hindus, it attracted Parsees, Christians, Sikhs, and even a few Muslims.[30] At least as importantly, it brought members of the western-educated elite of Indian society, such as Aiyar, Rao, and Sen into close contact with liberal members of the British community, such as Sinnett and Hume. The Society held annual conventions from 1881 and these gatherings provided a diverse group of sympathetic people with the opportunity to discuss the past, present, and future of India. Networks were formed, an understanding of how to deal with others was gained, and a growing sense of a common identity and common purpose was promoted. The importance of these networks can be seen at work in the formation of the Indian National Congress and again in the activities of the All-India Home Rule League.

The Formation of the Congress

From 1875 through to 1885 a number of young nationalists became increasingly disaffected with their older leaders. Their alienation first became apparent in 1876 when a group of young Bengalis, led by Surendranath Banerjea, formed the Indian Association of Calcutta.[31] They broke with the established British Indian Association of Bengal because they thought it was tied to the zamindars, who showed little, if any, desire to end British rule. Sen, the editor of the *Indian Daily Mirror*, was a prominent member of both the Theosophical Society and the Indian Association of Calcutta. Early in 1885, he first put forward a proposal for an all-India nationalist association, and then, together with Banerjea and others, began to organize a conference for that December to form just such an all-India body. The inspiration for Sen's proposal might well have come from Madras, which had been the venue for the 1884 annual convention of the Theosophical Society, during which Ranganath Rao argued that the society should formally discuss political issues as well as religious ones. Although Rao did not have his way, he managed to arrange a political discussion at a separate meeting across the road from the official convention. Theosophists, including Aiyar, Ananda Charlu, M. Viraraghavachariar, besides Rao himself, met as private individuals to promote a nationalist agenda. Soon afterwards they formed the Madras Mahajana Sabha, arguing that the established Madras Native Association had ceased to be of any value to the nationalist cause. Sen had attended some of the meetings leading up to the formation of the Madras Mahajana Sabha, and he surely must have had some knowledge of its plan to establish an all-India organization at a meeting scheduled to coincide with the next annual convention of the Theosophical Society. Later in 1885, Malabari, Telang and other nationalists, such as Pherozeshah Mehta and Dadabhai Naoroji, formed the Bombay Presidency Association as a more radical alternative to the older Bombay Association. Throughout India, theosophists were joining with other young nationalists to advance a more radical agenda, at the heart of which lay the idea of an all-India organization.

The single most important individual behind the formation of the Indian National Congress was, arguably, Hume. In 1878 Hume read various documents that convinced him that large sections of the Indian population were violently opposed to British rule and even plotted rebellion.[32] These documents were communications he had received, supposedly from the Mahatmas of which Blavatsky spoke, but presumably from Blavatsky herself. In one of the letters sent to Sinnett, the Mahatmas described how the Great White Brotherhood had controlled the Indian masses during the Rebellion of 1857 so as to preserve an imperial rule necessary apparently to bring India to her true place in the world.[33] Now the Mahatmas seemed to be directing Hume to maintain the correct balance between East and West.[34] Even after Hume turned against Blavatsky, he continued to believe in the Mahatmas. He thought that they had chosen to pass some of their understanding on to him, and, in particular, to warn him of an impending catastrophe so that he could ward off disaster. Hume set about averting disaster in two ways. First, he tried to convince Viceroy Ripon to reform the administration of India so as to make it more responsive to the Indian people.[35] Second, he tried to promote an all-India organization so as to give voice to nationalist concerns and aspirations.[36]

Although Hume helped to form the Bombay Presidency Association, he wanted in fact to create an all-India body, and throughout 1885 he used the Bombay group as a springboard from which to promote the idea of an Indian National Union. He soon acquired the backing of the Poona Sarvajanik Sabha as well as the Bombay group for an all-India political conference to be held in Poona during December 1885. His quarrel with Blavatsky meant, however, that he had to work harder to win over the theosophists of the Madras Mahajana Sabha and the Indian Association of Calcutta. By May, he had visited Madras to discuss his proposals for the Poona conference with the members of the Mahajana Sabha, and also to put forward his views on the way the Theosophical Society should develop. He convinced the local leaders to fall in with his plans for an Indian National Union. Next he travelled to Calcutta, where he seems to have contacted several prominent members of the Indian Association. Although Sen decided to give his backing to Hume, many others, under Banerjea's leadership, did not, preferring instead to go ahead with their alternative conference. An outbreak of cholera in Poona forced Hume to change the venue of his proposed conference, but, finally, in December 1885, the Indian National Union convened in Bombay.[37] Those present immediately renamed themselves the Indian National Congress, and when the Congress next met in December 1886, it did so in Calcutta, thus ensuring the adherence of Banerjea's alternative National Conference.[38]

The Indian National Congress was formed by nationalists from all over India under the leadership of a retired British official. Hume worked alongside people he had met at the annual conventions of the Theosophical Society—Malabari, Rao, and Sen—to arrange the founding conference of the Congress. The Theosophical Society helped to make it possible for Hume to meet and cooperate with these Indian nationalists, and had it not done so, the formation of an all-India political body would have been, at the very least, harder. 'No Indian could have started the Indian National Congress', wrote G.K. Gokhale; indeed, 'if the founder of the Congress had not been a great Englishman and distinguished ex-official, such was the distrust of political agitation in those days that the authorities would have at once found some way or other to suppress the movements.'[39]

The All-India Home Rule League

By 1914 the Indian National Congress had become an established organization. But the triumph of the moderates over the extremists had left it with a significantly restricted and rather non-confrontational political vision. When Besant entered the political arena, after years of devoting herself to religious, educational, and social work, she tried to foist a more radical position on to the Congress. She demanded self-government for India in the immediate future, and she wanted the Congress to advance this demand by heading a campaign of educative propaganda, a campaign using many of the techniques with which she had become familiar as a radical agitator in Britain. 'The Congress', she said, raised little 'enthusiasm' among Indians since it continued in the same groove, passing year after year similar resolutions and making little substantial progress'.[40] What the Congress needed to do, she continued, was to formulate, proclaim, and promote the views of educated India on all matters of public importance. More particularly, each year it needed to select various topics for discussion and then conduct an educative campaign around them. Politics, she concluded, had to become a permanent feature of the life of the Indian people, not a three-day event circumscribed by the annual Congress. All through 1914, Besant published, in her new daily paper, *New India*, a series of articles debating the role that the Congress should play. Many of the more vociferous articles in support of her views came from fellow theosophists such as Krishna Rao and Aiyar, although she also attracted support from other nationalists.[41] At the Madras Congress of 1914, Besant put forward a constitutional amendment in line with her views, but suffered defeat in the Subjects Committee.[42] Despite this defeat, her proposals continued to gain momentum, with, for example, young theosophists in Bombay, led by Jamnandas Dwarkadas, publishing a paper, *Young India*, to promote her programme.[43] When Besant failed once more to introduce changes at the Bombay Congress of 1915, she founded a new organization, the All-India Home Rule League.[44]

The League was formed on 3 September 1916 at a meeting in Gokhale Hall, Madras. George Arundale, a British theosophist who became organizing secretary of the League, gave a speech in which he said that Besant already had sent him on a tour of north India 'to draw recruits around the Home Rule flag, to help to organize educative propaganda, and above all else to send to the coming Congress, delegates pledged to make the policy of Home Rule the dominant policy of the National Congress.'[45] When Besant sent out home rule missionaries, they generally stayed with local theosophists who made the arrangements for the meetings they addressed.[46]

Besant and Arundale were not the only western theosophists to play prominent roles in the League: S.H. Burdett, a former suffragette, became his secretary; Miss Gmeiner, the headmistress of a girls' school, helped to establish the Delhi branch; Francesca Arundale was a leading figure in the Benaras branch. The League also drew heavily on the support of Indian theosophists. The Council of the League consisted of, besides Besant and Arundale, Ramaswami Aiyar, who served as recording secretary of the Society, B.P. Wadia, a Parsi and theosophist from Bombay who then lived in the society's headquarters at Adyar, and A. Rasul and Pandharinath Telang. Aiyar was not a theosophist, but a sympathizer.

Also, although membership of the League rose to about five times that of the Indian section of the Theosophical Society, Indian theosophists often provided the impetus behind, and core members of, the branches of the League: in Tanjore, Srinivasa Aiyar headed the local branches of the Society and the League; in Calicut, Manjeri Ramier held an office in both organizations, and sixty-eight of the seventy persons who founded the Bombay City branch of the League were members of the Society.[47] Clearly the two organizations became deeply entwined with one another: when Wadia visited Guntur in October 1916, he spent one day engaged in home rule work and another in theosophical work.[48] Many leading Leaguers were inspired by Besant's religious teachings as president of the Society. They saw participation in the League as an expression of their spiritual or theosophical commitments. Jamnadas Dwarkadas saw Besant as his 'adorable guru', describing his meeting with her as a greater landmark in his life than his marriage; his brother Kanchi saw himself as Besant's *chela,* describing his becoming a theosophist as 'the happiest and most important decision I ever made'.[49]

The League pursued its programme of educative propaganda vigorously through late 1916 and early 1917. When the governments of Bombay, the Central Provinces and Madras banned students from meetings, and the governments of Bombay, Madras and Punjab seemed to be close to banning home rule agitation as such, Besant denounced the government, and even spoke of meeting any ban with passive resistance.[50] In response, the government of Madras interned her, along with Arundale and Wadia, in June 1917. The internments stirred up even more of an outcry, until, in September, in an attempt to calm things down, she was released. By then Besant had become a nationalist heroine who was elected president at the Calcutta Congress in 1917. Although her popularity diminished rapidly thereafter, the home rule agitation had set the scene for Gandhi's entry on to the national stage.

CONCLUSION

Despite the Theosophical Society's avowedly apolitical nature, it clearly played an important role in the growth of Indian nationalism. Not only were individual theosophists, such as Hume, Besant and the Dwarkadas brothers key figures in the development of nationalist thought and organization; nor is it just a matter of many of the leading activists of the freedom struggle, including Gandhi and Nehru, having been influenced by theosophy; the key point is rather the general picture within which these details about individuals gain their significance, a general picture of theosophy as an integral part of the cultural and social context out of which the nationalist movement arose.

At first sight it might seem odd that a society emerged from the western occult tradition and became enmeshed with Indian culture and politics. Looking further, however, this oddity gives way to an understanding based on a recognition of how ideas forged in one context can take on a radically different political colouring when transposed to another one. Blavatsky might have developed theosophy largely as a reworking of the occult tradition in the light of a post-Darwinian crisis of faith, and her western followers, including Hume and Besant, might have turned to theosophy precisely because it seemed to resolve questions raised in them by this crisis of faith; but within India the most important theosophical doctrine was undoubtedly Blavatsky's identification of the universal religion with the Brahmanism of the Vedas. Because theosophy both eulogized the ancient faith of India and also interpreted this faith as incorporating modern scientific doctrines such as evolution, it had an obvious appeal to western-educated Indians looking for a way to reconcile their indigenous culture with the new learning. Moreover, despite Blavatsky's concern with avoiding politics, any set of doctrines that thus encouraged Indians to equate their ancient culture with the ideal was almost bound to have a radical political significance within the context of the Raj.

Theosophy was, of course, only one of several movements at the turn of the century that encouraged Indians to equate their ancient culture with the ideal. Other religious thinkers and movements, such as the Arya Samaj, the Ramakrishna Math and Mission, and Aurobindo eulogized Vedic Hinduism as a universal religion of unmatched purity that both incorporated the truths of modern science and sustained an idyllic society. Despite important differences between them, therefore, theosophy and these other movements did much to develop and promote an analysis of India's past, present, and future, that provided fertile soil for nationalism. India, they suggested, had a highly valuable indigenous culture that had flourished in an earlier golden age. Although this culture continued to provide the basis of a national identity, the golden age had ended as a result of the disruptive effects of foreign rule. Indians needed to revive this culture, purging it of later abuses and distortions, and thereby liberate themselves. In addition, and again despite important differences between them, theosophy and these other movements created networks of individuals, patterns of organization, and modes of behaviour that nationalists could draw on to create a political movement. The Indian National Congress and the All-India Home Rule League certainly drew for their formation, and at least some of their activities, on a social basis that had been established by the Theosophical Society.

NOTES

1. I thank the Leverhulme Trust for awarding me a Travel Abroad Studentship with which to pursue my research.

2. *The Theosophist*, October 1879.

3. H. Olcott, *Old Diary Leaves: The History of the Theosophical Society*, 6 vols, Theosophical Publishing House, Adyar, 1972–5; vol. 1, pp. 254–7. Biographies of Blavatsky include the eulogizing J. Fuller, *Blavatsky and her Teachers*, East-West Publications, London, 1988; and the condemnatory G. Williams, *Madame Blavatsky: Priestess of the Occult*, Lancer Books, New York, 1946.

4. Besant wrote two autobiographies. See A. Besant, *Autobiographical Sketches*, Freethought, London, 1885; and *An Autobiography*, Theosophical Publishing House, Adyar, 1983. The main biographies are: A. Nethercot, *The First Five Lives of Annie Besant* (1961) and *The Last Four Lives of Annie Besant* (1963), R. Hart Davis, London, and A. Taylor, *Annie Besant*, Oxford University Press, Oxford, 1992.

5. A. Besant, 'India's Mission among Nations', in *India: Essays and Addresses*, Theosophical Publishing Society, London, 1913, p. 3.

6. On the history of the Theosophical Society in the west, see B. Campbell, *Ancient Wisdom Revived: A History of the Theosophical Movement*, University of California Press, Berkeley, 1980; R. Ellwood, 'The American Theosophical

Synthesis', in H. Kerr and C. Crow (eds), *The Occult in America: New Historical Perspectives*, University of Illinois Press, Chicago, 1983, pp. 111–34; and P. Washington, *Madame Blavatsky's Baboon: Theosophy and the Emergence of the Western Guru*, Secker & Warburg, London, 1993.

7. H. Olcott, *People from the Other World*, American Publishing Company, Hartford, 1875. On the relation of theosophy to spiritualism, see J. Oppenheim, *The Other World: Spiritualism and Psychological Research in England, 1850–1914*, Cambridge University Press, Cambridge, 1985, pp. 159–97.

8. M. Bevir, 'The West Turns Eastward: Madame Blavatsky and the Transformation of the Occult Tradition', *Journal of the American Academy of Religion LXII* (1994), pp. 747–67.

9. H.P. Blavatsky, *Isis Unveiled: A Master-Key to the Mysteries of Ancient and Modern Science and Theology*, 2 vols, Theosophical Publishing House, Wheaton, Ill., 1972, vol. 2, p. 588.

10. See K. Johnson, *The Masters Revealed: Madam Blavatsky and the Myth of the Great White Lodge*, State University of New York, Albany, NY, 1994.

11. Blavatsky, *Isis Unveiled . . .*, vol. 1, p. 626.

12. A.P. Sinnett, *The Autobiography of Alfred Percy Sinnett*, Theosophical History Centre, London, 1986.

13. A.P. Sinnett, *The Occult World*, Trubner & Co., London, 1881.

14. Compare the role ascribed to theosophy in M. Gandhi, *An Autobiography*, in *Collected Works*, vol. 39, Publications Division, New Delhi, 1958–95; J. Nehru, *An Autobiography*, John Lane, London, 1936; and B. Pal, *Memories of My Life and Times*, vol. 1, Modern Book Agency, Calcutta, 1932.

15. Studies that emphasize the way these movements constitute a hiatus within the Hindu tradition include A. Bharati, 'The Hindu Renaissance and its Apologetic Patterns', *Journal of Asian Studies* 29 (1970), pp. 267–88; P. Hacker, 'Aspects of Neo-Hinduism as Contrasted with Surviving Traditional Hinduism', in W. Halfbass (ed.), *Philology and Confrontation: Paul Hacker on Traditional and Modern Vedanta*, University of New York Press, Albany, NY, 1995, pp. 229–55; and idem, *India and Europe: An Essay in Understanding*, State University of New York Press, Albany, NY, 1988, pp. 219ff.

16. Compare, G. Studdart-Kennedy, *British Christians, Indian Nationalists, and the Raj*, Oxford University Press, Delhi, 1991.

17. Compare the general construction of Hinduism within western Indology as described in R. Inden, *Imagining India*, Basil Blackwell, Oxford, 1990.

18. A. Besant, *What is Theosophy?* Theosophist Office, Adyar, 1912, p. 9. One of her earliest theosophical articles considered the relationship between karma and social action. See *Lucifer*, August 1889.

19. A. Besant, *The Basis of Morality*, Theosophical Publishing Society, Adyar, 1915, p. 26.

20. A. Besant, 'The Place of Politics in the Life of a Nation', in *India: Essays and Addresses*, p. 131.

21. Ibid., p. 25.

22. *The Theosophist*, September 1950. For the contemporary disquiet over the

morality of atonement, see J. Altholz, 'The Warfare of Conscience with Theology', in idem (ed.), *The Mind and Art of Victorian England*, University of Minnesota Press, 1976, pp. 58–77.

23. A. Besant, *The East and the West*, Theosophical Office, Adyar, 1908, pp. 22–3.

24. A. Besant, *How India Wrought for Freedom*, Theosophical Publishing Society, Adyar, 1915, pp. LV–LVI

25. A. Besant, 'East and West', in *India: Essays and Addresses*, p. 78.

26. On the dichotomy between the west as materialistic and India as spiritual, see U. King, *Indian Spirituality, Western Materialism: An Image and its Function in the Reinterpretation of Modern Hinduism*, Indian Social Institute, New Delhi, 1985.

27. Olcott, *Old Diary Leaves . . .*, vol. 2, pp. 213–14.

28. That these divisions within Indian society persisted during the nationalist era has since been emphasized by both the Cambridge School (A. Seal, *The Emergence of Indian Nationalism: Competition and Collaboration in the Late Nineteenth Century*, Cambridge University Press, London, 1968) and the Subaltern Studies movement (R. Guha (ed.), *Subaltern Studies: Writings on South Asian History and Society*, vol. 1, Oxford University Press, Delhi, 1982).

29. J. Jordens, *Dayananda Sarasvati: His Life and Ideas*, Oxford University Press, Delhi, 1978.

30. See 'Membership Lists', Archives of the Theosophical Society, Adyar, Madras. It is significant that various theosophists even complained that Besant's close identification with Hinduism transgressed the society's principle of remaining equally open to all faiths. See, for example, *The Theosophist*, March 1894.

31. S. Banerjea, *Nation in the Making: Being the Reminiscences of Fifty Years of Public Life*, H. Milford, London, 1925.

32. W. Wedderburn, *Allan Octavian Hume: Father of the Indian National Congress, 1829–1912*, Fisher & Unwin, London, 1913, pp. 78–83. Wedderburn, a friend of Hume's, somewhat glossed over the place of theosophy—especially the Mahatmas—in his account of Hume's political work, no doubt because he regarded Hume's attachment to them as superstitious and so disreputable.

33. Morya, *The Mahatma Letters to A.P. Sinnett*, Compiled by A.T. Barker, Fisher & Unwin, London, 1923, p. 324.

34. *Ripon Papers*, British Library, London.

35. Ibid.

36. Wedderburn, *Allan Octavian Hume*.

37. Reports of the Indian National Congress, 1885-6.

38. Ibid.

39. Wedderburn, *Allan Octavian Hume*, pp. 63–4.

40. *New India*, 17 October 1914.

41. *New India*, 22 and 24 October 1914.

42. 'Proceedings of the All-India Congress Committee Meeting held on the 30th December, 1914', Political Papers of Annie Besant, Archives of the Theosophical Society, part 2, file 13.

43. Other theosophists involved in forming *Young India* included: Shankarlal Banker, Kanji Dwarkadas, M.R. Jayakar, K.M. Munshi, Umar Sobhani, and Pandharinath Telang who became its editor.

44. See M. Bevir, 'The Formation of the All-India Home Rule League', *Indian Journal of Political Science* (3) 1991, pp. 1–16; and H. Owen, 'Toward Nation-Wide Agitation and Organization: The Home Rule Leagues 1915–18', in D. Low (ed.), *Soundings in Modern South Asian History,* Weidenfeld & Nicolson, London, 1968, pp. 159–95.

45. *New India,* 4 September 1916.

46. See various letters preserved in Political Papers of Annie Besant.

47. K. Dwarkadas, *India's Fight for Freedom 1913–17: An Eyewitness Story,* Popular Prakashan, Bombay, 1966, p. 35.

48. *New India,* 31 October 1916.

49. J. Dwarkadas, *Political Memoirs,* United Asia, Bombay, 1969, p. 175; and K. Dwarkadas, *India's Fight for Freedom.*

50. See, for example, *New India,* 4 June 1917.

Thinking Culture Through Counter-culture: The Case of Theosophists in India and Ceylon and their Ideas on Race and Hierarchy (1875–1947)

CARLA RISSEUW

People read, in articles on Census Reports in the daily press, remarks on the hill-tribes and other savages who still remain ensconced in some of the recesses of her vast extent, and think, more or less casually, that these are 'Indians'. Obviously these need not be considered when matters of self-governing nations are being discussed. Her people are 'natives,' 'coloured' and the words call up pictures of Hottentots and Kafirs, and others of that ilk. So the British nation blunders along after its wont, and risking the loss of the noblest opportunity a people have ever had of building a world-Empire so mighty that it could impose peace on the world, and in tending steadily toward a war of 'white' and 'coloured' in which Asia, indignant at long exploitation and injustice, shall be pitted against Europe and America—Besant 1914: 63.

Britain is a top-heavy country. Too much India and Ireland at the top; too little India and Ireland at the foundations. Too little real Britain, too much self-seeking Britain, at the foundations.—Besant, *The Theosophist*, September 1934: 650.

Yet India needs the intensive strength of modern Nationalism to give a purposive and dynamic vigour to that intuitive recognition of common humanity which the ancient recognition of One Life meant to the Hindu.—A. Ramaswami Aiyar, *The Theosophist*, July 1934: 40.

INTRODUCTION

THIS ESSAY DEALS WITH ideas on race and hierarchy within the theosophist philosophy during the latter part of the nineteenth and first half of the twentieth century. It is based on readings of the major journals of the school—the *Theosophist, Lucifer, Mahabodhi* (Ceylon) and

Adyar Bulletin (India)—from 1879 to 1947 as well as some major publications of its main European-American figures active in India and Ceylon—Helena Blavatsky, H.S. Olcott, Annie Besant, Margaret Cousins and James Cousins. These journals provide a wide array of articulate views on societies from which the theosophists came, as well as the societies they went to live in. They contain lively debates on many issues from which, here, one overarching theme of racial categorization and hierarchy is selected. In spite of many opposing views and debates, this theme seems to have been generally accepted as an underlying logic. It is also a crucial perspective in understanding how the theosophical leaders merged these 'racial notions' with their views on the need for nationalism and education in India and Ceylon. Their ideas at the time were often extremely progressive for the political climate of their societies of origin. They campaigned for Indian home rule long before any form of political autonomy was accepted by Britain and severely clashed with missionaries on their views on the type of education to be given to young Indians and Ceylonese. ('Let your coinage, as it were, your mental coinage, bear the imprint of your own nation': Besant, citing Olcott 1885: 104). Such political goals were fitting to the first principle of their organization: universal brotherhood of all human beings, irrespective of race, creed or colour; sex was added to the list three years later, in 1888.

At first glance the centrality of the concept of 'brotherhood' seems to mirror the idea of 'democracy', which had become prevalent. A politically critical organization, advocating a certain independence for colonized nations could be expected to take the idea of democracy further than established peers. This is, however, misleading, as theosophy stood equally for 'the question of birth', 'the value of breed' and critiqued the idea of democracy for having caused 'a confusion which has spread over the whole of the world' as it mystified the distinction between 'the lad of the manual labour class . . . (who) could be distinguished at sight from the lad of noble birth. He is of a different physical type, due to physical heredity' (Besant, *Adyar Bulletin,* June 1910: 170–1). Only some are of the material to 'lead', others must follow.

This hierarchical perspective was taken beyond class to 'race' and led to a matter-of-fact distinction between those dark-skinned people of Aryan stock and others (descendants of Lemurian stock), who at best are described as 'primitive peoples (who) have caught faint glimpses of astral experiences' (*The Theosophist,* April 1899: 448). One also comes across quite stark formulations such as '. . . A more dirty, stupid and brutal group of human beings I never saw: despite their being Muslims, it seemed to me that they must be capable of every cruelty and treachery in their own country, and one visit was quite enough to satisfy our curiosity.' The view record here is that of Olcott, after visiting 'Soudanese Negroes' on display at the Jardin des Plantes in Paris, with his sister and a friend *(The Theosophist,* April 1904: 388).

Not always are the descriptions of this nature. Many of them were more subtle. For example in *The Theosophist* of October 1901 (p. 55), a strong protest is articulated against the objections raised at the participation of a 'small number of Negro delegates to the Methodist Ecumenical conference'; in another context 'the Negroe' is acclaimed as 'he (who) has given us his music, his laughter and care-free spirit, his song' *(The Theosophist,* February:1939: 36), the article concluding that the 'warm-hearted Negroe race' has grown through interaction with the 'strong-minded, austere Caucasian people.' Within the proclaimed brotherhood, he remains the 'younger brother', in need of loving guidance and support from his 'older brothers'.

The theosophists did not talk only about 'race'. They held articulate views on education, nationhood, imperialism, socialism ('Socialism, in its ideal, . . . is true, but not a democratic idea, which is impossible.'—Besant cited in *The Theosophist,* February 1905: 303), feminism ('But for how long will feminism stop short of Humanism'—*The Theosophist,* November 1913: 228), womanhood, religion, science, vivisection, vegetarianism, war and the future of the societies they went to live in, which often contradicted the mainstream views back home. Further, James and Margaret Cousins brought in the often drawn parallels between the colonized East and their beloved Ireland, portrayed as 'a dreamy feminine person, beautiful to gaze upon, but devoid of the supreme Anglo-Saxon virtue of practicality . . . (who) insists on the right to speak her own language and govern herself' (J. Cousins, *The Theosophist,* October 1912: 35).

The articles in these journals further give a lively picture of the many Europeans and Americans (and also Australians and New Zealanders), who often joined the movement at middle age and of whom many were women. A typical example is Anna Kamensky, a woman of noble birth who had suffered during her life 'deprived of religion, torn with the agony over social and humanitarian problems' and who 'In the midst of a hopeless night of despair and anguish (experienced) the light of Theosophy dawn(ing) upon her, on hearing, in 1902 the lectures delivered in London by myself' ('Myself' was in this case Annie Besant, who reported Kamensky's case including her portrait, in *The Theosophist,* February 1911: 834–7). There were many like her, seeking a further purpose in life and experiencing a deep dissatisfaction with their own societies and philosophies.

Towards the end of the nineteenth century Theosophy was among the prominent movements opposing the Establishment in an era when many of the formerly unassailable pillars of certainty lost their appeal. Darwinist evolutionary thinking had made severe inroads into Christian belief, and led many to search for new philosophies and answers. It was a period when many new movements emerged.

The Theosophical Society (founded in 1875) occupied a prominent place within these counter-movements. It was also a counter-group which combined issues at home with activities, including those of a political nature, abroad; a striking example of criticism of the colonial empire and mainstream western thinking on relations between Europe and other continents. Between 1891 and 1935 it established around 45 branches in such widely differing countries as Great Britain, Holland, India, Ireland, United States, Ceylon, Australia, Vietnam, Indonesia and several countries in Africa and Latin America. It was by no means a marginal movement. For example in 1911, the year of the Foundation of the Order of the Star in the East,[1] Annie Besant's lectures at the Sorbonne were attracting audiences of over 4,000 people at a time (Webb 1971: 61).

Considering that the theosophy movement was a striking example of how western counter-thinking developed in relation to cultures outside the western world, it is relevant to analyse how its specific and central conceptualization of race came about. Especially as at the time, within the academic establishment, the scientific legitimacy of a hierarchy of races had become a reality, next to the already circulating popular myths of the 'Noble Savage'.

In many ways theosophy incorporated immense contradictions. On the one hand it was a remarkable counter-movement to colonialism: on the other its exponents maintained a philosophy deeply ingrained in the hierarchy of what they termed 'races', and identified closely with privileged classes in both East and West.

ELEMENTS OF COUNTER-CULTURE

What was it that the theosophists opposed? And what did they resist in the Establishment of their society?

In the *first* place colonialism in India and Ceylon, where leading exponents of their organization became involved (at various organizational levels) in (c)overt counter-movements to colonial rule. For example, in India Annie Besant played an important role in certain stages of anti-colonial agitation (the Home Rule League, between 1915 and 1919) and she was even elected as the leader of the National Congress, the main

Indian political body besides British rule at the time. She wrote extensively on her proposal for 'self-rule for India', as opposed to the 'other-rule' which Great Britain was imposing on India.[2] In Ceylon Colonel Olcott was very active on many fronts. The foundation of a network of Buddhist schools throughout the Buddhist part of the country is currently seen as his major achievement. He also substantially contributed to the various movements of Buddhist revival.[3]

Secondly, theosophy opposed the established view that the dark races and their cultures were inferior to the white race and its traditions. It created a differing racial categorization, reaching back to prehistory. Within this context, the theosophical doctrine emphasized the East, and especially the religious knowledge of India.

Thirdly, theosophists strongly condemned the materialism, technology, capitalist valuation of progress and the approach to control the environment—all elements of a philosophy of life which had become accepted in Europe and North America by the end of the nineteenth century. As an alternative they posed the superiority of the eastern spiritual and transcendental philosophies within which ample room was created for esoteric forces. The interest in the transcendental philosophies of the East was shared by various intellectual circles in the West, while a wider public appeal was emerging for the exoticism, perfumes, incenses and spices: 'A hint of a certain mysticism which did not have to be explained too much' (Webb 1971: 43). Closely linked to the resistance to the dominant values of their own culture was their opposing discourse on science and religion.

In science the theosophists opposed what they termed the overemphasis on rationality and the empirical basis of science:

The Western psychologists have . . . chopped man into minute threads. There is not . . . a bone, muscle, nerve, cell or ganglion, that they have not dissected, and fumbled over, and analysed. He [man] has not a feeling, an emotion, a cognition—not a single or complex intellectual process, that they have not pulled out, weighed in the scales of logic, tested with the resoluents [*sic*] of reason, ticketed, and laid away in the psychological herbaria. But I defy the whole of them, from Locke to Bastion, and their whole army of followers, to show you a single discovery that explains the psychic phenomena whose occurrence has been observed in India from the remotest ages, and the laws of whose causation are explained by the Aryan Sastras. (Olcott 1885:132; see also following pages)

According to their perspective, during the Age of Reason and even before, western culture, and especially western science, had lost something crucial, which was still 'intact', respected and maintained in others.

Theosophical opposition to the Christian religion is the best known. Together with other counter-movements of the time, it maintained that

Christianity could provide no answers for new and fundamental questions arising out of scientific discoveries. 'On the great question of individual immortality—on surviving consciousness—Christianity has long ceased to offer any conceptions by which it is thinkable to the modern intellect' (Olcott 1885: 75). This stand resulted in the Theosophical Society drawing extremely fierce opposition from the clergy 'at home', and even more from the missionaries abroad, who felt the core of their existence threatened by theories posing the universality of all religions, or even the superiority of others over Christianity.

If we point out to the natives of India that the form of Christianity taught by these zealots [missionaries in India] is becoming more and more discredited among the best religious thinkers of the West itself, our doing so belongs rather to a duty as educated Europeans than to any polemical position. (Olcott 1885: 32)

Theosophy, to a certain extent, also resisted the occidental, Christian perception of man as the superior being of the universe, which led it to counter the cultural values embodied in the conquest of nature and the utilitarian approach to other living beings. Many theosophists were vegetarians and active in organizations promoting vegetarianism and those opposing vivisection. This was a constant concern of the movement. In Australia for example, the theosophists started food kitchens to purify food habits (Roe 1986: 229). And when confronted with the anger of a close friend, G.B. Shaw, on her sudden turn to theosophy in middle age, Besant is said to have smilingly answered that she had become a vegetarian 'and that perhaps had enfeebled her mind' (*The Theosophist,* October 1917: 18). Theosophy also disagreed with emerging movements of Socialism and Communism. It saw these as too narrow and materialistic opposing forces, which neglected the valued 'spirituality' and the strength of existing philosophies of colonially dominated cultures.

A century later many of these issues are still part of current movements in the West, sharing the rejection of many of the fundamentals of superiority, still intact among exponents of the 'Establishment' (Barker 1990; Vanheste 1996). This gives a keener edge to our enquiry as to how and why the above-mentioned themes were adopted, succeeded or failed in obtaining legitimacy, and why many of them still appear so alive in western counter-movements today.

MEMBERSHIP

The theosophists not only profiled themselves through the many arenas of ideological resistance which they created or in which they participated.

Their philosophy, universal in outlook, overstepped the boundaries of nations and resulted in the global structure of their organization. In addition to the successful organizational structure on this scale, the extensive travels made by the members, received at each base by elaborate and supportive networks, and their innumerable journals and publications, the organization was also characterized by a membership drawn mostly from the upper classes. Many were aristocrats or middle class and usually well educated. The movement thus presents an interesting example of 'opposition to the establishment' or 'inner critique' among the privileged sections of society. Many were not members for life, but moved from one movement to another, as occurred often in a period in which doubt and change prevailed. Before Annie Besant joined the theosophists, her life was said to exemplify this trend, by the main biographer who titled his book 'The Eight Lives of Annie Besant' (Nethercott 1960).[4]

Several members of the organization, who were carefully promoted to leading positions, came from the colonized peoples themselves. Although this may not seem a striking point now, at the time within 'white society' this was a very 'forward' position, to use one of Annie Besant's favourite words. Many white-skinned members of the Order of the Star in the East needed time to digest the fact that the World Messiah (Krishnamurti) who was coming, was not white (see also Roe 1986: 152). In Ceylon Dharmapala was stimulated to take a leading role upon himself. Although neither of these men remained part of the Theosophical Society all their life, their role was crucial in determining the organization's public profile and the momentum it achieved in their countries. Further, theosophy firmly promoted the education of the privileged indigenous classes to prepare them for the leadership of their country.

The theosophical movement also had an impressive number of women in its ranks, who became lower and middle cadre as well as high-level leaders (see also Burton et al. 1994). When the movement was initiated in New York in 1875, two of the sixteen members were women, one of whom was the leader, Madame Blavatsky or HPB as she was called. In the flourishing Australian section of the organization women were predominant, although only a minority belonged to the group of officials (Roe 1986: 182-204). These women were not only from the privileged and educated sections of society, they often joined the Theosophical Society at mid-life, as wives, widows or single women: professionals, (kindergarten) teachers, journalists and artists. They do not seem to have been very committed to traditional female roles. Many were childless or remained unmarried (Roe 1986: 194).[5] Women's contribution to the movement extends to more than providing two of its most famous leaders (Blavatsky and Besant). It is found especially in the middle and senior staff levels. Many women worked devotedly for ten to thirty years on projects assigned to them within the organization. For example Musaeus Higgings, an American widow successfully headed the first Buddhist girl's college in Ceylon for thirty-three years. Irish-born Margaret Cousins was for over thirty years involved in Indian women's organizations, their struggle for franchise, their education and was editor of several Indian women's journals. Cousins was also a major exponent of the view that Indian womanhood—though 'a flower of humanity', especially in comparison with the nervous, restless life of the western woman—was in urgent need of awakening (*The Theosophist,* November 1913: 222; also Cousins 1922, 1924; and J. and M. Cousins 1950).

A third characteristic of the support base of the theosophical movement was that a great number of sympathizers with the Irish freedom struggle from Ireland joined its ranks or remained strong supporters throughout their lives. Several of them fled to the colonies from where they contributed to counter-movements against colonialism (Davis 1986).

Finally, the movement did not reject members and even leaders, who were privately accused of homosexual practices (Dharmapala), or stood by them as far as possible during public accusations in print or court. This is illustrated in Besant's reluctance to remove Leadbeater, as head of the Esoteric Section of the Society at Adyar, after public accusations and a public trial on his sexual relations with young men under his supervision (Roe 1986: 214). Within a few years he was reinstated into the Society. This again is an indication of the depth of the opposition shown by the theosophists to the Victorian values of the time and the damaging assaults of their opponents on the organization.

RESISTANCES WITHIN RESISTANCE

Thus on the level of discourse and practice, one can designate theosophy as an example of a counter-culture. It appealed to what Roe termed 'the Great Unsatisfied'. Neither religion nor science gave answers to fundamental questions. 'There were many late Victorians trapped between the will and the incapacity to believe' (Roe 1986: 191). Theosophy gave them an organization to shape their questions and develop their answers. It was a substantial resistance to colonial hegemony and the foundations on which the superiority of the British empire and, more generally, the white race was based. This also explains why theosophists were and are viewed as highly controversial in many different circles. Theosophy seldom became respectable, and even as late as 1905 the Australian sections still discussed whether contributors to theosophical journals should be allowed to omit their names (Roe 1986: 136). Their opponents were to be found among colonial administrators, scientists, orientalists like Max Müller, Christian missionaries, political activists in the colonized countries who centred more on the masses rather than solely on the elite (Mahatma Gandhi), feminists as well as Socialists and Marxists both in the West and the colonized countries. As a movement they appear to have opposed 'too much at once' and even groups who opposed each other could each find their own particular axe to grind with the theosophists.

Within this resistance to the dominant thinking of their time, other resistances were fought out, as for example the great number of women who could acquire a certain degree of public space for their ideas. Likewise leaders of the colonized elite in India and Ceylon could make use of the organization theosophy provided, as a base to gain experience in opposing colonialism, to develop their vision of the future and often at later stages to break again with the Society (See also in this volume the contribution of Mark Bevir).[6]

There are marked variations in judgements on the theosophists and their leaders in different parts of the world. In the western world they failed to maintain the prominence enjoyed during the period 1880–1920: no public spaces such as streets, libraries, etc. are named after them and no statues were erected in their memory. No theosophical leader would now hope to draw crowds and get coverage on the front pages of leading newspapers as Annie Besant did in every part of the world she visited.

The situation is different in India and Sri Lanka. For instance one cannot visit Chennai (formerly Madras) without experiencing the presence of Annie Besant. One of the main avenues is simply known as 'A.B. Marg', and in the midst of traffic, her imposing statue stands, showing her gazing solemnly towards the sea. Likewise in Sri Lanka Colonel Olcott has his statue on a roundabout in Galle (south Sri Lanka), while among the middle classes the theosophists are still respectfully (if a little vaguely) remembered for their contribution to the start of a network of Buddhist schools.[7]

People know far less of issues other than colonialism, which the theosophists opposed, although especially in India their current elitism—more prominent than in the past—is often deplored. Today scholars are assessing the impact of the organization on their own anti-colonial movements (Gombrich and Obeyesekere 1988; Obeyesekere, 1997).

As was mentioned earlier, the focus in this article lies in the discourse of opposition as it was shaped by the theosophists in India and Ceylon.

To what extent did they oppose the dominant values of their society and more, specifically, which tenets of the orthodoxy of thought did they retain? The relevance of this approach is found in the re-emergence today of many of the issues raised by the theosophists. The various New Age movements are a prime example, as also the spiritual dimension of movements within feminist circles of the USA, spiritual organizations in USA and Europe, alternative food circuits, alternative healing systems, vegetarianism, alternative educational systems (Rudolf Steiner) and rising concern for the environment (Barker 1989; Vanheste 1996). This raises the question whether there is some kind of continuum or at least pendulum of values, whereby one finds elements of late-nineteenth-century progressive thought repeated in specific new forms of counter-thinking during the twentieth century.

HISTORICAL ROOTS OF THEOSOPHY AND THE PLACE OF THE OCCULT IN COUNTER-MOVEMENTS IN THE EUROPEAN TRADITION

As one delves deeper into the meaning of this re-occurrence of counter-values in western society, one comes across writers localizing the emergence of opposition to rationality. James Webb is one of these authors whose work centred on the 'widespread flight from reason' (1971, 1976), which took place from the mid-nineteenth century in Europe. This 'crisis of consciousness', in opposition to 'civilized society' was articulated by intellectuals and artists who found a hearing among a growing public. Webb describes sympathizers of this phenomenon as 'the Bohemia . . . a land without geography . . . whose . . . inhabitants are spread among many nations' (1971: 94).

In Webb's view, besides the political and social revolutions (as in 1789), the bourgeoisie of Western Europe and USA were rocked by upheavals of another kind:

An artistic rebellion was brewing, impatient with what was. Society, considered as it had been in the Age of Reason, as it was in the scientific age, implied naturalism, rationalism, a fixed code of behaviour; this state of affairs by which the bourgeois made his money and sold his soul through a virtuous cynicism was simply unacceptable. With a seriousness which is difficult for 20th-century man to realize, the Bohemians, in the midst of their posing and their legendary debauch, set out to find their own solutions. [. . .]

They set out, therefore, with assumptions which were anti-rationalist and anti-materialist, to produce anti-naturalist art. Because this approach was based on the total rejection of the world it is legitimate to call it 'spiritual' (1971: 101–2).

Webb traces these counter-movements to the existence of the 'occult' and its long history of repression in western civilization, which started long before the mentioned pendulum of opposing values for the nineteenth and twentieth centuries. He argues that the nature of the widespread and varying counter-reactions to dominant culture cannot be understood without understanding the largely ignored element of European history, namely the 'occult'. The occult is defined as knowledge actively rejected by an Establishment culture, or knowledge that voluntarily exiles itself.

This trend is traced back far beyond the Age of Enlightenment to the fourth century of western civilization. Webb sees it as a specific quality of European history that it produces 'an establishment' which can last relatively long periods of time, but 'allowed the constant replenishing of the forces of subversion' (ibid.: 120)

Even in the fifth century BC there already existed a deep chasm between the rationalism of the Greek intellectuals and a body of popular beliefs, and in the third century BC, when rationalist thinking became prominent many counter-perceptions emerged. These led to the formation of numerous secret traditions, long since forgotten, especially after Christianity became the established religion by the third century. As examples Webb cites the Mithras cult, Neo-Platonism, Gnosticism, Hermetism and the Mystery religions (ibid.: 121-2).

These cults, varied in form and time, all contained the element of the incorporation of self-knowledge, of the divine via possession of direct mystical experience, or through a secret body or doctrine shared with initiates. These counter-movements met with violent resistance from the established philosophies and religions.[8]

All these repressed traditions shared *a reverence for the East* as the source of wisdom. The emphasis on, and involvement in, the East was therefore no invention of theosophy and other nineteenth-century counter-movements (Webb 1971: 129). Webb explains this emphasis as being due to the deep alienation of Greek thought from the miraculous and the non-rational, which therefore had to seek a base in the religions of the East, while astrological conceptions were derived from Assyria and Babylon.[9]

The idea that Greek rationalism did not provide all the answers continued in the Christian era, together with a glorification of irrational peoples and their ascribed primitive ability to communicate with the divine. Initially these qualities were located in Egypt, Chaldea (Assyria and Babylon) and with the former Druids of Ireland; but in course of time, with the increasing knowledge of the Orient, the East, and especially India, superseded them as the source of superior wisdom (ibid.).

Webb notes several comparable movements during the Middle Ages and Renaissance, fiercely repressed, but which together with the greater availability of Aristotle[10] in the twelfth century, produced what Webb terms 'a certain giddiness and panic in the individual', as they challenged the all-embracing certainties of medieval Christianity.

During the Enlightenment (eighteenth century) science gained prominence as a source of knowledge, which further weakened the Church as a worldly power, resulting in its requiring more State support. The debate between Establishment and Underground turned more to social than religious or philosophical questions, but the occult did not die out completely. The Age of Reason, being an age of scepticism and disillusionment, did manage to dislodge the position of the occult, but it also led to a renewed search for the hidden place of a higher wisdom.

The eighteenth and nineteenth centuries also further expanded the 'discovery' of the East, and several writers and commentators noted how the Hindu doctrine bore 'a wonderful resemblance to Plato'.[11] It was on the wave of the scientific discovery of the East, the establishment of Orientalist studies and the founding of Asiatic Societies that the occultist traditions could once more successfully resurrect their reverence for the East as the source of superior wisdom, like in the distant past (Webb 1971: 148). During this period the occultist traditions were infused in many ways by elements in which the new rationalist establishment found no place. Blavatsky, who succeeded in blending occultist and Darwinist thought when she developed her racial theories, is a prime example of this trend.

A specifically new element of counter-movements such as theosophy was that for the first time in European history this old and diversified trend of European counter-thinking was expressed in the form of an organization which established itself in the Orient itself. Within the then political context, this was made possible by the colonial control of the British empire over countries like Ceylon and India.

In the next section the specific blend of occultism and Darwinism, leading to the theosophical philosophy of hierarchy, race and evolution, is discussed in more detail, in order to understand the philosophical base of the 'racial logic'. It will also help to clarify why theosophy could be so vehement in the later political struggle to gain acceptance for Indian gentlemen/citizens as equal members of the British empire, while remaining so lukewarm about the position of other 'races' within that same empire (see the first citation of Besant at the start of this essay).

THE THEOSOPHICAL PHILOSOPHY OF HIERARCHY, RACE AND EVOLUTION

The theme of race appears as a central concept in the philosophy, first formulated in *The Secret Doctrine* (1888) by Madame Blavatsky, and regularly re-explained in the many periodicals and emphasized by the leaders during their major addresses. It is also a constant theme, appearing from the first editions of their publications through to the later years. Several examples have already been given, and such references abound in theosophical publications during the whole period of analysis. References to the savages of darkest Africa in need of 'a civilizer' (*The Theosophist*, May 1913: 157) to 'Coloured men of a savage type, Australian, Red American Indian, Kaffir, etc. (who) are wiped out sooner or later, for they cannot effectively resist' (Besant 1914: 72), to the brotherly support for the South African youth movement, in which one should never forget one's duty to assist the native on the path of his development 'from savage to civilized man' (*The Theosophist*, February 1935: 454–6), to the questioned need to educate the Kaffir (*The Theosophist*, August 1904: 700–2), to the Maori, who through his inferior breeding, worsened by intermarriage, will subsequently lose his reproductive powers, and who described his life as Hell while being sympathetically listened to by Mabel Hornes (*The Theosophist*, May 1932: 174) and many such others contrast with the strongly supportive views articulated on 'Indian gentlemen and their need for the elementary rights of citizens.' (*The Theosophist*, May 1913: 57). See also Besant : 'The Hindu is as pure, noble and right-thinking a gentleman as any who are to be found in the West. Man for man, any noble English type can be matched in India (*The Theosophist*, October 1912: 134). Besant and her followers agitated strongly against colonial measures evicting Indians from other colonies as South Africa, Australia, New Zealand and British Colombia (Besant 1914).

This perspective on racial difference is also advocated by those who later dissociated themselves from theosophy and started their own movements such as the well-known case of Rudolf Steiner, whose anthroposophical schools and organizations are still found in many European countries. Therefore it is surprising that only a few critics then or later, have correlated the implications of their racial philosophy with their emphasis on universal brotherhood. Not that this racial philosophy should be equated simplistically with notions of 'racism' as the concept is viewed a century later. It is based on a complex religious and evolutionary philosophy of the interaction of mind and matter, the rudiments of which will be described here briefly. This summary is based largely on Annie Besant's 'The Pedigree of Man', a central lecture at the twenty-eight annual meeting at Adyar in 1903, published in 1905. Further elaboration and explanation was provided by A. Schwartz as an *aide-memoire* for students of her work (*The Theosophist*, June 1905: 545–87). Schwartz, a well-known member, at regular intervals held study classes on this issue for a theosophical hearing (*Adyar Bulletin*, October 1908: 292). Schwartz, described as an 'ardent' friend of Olcott (*Adyar Bulletin*, March 1908: 94) was an industrialist (Volkart Brothers, dealing in coconut and coir articles) from Ceylon. He was the treasurer at Adyar, head office Theosophical Society, 1908 to 1933, and secretary treasurer of the Olcott Free Schools for which he also donated substantial financial support (*The Theosophist*, June 1905: 545). His memorial plaque is still seen in the Musaeus Girls College in Colombo.

Besant's speech was translated into several languages, and would have contributed to the popularizing of these theories.[12] But as such it was not new. Blavatsky had originally elaborated on this idea and, much earlier in time, one can easily find the same issue addressed in the major theosophical journals (for example, see *The Theosophist*, October 1885: 76; de Purucker 1940).

Besant based her theory on Blavatsky's *The Secret Doctrine* and followed her definition of man, who is seen as the link between the divine and the animal:

Man is that being in the universe, in whatever part of the universe he may be and whatever form he may have, in whom the highest spirit (the Monad) and lowest matter are joined together by intelligence, thus ultimately making a manifested God, who will go forth conquering and to conquer, through the illimitable future that stretches before him. . . . Every being in this universe has to pass through the human kingdom; if he has passed beyond it, he must have passed through it; if he has not reached it, he will have to pass through it in the future (see Schwartz 1905: 546).

Besant further distinguishes three great lines of evolution: (a) the spiritual or monadic; (b) the physical at the other pole of human nature; and (c) the intellectual, which links the spiritual and the physical through constant struggle between the two poles. Besant contrasts western thinking with eastern thinking on the mind and the body, the latter being a mere temporary 'coat of skin' in eastern philosophy.[13] The struggle consists of the attempts of the spiritual to sink, descend into matter (the physical) and impart its superior qualities to it, and in matter attempting to rise up to the higher qualities of the spiritual. This is worked out in a scheme of evolution, encompassing millions of years, which is elaborately staged in a wide, cosmic perception of 'the Great Spiritual Hierarchies (I'shvara, the Logos) and the seven planetary Logoi' (Schwartz 1905: 546). The evolution of the planetary Logos is conceived within seven planetary chains, further influenced by corresponding globes.[14] Within these planetary chains further are distinguished the so-called rounds evolving one kingdom of nature to the highest perfection of its own type. The future types not belonging to the round, are at present only found in their embryonic stage. Besant assessed the historical moment of her age to be placed in the fourth planetary chain in its fourth round and on its fourth globe. The seven planetary logoi are further expressed in the twelve creative hierarchies, of which the first five have already passed away. The human monads count as one of the twelve creative hierarchies, and are found in the fourth one of the seven, with which the present evolution is concerned.

Born within Is'vara, as the centre of His Life, the Monads enter the streams which from the three (Logal) divide into seven (Planetary Logoi) and each group takes on the colour belonging to the Planetary Logos into whom it flowed, until within each Planetary Logos, the seven rays of colour are seen (Besant, 1904.: 23, 24, quoted in Schwartz.: 547).

Subsequently the monads start their descent through the creative hierarchies, seven of which assist the monad in obtaining their 'principles'. The first hierarchy awakens the will aspect of the monad, the second his wisdom, the third his activity, the fourth are the monads themselves. The fifth hierarchy guides the monad to the *nirvanic* atom; the sixth guides him to *buddhic* and *manasic* Atoms and also to the permanent mental unit and permanent astral atom, while the last and seventh hierarchy guides the monad in obtaining a permanent physical atom (Besant, ibid.: 25/26, quoted in Schwartz).

Via a series of tables Schwartz translated for the general theosophical reader, the complex evolutionary progress of the monads as they pass through the globes and rounds of each planetary chain (see Schwartz 1905: 548–9). Thus one can find monads within several evolutionary chains existing during the same time span.

THE SEVEN RACES

The human kingdom is further diversified into a hierarchical conceptualization of the 'seven races of men evolving on our earth' (Schwartz 1905: 550). The following short outline will have to serve as an indication of the philosophical scope on which the distinctions between the seven races are based. Further elaboration can be found in the cited literature. The average theosophical member would not have been aware of the full complexity of the theory and would not have been allowed to enter the hierarchy as member of the 'esoteric inner circle' of those who understood. He or she tended to accept the philosophical wisdom of this basis of theosophical philosophy, even if certain parts remained obscure. He would also be offered more simplistic versions, as in Annie Besant's speeches or her writings on the theme, even in 1898), or Schwartz's *aide-memoire* and his study classes.[15]

The First Race: The Race of the Gods

This race did not yet possess the human form, and its members are described as 'huge, filamentous, sexless Bhūtas', with a consciousness which could only slightly affect their clumsy bodies. Their consciousness existed on an *atmic* level and they were sometimes termed the race of the gods, and although they can stand, walk, run, recline or fly, they are still a shadow with no sense *(chaya)*. They possessed hearing and reproduced themselves through fission or 'budding'. They were not diversified into identifiable sub-races and emerged on earth after aeons of terrible turmoil and gigantic convulsions of nature, during which the first land appeared on Mount Meru, as the cap of the North Pole is termed.

The Second Race

These beings are built up out of denser particles of matter, forming a stiffer shell on the outside. They are golden-yellow, have gorgeously hued forms often tree-like in shape—some already approaching animal forms having a semi-human outline—and while drifting, floating, climbing they cry to each other in flute-like notes. They still multiply by fission but can also be sweat-born with adumbrations of the two sexes and maybe termed androgynes.

It is from the germs thrown off by these second race 'men' that the mammalian kingdom gradually developed. They occupied a continent, formed during the first race, named Hyperborean or Plaksha. Roughly this encompassed an area stretching from northern Asia and Greenland to a great sea now the site of the Gobi desert, covering Spitsbergen, Norway, Sweden and Great Britain. The climate at the time was tropical.

The Third Race: The Lemurians

The third race of man had the human shape but was of gigantic proportions powerful enough to hold his own among the huge animals of his time. His colour was red with shades; the head had a retreating forehead, flattened nose and heavy jaws projecting. These men were like 'Divine Androgynes' and had one large eye on their forehead. They responded to sight, in addition to hearing and touch of the former two races.

They were the first race to be divided into three types, with seven sub-races as they developed further. The first type, containing the first two sub-races, was still sweat-born. The second type, with the third and the fourth sub-race, produced hermaphrodites, fully developed at birth. 'Their forms became the vehicles of the "Lords of Wisdom" from the Venus Chain, who came before the separation of the sexes 18 million years ago' (Schwartz 1905: 552, citing Besant: 1904: 77, 78 and 102).

The fourth sub-race was still egg-born, but one sex began to dominate the other, when males and females were born. The infants became helpless and by the end of the fourth sub-race they could no longer emerge from the egg and walk immediately. The third type, containing the fifth, sixth and seventh sub-race developed the human evolution further. The fifth sub-race was still egg-born, gradually the egg being retained longer by the mother and the child becoming helpless and feeble. With the sixth and seventh sub-race sexual reproduction became universal while the one eye sank back into the forehead to be replaced with two.

These last exponents of the seventh sub-race were obvious savages in form, but responded quickly to impulses sent out by the divine kings (*pitris*), under whose guidance they built mighty cities and temples of which fragments still remain. Their continent, Lemuria, has also disappeared. It stretched from the Himalayas to Ceylon, Tasmania, Australia and Easter Island, westward to Madagascar and part of Africa. A great volcanic outburst destroyed Lemuria, leaving only some fragments such as Australia, Madagascar and Easter Island.

Apart from the volcanic destruction, the Lemurians had degenerated as their sexual passions became strong after the separation of the sexes. The solar pitris began mating with female inferiors and producing beings inferior to themselves. The purer forms moved northward while the lower forms moved south, east and west. They were destined to become the fathers of the fourth race of Atlanteans. In contrast to the previous two races, descendants of the Lemurians (the seventh sub-race) still exist as the aboriginal Australians and Tasmanians. Several other peoples are recognized as descendants from other combinations, as for instance the seventh Lemurian sub-race with sub-races of the Atlanteans as ancestors of the Malays, Papuans and the Dravidians of south India. Furthermore all African peoples were conceived to be descendants of the Lemurian race.

The Fourth Race: The Atlantean

The third race gave birth to the fourth approximately eight million years ago towards the latter part of the secondary age.

The most suitable types were chosen out of the Third race by the Manu of the Fourth and were led northwards to the Imperishable Sacred Land, to be isolated and evolved, and to settle, on leaving the cradle of races, on the northern parts of Asia, unaffected by the great Lemurian catastrophes. (Schwartz 1905: 553)

They were divided into seven sub-races known as:

Rmoahal (1), fair in colour, who drove the Lemurians from the land they settled. They still possessed the third eye, although two ordinary physical eyes were developing. 'The Astral world was not yet shut from the general vision' (Schwartz 1905: Table J). A quietly flourishing civilization, following the Divine Rulers, which was destroyed four million years ago by a huge convulsion, and the remaining descendants declined into barbarism.

Tliavatli (2), yellow in colour, grew up on land beneath the Atlantic Ocean. The most peaceful of the Atlantean civilizations, led once more by the divine kings. A great cataclysm destroyed their country and their 'glorious' civilization, leaving the descendants to intermarry with the Lemurians, thus giving rise to the Dravidian people (Besant 1904: 118, 123–4).

Toltec (3) were handsome with well-cut features, around twenty-seven feet tall and red-and-brown in colour. They were strong enough to bend a bar of iron. They had acquired taste, although no sense of smell. Their civilization was versed in chemistry, agriculture and alchemy and their great architecture was expressed in the famous 'City of the Golden Gates'. Their civilization spread from Atlantis to North and South America and Egypt. After many wars and victories, the white emperor was driven from the City of Golden Gates and replaced by the dark emperor. Finally, 50,000 years after the pollution of the Golden Temple, the empire was destroyed by a catastrophe some 850,000 years ago (Besant 1904: 118, 132–43).

Turanian (4) were the *rakshasas*, ferocious and brutal and their conflicts with the young fifth race are recorded in Indian history.

Semitic (5) were a turbulent, fighting people, and are the distant ancestors of the Jewish people. From one of their families, selected by Vaivasvata Manu, came the seeds of the fifth race, but it was rejected again because of its lack of plasticity.

Akkadian (6) emerged after the destruction of two-thirds of the Toltec civilization and the Etruscans and Carthaginians were derived from their root.

Mongolian (7) developed from the Turanian, fourth sub-race, and their descendants are the inland Chinese, the Malays, Tibetans,

Hungarians and Finns. Some of their offshoots mingled with the Toltecs and North Americans, being the reason why the North American Indians have some Mongolian blood. The Japanese are considered to be one of their latest offshoots. Many of the sub-race travelled westward, settling in Asia Minor, Greece and adjoining countries. There they mixed with the fifth sub-race, giving rise to the Greek and Phoenician cultures.

The Fifth Race: The Aryans

The fifth race evolved under Buddha-Mercury and its chief achievement was the development of the mind. About a million years ago Vaivasvata Manu selected from the fifth Atlantean sub-race, the Semitic, the seeds of the fifth race leading them to the imperishable sacred land. The Manu laboured for years to shape future humanity. The fifth sense of smell was added to this race, which was formed as they are currently known. This race had the brightest intelligence and the purest character, and were led southward by Manu to Central Asia where they developed their age-old civilization. At the same time the earth underwent many changes, shaping the continents as they are currently known: Europe, Asia, Africa, America and Australia.

The Aryans are divided into five Sub-Races as follows:

The Aryan (1) settled 850,000 years ago in northern India. They had already been built into the fourfold orders by the Manu, shaping their bodies subtly to each caste. They received the Zodiac directly from the 'sons of Will and Yoga', who came among them as teachers and from whom originated the 24 Buddhas, worshipped by the Jains as the 24 Tirthankaras (Besant 1904: 147).

The Aryo-Semitic (2) migrated from Central Asia via Afghanistan into Arabia and Syria. They intermingled with the Greeks, Egyptians, the Chinese, everywhere giving rise to great civilizations. 'They followed Saboeanism, the worship of beings who rule the celestial bodies, the star-angels, and the Magi of Chaldea were astronomers and astrologers profoundly versed in the science of the celestial bodies (Schwartz 1905: Table K).

The Iranian (3) were led by Zarathustra to the north and east, where they settled in Afghanistan and Persia, some pushing on to Egypt and Arabia. They were also famous for their alchemists.

The Keltic (4), led by Orpheus, migrated westward: first to Greece, then Italy, across France to Ireland and Scotland, 'peopling also the younger England' (Besant 1904: 150).

The Teutonic (5) migrated westward and occupied Central Europe, from where they are currently spreading over the world. 'It has occupied the greater part of North America, it has seized Australia and New Zealand and is destined to build a world-empire and to sway the destinies of civilization' (Besant 1904: 150, 151).

The Sixth and Seventh Sub-races

The sixth and Seventh sub-races, and the so-called root-races (each having seven sub-races) have not yet emerged. They are subjects of much speculation by theosophical philosophers. For a lengthier account, see *The Beginnings of the Sixth Root Race* by C.W. Leadbeater, Theosophical Publishing House, Adyar, 1954.

FAMILIAR AND UNFAMILIAR

It would be noted that this listing of the rise and fall of races and their sub-racial types does not give the philosophical sources on which the 'secret doctrine' based itself. Additionally, the exposition sounds fantastic to the layman, at the same time carrying elements of the familiar. One can well imagine an average theosophical member, not part of the Esoteric Circle, getting a feel for such philosophy: The more the races develop, the more their mind is developed; the mind is placed above the body and the site of spiritual superiority is placed in India, as had been done by counter-movements in the West for centuries. Lower intelligence leads to licentiousness and destruction. Male is superior to female. Darker tanned kings lose to lighter skinned ones. Those races having the most developed mind were and still are considered by many to be superior. The Teutonic race is destined to conquer the world. The north Indian Aryan is superior to the south Indian, whose Dravidian ancestry links him to the Lemurians, a lower and former race. The Semitics have a dubious position, which links to Christian notions. The descendants of the Lemurians, who have not been mixed with other races, such as Africans, Australian aborigines, Tasmanians and others are considered less intelligent than the descendants of the fifth race, among whom the Europeans and north Indians are ranked. Thus although the esoteric philosophy of theosophy opposed Christianity and western science, many similar lines of thought are reproduced in other forms. Destruction, it may be noted, always ends one racial civilization.[16] The phrase 'racial civilization' is used here, as it is apparent that theosophy uses the concept of race, in a wider context, than that of physical characteristics alone. While great emphasis is placed on the appearance of each race, these outer characteristics are unalterably linked to inner characteristics, merging exponents of each race to the civilization they create.

IN RETROSPECT

This overview indicates that the earlier mentioned contrasts in the theosophical perceptions of differences between 'the darker races' contained at their base a worked-out philosophy, which explains an underlying logic contained in the earlier mentioned individual citations. The theosophists had an all-encompassing vision of the universe and humanity, which fused accidental notions on evolution with interpretations of (eastern) religions, which was to lay the philosophical basis for their activities outside their own society.

Although a review of their various journals reveals the variety of opinions held by theosophists on certain themes, their logic and argumentation always starts from the philosophy on racial evolution as outlined above and provides them with an undisputed logic to differentiate between descendants of Aryans (north Indians) and Lemurians (Africans) for example, and also to distinguish between 'old' and 'new' souls. This philosophy is fundamental to their interpretation of the concept of 'race' and embedded in a hierarchical outlook where evolution and reincarnation seem to meet. Their perspective was, and still is, unacceptable to the establishment of their own societies. In religious, scientific and (left-wing) political circles their approach is rejected and ridiculed.

This essay began with a mention of how in the West theosophy formed a counter-culture which opposed too much at once. This caused different circles to find plausible reasons for rejecting the movement. In each case, theosophy attacked the essentials rather than secondary issues, which seems to have left the Society with too few associates to enable it to become a counter-movement of substance in the West. Only the 'doubters', the 'seekers' of each circle joined them, many of whom seemed to have originated from the privileged classes. In this sense they continued a far older tradition of what Webb termed 'the Bohemia', the resistance to the Establishment as it existed in western society. At the same time, their theory shared many of the basics of the notion of superiority inherent to the imperial project and other dominant cultural themes within the cultures of origin. A hierarchy between spirit and body, between races and between the sexes is maintained.[17] Thus although the major theosophical leaders attempted dramatically to shake occidental philosophical fundamentals—and in many respects succeeded—they also appear to have reintroduced the same fundamentals at another level. The right race, the right parentage and the right education retained their importance in securing a privileged position in society. The only point of difference between the imperial/Victorian culture and counter-culture was in the interpretation of which people the 'right race' consisted of.

In contrast, the contribution of the theosophy movement to the emergence of anti-colonial movements in India and Ceylon appears more directly subversive (see Mark Bevir in this volume). Despite the ridicule which the movement faced 'at home', it did contribute substantially to the emergence of anti-colonial agitation in Ceylon and India. In the West the disparaging views on the theosophical theory have overshadowed its contribution to the movement against colonialism. In the East, although the theosophists have become a marginal societal phenomenon, they are remembered with respect and affection, even by those who disagree with them. They are still remembered for their practical contribution to the organization of education and political agitation. Also, their position on the spiritual superiority of eastern religions and culture over that of the colonizers is remembered with nostalgia. In this respect, their counter-movement could gain enough legitimacy to retain a historical place in the struggle for independence. In practice their counter-hegemony to colonialism was directly subversive only in the context of certain eastern colonized societies. In relation to other societies colonized by the British (West), as for example Australia, New Zealand, Africa and North America, their subversive role needs to be reassessed. Their central value of 'universal brotherhood' irrespective of race, creed, colour and sex was opposed to colonialism in principle, but in the notion of universal brotherhood itself there were differences of degree.

In what respect the ideas of the theosophists were taken over and reshaped within specific nationalist struggles by Hindus (in India) and Buddhists (in Ceylon) associated with them is another issue. The third quote at the beginning of this essay indicates the seeds of nationalism, but further analysis is beyond the scope of this essay. A glance at a major work of a leading nationalist, Dharmapala (1965), will show how Ceylonese nationalism was associated with articulate anti-Tamil perceptions, many of which are still alive in certain circles.

Returning to the question of counter-culture in the West, one is struck by the parallels with counter-movements there a century later. In the varied brands of 'New Age movements', still very much alive, are comparable views on the mystic and superior sources of the East, vegetarianism, environment, 'spirituality', ideals of universal humankind, and a recurring critique of science, Christian religion and the narrowness of Marxist, socialist or feminist theorizing. By contrast, the notion of a hierarchy of race has become taboo. 'Racism' has been coined as a negative label, which no one, either of the dominant cultures or of counter-cultures, wants to bear. Just the same, if at all one attempted to 'deconstruct' ideas on race, and question preconceptions held, for example, on 'Africans' and 'Asians', one would probably stumble on notions which uncomfortable parallels, albeit diluted, with the counter-ideas held a century earlier.

In the current texts of theosophists and Steiner-followers, one does not find a formulated political distancing from the texts of their leaders. The strategy followed has been one more of glossing over racial interpretations, and making slight (undocumented) changes in the original texts in reprints. The strategy has drawn fire (Moerland 1986; Jeurissen 1996; Zander 1996; de Tollenaere 1996; de Roode et al. 1986), and has at times been defended (Voorham 1989a and b; Kegel 1989), but the result has been to limit recognition and success of the movements. The notion of hierarchy and racial superiority, in differing ways part of the mainstream culture as also of the counter-culture of a century earlier, in spite of losing public legitimacy, seems to have lost little of its uncomfortable potency. Apart from the current followers of theosophists, the question also arises to what extent the more recently formed New Age movements, sharing in the earlier mentioned pendulum of values have, retained notions of hierarchy and racial superiority in their philosophical edifices. The answer would shed interesting light on the question whether counter-ideas and counter-cultures transform themselves, and if and how they succeed in thinking beyond their (counter)-culture.

NOTES

The funding of this study was provided by the Third World Center, University of Nijmegen. I also want to thank Antony Copley, Gananath Obeyesekere and Gerrit Huizer for their interest and valuable comments made on earlier drafts of this article as well as Herman de Tollenaere for his help in locating sources.

1. Annie Besant first published her lectures on the coming race and the coming of 'some mighty teacher' who would change the world, in 1910. In the same year Leadbeater announced that he had found this world teacher in the form of a Brahmin boy from Madras (born 1895). After Besant endorsed his idea, the boy, Krishnamurti, was further educated by the theosophists and legally adopted by Annie Besant. In order to prepare for his coming theosophical teachers of the Central Hindu College, Benares, created a preparatory 'Order of the Star in the East' (OSE). By 1914 the order had developed, with several activities and paraphernalia such as badges, ribbons, journal, etc. and had a wide following both inside and outside the Theosophical Society. Krishnamurti was named the Outer Head and formally edited the journal, although in practice the work was done mostly by other theosophists such as Mary Lutyens (1975). In 1929 Krishnamurti was to dramatically dissolve the order at its yearly conference in Ommen, Holland.

2. See: *How India Wrought for Freedom. The Story of the National Congress told from Official Records* (1915); *India and the Empire, a lecture and various papers on Indian grievances* (1914); *India or Nation, a Plea for Indian Self-Government* (1915);

The Birth of New India (1917); *Coercion and Resistance in India,* Home Rule League, London (1919); Shall India Live or Die?(1926); *India–Bond or Free: A World Problem* (1926).

3. The anti-colonial opposition of the theosophists was not couched in a conceptual framework of the independence of nations, as was later adopted by the major leading local politicians in their struggle for independence.

4. According to C.L. Wessinger (1988: 1) this title suggests a disjointedness, which does not really reflect Besant's life. Like her counterparts she was searching for new answers, which led her to join new movements. But her questions and her line of thought displayed a certain continuity, which is overlooked when one focuses on her outward activities alone.

5. See, for example, A. Linklater (1980).

6. H. de Tollenaere in his valuable study, (1996) analyses the country of origin of the contributors to *The Theosophist.* His figures show that between October 1912 and September 1917, 8.8 per cent of the contributors were Indian men. From April 1934 to March 1939, 34.9 per cent were Indian men and another 1.4 per cent were Indian women (pp. 390–1). These figures indicate a substantial and possibly growing contribution of Indian authors to theosophical publications. The reasons for their sympathies and the manner in which the ideas and activities of the Theosophical Society fitted into their own (political) agenda is an interesting topic of study, which this essay cannot cover.

7. A system which continued till after independence, when it was taken over by the government and forms the basis of the current educational system.

8. For example Gnosticism was fundamentally opposed by Christianity. It claimed that the human soul was imprisoned in a world of matter, and that the true home of the spirit was outside the whole system of cosmic order. Added to this was the notion that Gnosis (knowledge) ensures salvation, in the realization that one contains a spark of God which can lead to an awakening from the half-life led on earth to a full consciousness of divinity within oneself.

9. F. Cumont, *The Oriental Religions in Roman Paganism,* Chicago, 1911, cited by Webb (1971 : 129).

10. Aristotle became available in the twelfth century. Within his emphasis on philosophical speculation and a method a careful observation, he likewise formed a serious threat to the existence of the established order.

11. Quoted in S.N. Mukherjee, *Sir William Jones, the Pioneer Orientalist,* Cambridge, 1968, p. 78, quoted in Webb 1976: 148.

12. In Dutch it was published in 1909 by the N.V. Theosophische Uitgeversmaatschappij, Amsterdam, translated by C. Streubel.

13. [S]ome Indians will never speak of bodily wants as theirs: they say: "My body is hungry", "My body is tired"—not "I am tired". And though in our ears the phrase may sound fantastic, it is truer to facts than self-identification with our body' (*Reincarnation:* 13)

14. Globes A and G (as named by Schwartz) are archetypal of subtle mental matter; Globes B and F are creative, of denser mental matter, Globes C and E are formative, of astral matter, while Globe D provides the physical, termed the turning-point.

15. I could find no critique on Schwartz's presentation, except for one reference in *The Theosophist* of 1903 (August, p. 695) where he is rebuked for having made one serious mistake in classing the Australian aborigines and the American Red Indians with the natives of India: '[T]here can be no comparison whatever in the minds of well-informed people, for the two former are scarcely above the savage stage, if they can be said to be at all above it, while the latter are the custodians of great religious teachings which are spreading all over the world, and contain among their numbers some of the finest thinkers and logicians of the modern world.' Schwartz refers to Besant's 1905 publication *The Pedigree of Man*. For a longer analysis of the same ideas, see *Man, Whether, How and Whither, a Record of a Clairvoyant Investigation* by A. Besant and C.W. Leadbea:er, Theosophical Publishing House, Adyar, 1913. Also published by the Theosophical Society, London the same year.

16. This perception on destruction of civilizations is closely linked to the theosophical view on war, which they do not ultimately oppose.

17. In the case of maintaining a hierarchy between the sexes, a distinction needs to be made between ideal and practice. Within theosophical thinking itself, the masculine was valued and all the guiding spiritual figures were masculine. Nevertheless theosophy as an organization provided a much wider social space for women than the mainstream society of the time.

BIBLIOGRAPHY

Barker, E., 1989. New Religious Movements, A Practical Introduction, London.
Besant, A., 1986. *Man and his Bodies. Theosophical Manual,* no. 11, Theosophical Publishing Society. London.
————, 1898. *Reincarnation, Theosophical Memorials,* no. 11, Madras.
————, 1905. *The Pedigree of Man,* Theosophical Publishing House, Adyar.
————, 1914. *India and the Empire, a lecture and various papers on Indian grievances,* Theosophical Publishing Society, London.
————, 1915a. *How India Wrought for Freedom. The Story of the National Congress told from Official Records,* Theosophical Publishing House, Adyar.
————, 1915b. *India: A Nation. A Plea for Indian Self-government,* Home Rule for India League, London.
————, 1917. *The Birth of New India.* Theosophical Publishing House, Adyar.
————, 1926a. *India Bond or Free, a World Problem,* G.P. Sons, London.
————, 1926b. *Shall India Live or Die?* National Home Rule League, Madras.
————, 1947. *Onze beschaving op haar dode punt en de oplossing. 5 lezingen gehouden te London in Juni 1924.* Theosophische Vereniging, Amsterdam (Civilization deadlocks and its keys).
———— and C.W. Leadbeater, 1913. *Man Whether, How and Whither: A Record of a Chairvoyant Investigation,* Theosophical Publishing House, Adyar.
Blavatsky, H.P., 1908. *The Secret Doctrine,* London.
Burton, A. 1994, 'Rules of Thumb: British history and "imperial culture" in nineteenth- and twentieth-century Britain, *Women's History Review* 3(4).

Cousins, M., 1922. *The Awakening of Asian Womanhood,* Madras.
———, M, 1924. *What Women Have Gained from Reforms,* National Conference Series no. 7, Madras.
———, J. and M. Cousins, 1950. *We Two Together,* Madras.
Davis, R., 1986. 'The Influence of the Irish Revolution on Indian Nationalism', *Journal of South Asian Studies,* 55ff.
de Purucker, G., 1940. *The Esoteric Tradition,* Pasadena.
de Roode, A., E. van der Tuin and G. Zondergeld, 1986. Anthroposofisch Racisme, Nijmegen.
de Tollenaere, H., 1996. *The Politics of Divine Wisdom, Theosophy and labour, national, and women's movements in Indonesia and South Asia 1875–1947,* Nijmegen.
Dharmapala, A., 1965. *Return to Righteousness,* ed. by A. Guruge, Colombo.
Gombrich, R. and Obeyesekere, G., 1988. *Buddhism Transformed, Religious Change in Sri Lanka,* Princeton.
Jeurissen, T., 1996. *Uit de vrije school geklapt, Over antroposofie en racisme, een stellingname,* Sittard.
Kegel, K., 1989. '*Ik weet niet wat ze bedoelen*' Bram Moerland wil '*racistisch interpreteren*', September–October, 136–8.
Linklater, A., 1980. *An Unhusbanded Life, Charlotte Despard, Suffragette, Socialist and Sinn Feiner,* London.
Lutyens, M., 1975. *Krishnamurti, The Years of Awakening,* London.
Moerland, B., 1989. *Over het racisme van Steiner en Blavatsky, Rassenleer met Charisma.,* Den Haag.
Nethercott, A., 1960. *The First Five Lives of Annie Besant,* Chicago.
———, 1963. *The Last Four Lives of Annie Besant,* London.
Obeyesekere, G., 1997. Public lecture on Theosophists and Colonel W.S. Olcott in particular in Sri Lanka, held at IIAS, Leiden University, March.
Olcott, H, 1885. *Old Diary Leaves, Second Series,* 1878/83, Madras.
Roe, J., 1986. *Beyond Belief, Theosophy in Australia 1879–1939,* Kensington, Australia.
Schwartz, A., 1905. 'Notes on the Pedigree of Man', *The Theosophist,* June, 545ff.
Vanheste, T., 1996. *Copernicus is ziek. Een geschiedenis van het New-Age denken over natuurwetenschap.* Amsterdam.
Voorham, B., 1989a. '*H.P. Blavatsky verdedigd, als fel tegenstandster van racisme*'. *Lucifer,* March–April, 36–42.
———, 1989b. '*Waarheid of lielheid*', Lucifer, September–October, 139–43.
Webb, J., 1971. *The Flight from Reason,* vol. 1, *The Age of the Irrational,* London (published in USA as *The Occult Underground,* 1974).
———, 1976. *The Occult Establishment,* Illinois.
Wessinger, C.L., 1988. *Annie Besant and Progressive Messianism,* Queenston.
Zander, H., 1996. '*Sozialdarwinistische Rassentheorien aus dem okkulten Untergrund des Kaiserreichs,*' in *Handbhch zur 'V'Ikischen Bewegung' 1871–1918,* London.

Sri Aurobindo

'The Error of All "Churches"'
Religion and Spirituality in Communities
Founded or 'Inspired' by Sri Aurobindo

PETER HEEHS

I T IS IRONIC THAT the name of Sri Aurobindo is often included in
lists of founders of 'new religious movements' in India.[1] He did not
consider himself religious, denied that he had founded or wished to
found a new religion, and was convinced that religious movements were
doomed to failure. Nevertheless, there is some justification for speaking
of his work as part of the development of new religious forms and
activities that was a significant aspect of nineteenth-and twentieth-century
Indian life. Aurobindo was familiar with at least four of the recognized
'new religious movements', and conceived his aim in terms broadly
similar to theirs: a restatement of the truths of Veda and Vedanta and the
formulation of a method of spiritual practice for bringing about individual
and social change.[2]

This essay is an attempt to trace the origin and development of
communities founded or 'inspired' by Aurobindo, and to determine
their relationship to incontestably religious bodies and movements. In
the first section I provide a sketch of Aurobindo's life, giving special
attention to the development of his ideas on religion and spirituality—
terms that he distinguished. In section 2, I sketch the genesis of his
ashram, which he intended to be an experiment in individual and
collective spiritual life, and examine documents in which Aurobindo

In the interests of full disclosure the author would like to state that he is a
member of the Sri Aurobindo Ashram Archives and Research Library. His
research is carried out and published independently. He alone is responsible for
all observations and judgements in this paper.

wrote on collective spiritual practice. Finally, in section 3, I consider the apparent similarities between groups founded or 'inspired' by Aurobindo and movements that are avowedly religious, and suggest that the apparent discrepancy between Aurobindo's intentions and the actual status of such groups might be resolved by looking at them from a developmental point of view.

FROM ATHEISM TO VEDANTA

Although sometimes regarded as a proponent of reformed or even of orthodox Hinduism, Aurobindo was not brought up as a Hindu and never practised the religion in the ordinary way. Born in Calcutta in 1872, Aurobindo Ghose received an entirely western education at Loreto Convent School, Darjeeling, St Paul's School, London, and King's College, Cambridge. His father, a rationalist physician who abandoned first Hinduism and then Brahmoism, saw to it that his sons received no religious training. He asked their English guardian, a Congregationalist minister in Manchester, to let them make up their own minds about religion when they came of age. Aurobindo read the Bible in this man's house, but was 'repelled rather than attracted' by Christianity, being 'disgusted' in particular by 'the hideous story of persecution staining medieval Christianity and the narrowness and intolerance even of its later developments'. Before leaving England he drew back from religion altogether and 'after a short period of complete atheism, he accepted the Agnostic attitude'.[3]

Wishing his sons to imbibe the virtues of the English culture he then admired, Aurobindo's father asked their guardian not to let them 'make the acquaintance of any Indian or undergo any Indian influence'.[4] As a result Aurobindo knew virtually nothing of the country of his birth till he went to Cambridge. There, along with Greek and Latin, he studied Sanskrit and Bengali, and read translations of the *Ramayana,* the Upanishads and other texts. This bookish discovery of a somewhat romanticized India, together with a growing disenchantment with English life—its ugliness, its utilitarianism, its reliance on physical and social machinery—helped him avoid the anglophilia affected by other British-educated Indians. When he returned to India in 1893, he plunged into the study of Bengali and Sanskrit literature, and translated passages of several classical texts. His own writings of this period exhibit a tension between his European cultural formation and a temperamental preference for India and its people. Many of his poems are based on Indian mythological themes, but the manner is that of English writers of the late nineteenth century. His essays condemn European materialism and heap praise on the Indian way of life, but do so in the style (and with many of the preconceptions) of a Carlyle or Arnold.*

At this time Aurobindo's interests were chiefly literary. He encountered Hinduism through its texts. In the *Mahabharata* and *Ramayana* he found the epic grandeur he admired in Homer, in Kalidasa a poetic craft comparable to Shakespeare's; but he believed the cultural framework within which the Indian poets worked was incomparably deeper and wider than that of Greece or England. Attracted by this 'Hindu' culture,[5] Aurobindo began, around the turn of the century, to speak of himself as a Hindu. This was part of a wholesale adoption of Indian cultural forms, and wholesale rejection of those of the West. This included a rejection even of the Brahmo Samaj, the creed of his maternal relatives, which he considered a bastard cross between European rationalism and Indian religion.[6] When he got married in 1901 he insisted on having a Hindu ceremony; but this was perhaps the only time in his life he took part in a traditional Hindu rite. According to his brother, he rarely entered a temple and, if he did, he never bowed his head to the image.

Around 1904 Aurobindo became interested in the Vedanta philosophy. From this point, Hinduism was for him 'the religion of Vedanta':

For at the root of all we Hindus have done, thought and said through these thousands of years of [our] race-history, behind all we seek to be, there lies concealed, the fount of our philosophies, the bedrock of our religions, the kernel of our thought, the explanation of our ethics and society, the summary of our civilization, the rivet of our nationality, this one marvellous inheritance of ours, the Vedanta.[7]

According to Aurobindo, what distinguished Vedanta from other philosophies was that it was based not on reasoning but on spiritual experience.* He had had already some spontaneous experiences that he later referred

*In writing about Aurobindo's experiences, my only documents are his own accounts of them. No other first-hand documentation of a subjective experience could exist. Aurobindo's accounts are found in his diary, in letters, and in reports of his talks, all of which I have examined and determined to be authentic. Questions of the verticality of these experiences and of the correctness of Aurobindo's interpretations of them do not fall within the scope of this paper. There is enough cross-cultural evidence of the existence of spiritual experiences to permit the historian of religion to use accounts of them as data. For considerations of their epistemic value, see for example William James, *The Varieties of Religious Experience*, Collier, New York, 1961 (1902), and William P. Alston, *Perceiving God: The Epistemology of Religious Experience*) Cornell University Press, Ithaca, NY, 1991.

to as 'preliminary' spiritual experiences. By 1905 he had resolved to obtain the experiences described in the *Gita* and Upanishads by following the guidance given in those texts. He would, he wrote his wife in August 1905, have nothing to do with conventional religious observances; but 'by whatever means' would 'have the direct vision of God'.[8]

Around this same time Aurobindo was becoming involved in revolutionary activities. From his school days he had been convinced that the British had no right to rule India. A low commercial culture was imposing itself on a great spiritual one by means of the account book and the sword. He sympathized with the Irish who, similarly endowed, were similarly victimized. At Cambridge he supported Home Rule and wrote poems on Parnell. His first published writings after his return to India were critiques of the Indian National Congress, which he considered elitist, spineless and ineffective. Around 1902 he made some tentative attempts at organizing a group he hoped would eventually engage in militant opposition to the Raj. Little was accomplished until the agitation against the partition of Bengal (1905) created conditions that made it possible for this group, led now by Aurobindo's brother, to attract men willing to engage in covert revolutionary activity.

Aurobindo saw no contradiction between revolution and spiritual practice.[9] Part of his reason for taking up yoga was to obtain spiritual power to help him liberate his homeland. India's freedom was necessary for the resurgence of Indian culture and the triumph of the values it enshrined. Around this time he wrote a pamphlet proposing the formation of an order of political sannyasis or monks who would work for the uplift of India. He sought out real sannyasis as well, and from one of them received a *stotra* (hymn or spell) meant to drive the British from India. 'It was a very violent stotra with *jahi, jahi* [slay, slay] in it', he later reminisced. 'I used to repeat it, it did not give any results.'[10]

Reaching a standstill in his yogic practice in 1908, Aurobindo took the advice of a guru, who showed him how to silence the activities of his mind. This opened him to the experience of the impersonal Brahman or Absolute. This was, he later said, the first fundamental realization of his yoga. A few months later, while in jail awaiting trial for conspiring to wage war against the King, he had the complementary realization of the personal Godhead:

I looked at the jail that secluded me from men, and it was no longer by its high walls that I was imprisoned; no, it was Vasudeva who surrounded me. I walked under the branches of the tree in front of my cell but it was not the tree, I knew it was Vasudeva, it was Sri Krishna whom I saw standing there and holding over me his shade.[11]

A year later Aurobindo spoke of this experience as embodying 'the central truth of the Hindu religion'. At that time he gave the name 'Hinduism' or *sanatana dharma* ('eternal religion') to the sum of experiences, experience-based conceptions and experience-oriented practices that made up 'the religion based on Vedanta'. He called this

the Hindu Religion only because the Hindu nation has kept it, because in this Peninsula it grew up in the seclusion of the sea and the Himalayas, because in this sacred and ancient land it was given as a charge to the Aryan race to preserve through the ages. But it is not circumscribed by the confines of the single country. It does not belong particularly and for ever to a bounded part of the world. That which we call the Hindu religion is really the eternal religion which embraces all others. If a religion is not universal it cannot be eternal. A narrow religion, an exclusive religion can only live for a limited time and a limited purpose. This is the one religion that can triumph over materialism by including and anticipating the discoveries of science and the speculations of philosophy.[12]

This passage from a frequently reprinted and cited speech deserves special attention because it illustrates the ambiguities and difficulties of the term 'Hinduism', which Aurobindo was soon to discard. He began by using 'Hindu' in the geographical sense, which is of course how this Persian word originally was used. He then equated 'Hindu' with 'Aryan', a term that then had ethnological as well as linguistic connotations.[13] He went on to state that the religion of the Aryans was not confined to a single country; it was 'eternal' and 'universal', not 'narrow' and sectarian'. By universal he would appear to mean something like 'valid for all human beings', by non-sectarian, 'not confined to a specific set of doctrines or practices'. But the general tenor of what follows, together with the earlier statement that Hinduism was 'the religion of Vedanta' suggests that the 'universal religion' is the same as or has a special relation with the specific set of beliefs and practices spoken of in the Vedantic texts. This problem would not arise if 'Vedanta' was taken to mean a set of concepts and practices based on universal experiences that happen to be adequately described in the Upanishads, but are well described in other texts as well. Aurobindo conceded this when he wrote, in an article published along with the speech, that the sanatana dharma included among its scriptures non-Vedantic texts such as the Puranas and Tantras, 'nor could it reject the Bible or the Koran'.[14] Why then call the universal religion 'Hinduism', a term associated with a particular part of the world and a diverse but generally distinguishable set of beliefs and practices? Why call it sanatana dharma when that phrase is commonly used to describe that same set of beliefs and practices (it became popular in the nineteenth century as a Sanskrit substitute for the English word 'Hinduism'). The claim that this 'eternal religion' embraces all others has a decidedly ethnocentric ring. The whole passage could be taken as a good example of what scholars of religion call Hindu 'inclusivism', a different thing from universality.[15]

It may have been considerations of this kind that caused Aurobindo to drop the terms 'Hindu' and 'sanatana dharma' from his vocabulary from around 1912. In his mature works on philosophy and yoga, most of which were written between 1914 and 1920, he never referred to himself or his world-view as 'Hindu' even in the broad sense of 'the religion of Vedanta'. At times openly critical of the superficiality and hypocrisy of the popular religion, he nevertheless considered Hinduism a storehouse of profound texts and practices, notably the spiritual practices described in the Vedas, Upanishads, Gita and Tantras. All religions had 'helped mankind', he wrote; among them, Hinduism had opened 'the largest and profoundest spiritual possibilities'. But no religion had been able to 'spiritualise mankind. For that there is needed not cult and creed, but a sustained and all-comprehending effort at spiritual self-evolution.'[16]

To understand this passage, and to get to the root of Aurobindo's ideas on religion and yoga, one must take into account his distinction between formal religion or 'religionism' and true religion or 'spirituality'. He explained this distinction in another passage written around the same time:

True religion is spiritual religion, that which seeks to live in the spirit, in what is beyond the intellect, beyond the aesthetic and ethical and practical being of man, and to inform and govern these members of our being by the higher light and law of the spirit. Religionism, on the contrary, entrenches itself in some narrow pietistic exaltation of the lower members or lays exclusive stress on intellectual dogmas, forms and ceremonies, on some fixed and rigid moral code, on some religion-political or religion-social system. . . .

In spirituality, then . . . we must seek for the directing light and the harmonizing law, and in religion only in proportion as it identifies itself with this spirituality.[17]

In this view, those who practise 'religion' are content with intellectual, aesthetic and ethical uplift. They guide their lives by reference to religious texts or teachings. Those who practise 'spirituality' put themselves in contact with the divine principle or 'spirit', or at least attempt to do so, guiding their lives not by mental dogmas or ethical rules but by the spirit's 'directing light'. This contact is achieved by means of those experiences called mystic or spiritual. Since such experiences are necessarily subjective and individual, spiritual seekers have no need of church, priesthood, or any other intermediary between them and the divine principle. Such intermediaries are characteristic of religion. Viewed from the spiritual point of view, their purpose is to help individuals to put themselves in contact with the teachings and practices of past spiritual adepts, in order to prepare them for their own direct contact.

SETTING UP A 'LABORATORY'

Aurobindo practised yoga for more than fifteen years before he took an active interest in collective practice. From the beginning, he later wrote, his yoga 'had always been personal and apart.'[18] Even in jail, when he was thrown together with young men interested in yoga, he kept to himself as much as he could. After his release he spoke of his spiritual experiences in public on one occasion,[19] and frequently wrote on spiritual subjects in his weekly newspaper. At this juncture some began thinking of him as a religious or spiritual figure,[20] but he did not put himself forward as such and took no disciples. There is an intriguing bit of hearsay reported by the police in 1909 that he was planning to buy land in a place east of Calcutta in order to 'start an Asram . . . and live there and practise yoga'.[21] If the report is true, nothing came of the plans. Two months later he left Calcutta for the nearby French enclave of Chandernagore and a few weeks after that went to Pondicherry, another French enclave in southern India. Here he remained incognito for several months before announcing that he had retired to Pondicherry 'in order to pursue his yoga undisturbed by political action or pursuit'.[22] This marked the end of his political career and the beginning of a forty-year period of yogic practice.

Even in his retirement Aurobindo refused the role of a guru. In 1911 he published a letter informing the 'pilgrims' who were flocking to see him that he would meet no unknown admirers but only a few local friends and selected visitors. For a while, as an exception, he treated a young man of Chandernagore as a disciple, encouraging or at least not opposing him in his efforts to set up a spiritual collective. This experiment turned out badly and was not repeated. With the few youths, mostly former revolutionaries, who had gathered around him he had, he wrote, 'the relation of friends and companions rather than a Guru and disciples'.[23] The young men spent more of their time playing football than meditating.

One of the first to look on Aurobindo chiefly in spiritual terms was Mirra Richard. Born in Paris in 1878 of non-observant middle-eastern Jewish parents, Mirra received no religious upbringing. Inclined to spirituality (in Aurobindo's sense) from an early age, she became associated with groups of practitioners in France and Algeria during her twenties and thirties. In 1910 her husband Paul Richard met Aurobindo in Pondicherry. Four years later Paul returned with Mirra. According to her own account, as she stood before Aurobindo she 'at once knew that it was he, the Divine'.[24]

The Richards left India after the outbreak of the First World War, and did not return until 1920. Paul soon left again; Mirra remained with Aurobindo. Meanwhile there had been (as Aurobindo later wrote) a 'gradual development of spiritual relations' between him and the young men staying with him. Within this nascent community, Mirra assumed a special place. In 1926 Aurobindo withdrew from outward contacts and put the direction of the day-to-day running of the community in the hands of Mirra, now called 'the Mother'. In this way, he later wrote, his 'ashram was founded or rather founded itself.'[25]

This account, based on documents written after the event, gives the impression that before the 1920s Aurobindo had no interest in collective yoga and no desire to found a spiritual community. Contemporary letters show that this was not the case. As early as 1911 he wrote that he needed to remain in retirement not only 'to complete [his] own yoga' but also to 'build up other souls' around him.[26] The next year he informed two correspondents that he had a four-part work or mission in life: (1) to write a new explanation of the Veda and Vedanta, (2) to perfect and give to others a new system of yoga, (3) to help restore India 'to its proper place in the world', and (4) to remodel human society in order to make possible a 'perfect humanity'. He regarded his 'little colony' in Pondicherry as 'a seed plot, a laboratory' that would help him accomplish the second of these four aims, 'making men for the new age by imparting whatever Siddhi [perfection in yoga] I get to those who are chosen.'[27]

A year or two after writing these letters, Aurobindo launched a monthly journal in which he published, over the course of seven years, the equivalent of a dozen books of philosophy, yoga, Vedic and Vedantic commentary, social theory, etc. At the same time he began the 'experiment' of transmitting his method of practice to the young men staying with him. He was thus, by his own reckoning, well on his way to accomplishing the first two parts of the fourfold mission outlined in the passage quoted above. He considered the third or political aim to be already accomplished (an assessment, it must be admitted, that facts on the ground scarcely justified at that time). As a result he ceased to occupy himself with politics. What remained was the fourth or social part of the mission. This would be, he wrote, a work 'of spiritual, social, cultural and economic reconstruction of an almost revolutionary kind', of which his 'laboratory experiment' was a small prototype'.[28]

For a while he seems to have thought that this work might include the formation of a public society. One day in 1914 he jotted down in his diary: 'A Society to be formed like the Theosophical Society which will support and popularize the Knowledge & the writings which express it.'[29] A month or two later he and Mirra Richard actually started a discussion group, modelled on groups she had belonged to in Paris. This never had more than a handful of members, and disappeared without a trace even before the Richards left India in 1915.

Aurobindo's general lack of enthusiasm for organized groups is expressed in several of his writings of the 1914–20 period. 'The effective power' behind any great change in the workings of society (such as he proposed) was always 'an individual or a limited number of individuals'. The mass could only follow the pioneers' lead. But the participation of the mass—a body 'capable of receiving and effectively assimilating'—was necessary; otherwise the individual's work could have no permanent effect.[30] He observed that the usual way of reaching the mass was establishing 'spiritualized communities'. These however tended towards 'the creation of the religious temperament, the most outward form of spirituality'.[31] The result was an attempt of the new impulse to impose itself on society 'by the old familiar apparatus and the imperfect means of a religious movement', with predictable results:

A religious movement brings usually excitement and aspiration that communicates itself to a large number of individuals and there is as a result a temporary uplifting and an effective formation, partly spiritual, partly ethical, partly dogmatic in its nature. But the wave after a generation or two or at most a few generations begins to subside; the formation remains.[32]

The end result of such a development, he wrote elsewhere, is 'a Church, a hierarchy, a fixed and unprogressive type of ethical living, a set of crystallized dogmas, ostentations, ceremonials, sanctified superstitions, an elaborate machinery for the salvation of mankind'.[33]

As his ashram began to take shape after 1926, Aurobindo tried to steer it away from the conventionalism he observed in past and present spiritual communities. He avoided setting rules, discouraged mechanical observances, and abjured proselytism. In a humorous letter of 1934, he remarked that he did not 'believe in advertisement except for books etc., and in propaganda except for politics and patent medicines'. In 'serious work' propaganda was 'a poison' resulting either in 'a boom or a stunt' or else 'a movement', and

a movement in the case of a work like mine means the founding of a school or a sect or some other damned nonsense. It means that hundreds and thousands of useless people join in and corrupt the work or reduce it to a pompous farce from which the Truth that was coming down recedes into secrecy and silence.[34]

The last sentence refers to the 'truth-consciousness' or 'supermind' that in Aurobindo's philosophy is the dynamic force behind the cosmic process of evolution. He was confident that this power would do what was necessary to accomplish the work of individual and social transformation he envisaged. His own part was to assist this 'higher force' by receiving its influx, thus opening the way for its more general manifestation. 'A way to be opened that is still blocked, not a religion to be founded', was his 'conception of the matter', he wrote in a letter.[35]

If, as he intended, this transformation was eventually to have an effect on humanity, the participation of a few men and women would be helpful, perhaps necessary; on the other hand, the involvement of great numbers would be counterproductive. 'Nothing depends on the number', he wrote in a letter of 1934:

The numbers of Buddhism or Christianity were so great because the majority professed it as a creed without its making the least difference to their external life. If the new [supramental] consciousness were satisfied with that, it could also and much more easily command homage and acceptance by the whole earth. It is because it is a greater consciousness, the Truth-Consciousness, that it will insist on a real change.[36]

Between 1926 and 1934 the number of people staying in what was now known as the Sri Aurobindo Ashram grew from two dozen to around 150. There was a jump during the Second World War when people living in the war zone clamoured for admission; but even then numbers did not exceed 400. Members (called sadhaks) spent their time meditating, studying, working and engaging in devotional practices. Meditation and study were regarded as parts of the yoga of knowledge, work done with the right attitude part of the yoga of works, and devotional practices part of the yoga of bhakti.[37] Various forms of collective concentration and devotion grew up, often untraditional and informal, such as a ritualized distribution of soup. Some more traditional practices, such as darshan or 'viewing' the teachers,[38] also became part of the yearly routine. But Aurobindo avoided establishing specific forms of practice, stressing that each sadhak should develop his or her own inner relationship with the divine principle.

Although Aurobindo took no active steps to attract a larger following, many people, drawn by his writing or reputation, expressed a desire to join the ashram. Most were turned away. Some individuals formed groups for study or practice in other cities; Aurobindo did not oppose this, but did not permit anything like the Brahmo Samaj's 'missionary' work, the Theosophical Society's membership, or the Arya Samaj's shuddhi.

After Aurobindo's death in 1950, the ashram continued under the direction of the Mother. In the years that followed there was a slow but steady growth in the number of ashramites. The Mother also permitted the formation of organizations meant to promulgate the ideas of Sri Aurobindo and herself, and to engage in educational and cultural activities. The most notable of these organizations is Auroville, an experimental community that has undergone considerable development since its foundation in 1968. Millions of trees have been planted, hundreds of hectares brought under cultivation, and houses, schools and small-scale industries constructed and maintained by more than a thousand men, women and children. More organizations 'inspired' by Sri Aurobindo and the Mother have been founded since her death in 1973.

On the basis of the developments and texts discussed above, one would have little reason to conclude that the Sri Aurobindo Ashram and related groups were set up as a religious movement. Aurobindo's intention was to provide a field where people could pursue 'spiritual' (as distinct from 'religious') self-development.

THE ASHRAM AND OTHER COMMUNITIES AND MOVEMENTS VIEWED DEVELOPMENTALLY

Spiritual and religious movements are not immutable doctrines but processes—they are not called 'movements' for nothing. It will be best therefore to use a developmental yardstick to measure them. Many such are available, for instance the various cyclical theories of human development illustrating the growth, degeneration and sometimes also regeneration of social formations and institutions. In a book devoted to 'the psychology of human development', Aurobindo himself made use of a modification of the cyclic theory of history proposed by the German scholar Karl Lamprecht. It will be both interesting and instructive to apply this theory, which Aurobindo used to arrive at significant insights into various social groupings, to groups he himself founded or is said to have 'inspired'.

Expanding Lamprecht's five-part cycle, Aurobindo theorized that religions, like other human institutions, pass through a cycle of six stages: typical, conventional, individualistic, subjective and spiritual. In India, he said, the symbolic stage was represented by the Vedic religion, in which the rite of sacrifice was an outward enactment of psychological self-offering to the divine. During the epic period religion became 'a mystic sanction for the ethical motive and discipline'. This was followed by a stage where 'the outward expressions of the spirit or the ideal, become more important than the ideal'. During the thousand years that this period lasted in India there were numerous attempts to break loose from the pervading conventionalism—new religious impulses, 'movements' if one prefers, such as the bhakti cults of Tamil Nadu and the Deccan, the Kabir panth, Sikhism, the religion of Chaitanya, etc., but

the efforts of the saints and religious reformers become progressively more scattered, brief and superficial in their actual effects. . . . [I]n a generation or two the iron grip of that conventionalism has always fallen on the new movements and annexed the names of its founders.[39]

In another essay from roughly the same period, Aurobindo wrote that the 'new religions' (his term) of the previous ninety years—the Brahmo Samaj, Arya Samaj, Ramakrishna movement, neo-Vaishnavism, new movements within Islam—were an attempt of 'the Indian spiritual mind' to recover its past and turn towards its future.[40] Viewed within the framework of his six stages, these new religions might be seen as originating in an individualistic revolt against Hindu conventionality. Their founders, men with a strong subjective turn, some of whom achieved remarkable heights of mystical experience, left behind new forms of discipline and worship which have helped some of their followers make spiritual progress. Yet Aurobindo does not seem to have thought that these groups as a whole were able to escape the fate of the earlier 'new religions' of India. He thought, for example, that Keshab Sen and the Sadharan Brahmo Samaj were of no interest to the generation turned towards the future.[41] A series of unpublished articles on theosophy show that he felt the same way about that movement.[42] As for the Ramakrishna Mission, he felt that even the experience and teaching of Ramakrishna and Vivekananda, both of whom he admired and whose influence he acknowledged, had not prevented it from falling into the usual error—keeping 'too much to the forms' of the founders, and not remaining 'open to new outpourings of their spirit—the error of all "Churches" and organized religious bodies.'[43]

So far as I know Aurobindo never commented publicly about how his own community measured up on the scale of authenticity and conventionality. When he instituted forms of collective practice, he took steps to insure that they did not become a mechanical observance; but he was aware that much depended on how his followers responded to his lead. If he was optimistic about the future, it was not because he thought his followers would act in the right way, but because he believed that the power of the supermind would do what was necessary to bring about the preordained result: the beginning of a new cycle of humanity or rather superhumanity, the establishment of a 'gnostic society'. Confident that this would come within his lifetime or at least within the lifetime of the Mother, he left no contingency plan to be put into effect in case it did not. The statement quoted at the end of the previous paragraph may serve as one. The way to avoid or overcome conventionalism 'the error of all "Churches" ', is to remain open to 'new outpourings' of the founders' spirit. Accepting this suggestion would mean going beyond the 'forms' and trying to seize on the 'spirit' of their teachings—a risky endeavour, given the likelihood of misunderstanding, misinterpretation and misapplication—but perhaps a necessary one. In a passage already quoted, Aurobindo gave one or two generations as the period of vigour of a new spiritual impulse, the time it took for it to be overcome by conventions. This is about the time that has elapsed since his death.

In Aurobindo's six-phase developmental cycle, the conventional stage is followed by one of individuality, that in turn by a period of subjective self-discovery, and that, finally by an age of unending spiritual evolution. Writing in 1918 of the 'advent of the spiritual age', he affirmed:

Therefore, while many new spiritual waves with their strong special motives and disciplines must necessarily be the forerunners of a spiritual age, yet their claims must be subordinated in the general mind of the race and of its spiritual leaders to the recognition that all motives and disciplines are valued and yet none entirely valid since they are means and not the one thing to be done. The one thing essential must take precedence, the conversion of the whole life of the human being to the lead of the Spirit.[4]

While he does not specifically link this passage to his own work or to the religious movements of nineteenth-century India, one could take it as presenting an alternative to the religiosity that many believe to be the inevitable destiny of all new spiritual teachings.

NOTES

1. For example, the *Encyclopaedia Britannica*, that great compendium of *idées reçues* counts the Aurobindo Ashram, along with the Ramakrishna Mission and the Theosophical Society, among 'new religious movements' (1977, *Macropaedia* 8: 918). See also, for example, F. Robinson (ed.), *The Cambridge Encyclopedia of India, Pakistan, Bangladesh, Sri Lanka* (Cambridge: Cambridge University Press, 1989), p. 347.

2. Aurobindo acknowledged the influence of Ramakrishna and Vivekananda, bestowed qualified praise on Dayananda, and wrote critically of the Brahmo Samaj and Theosophical Society. References to each of these movements occur in the body of the text.

3. Sri Aurobindo, 'Sri Aurobindo on Himself', *Sri Aurobindo: Archives and Research* 1, 2 (1977), p. 88.

4. Sri Aurobindo, *On Himself*, Aurobindo Ashram, Pondicherry, 1972, p. 1.

5. It is significant that Aurobindo wrote of Kalidasa as a 'Hindu' poet knowing full well that the dramatist's religious beliefs were conventional and that temperamentally he was a typical *homme moyen sensuel*. Here, as elsewhere, Aurobindo used 'Hindu' in the current sense of 'indigenous Indian', exclusive of Muslim and Christian influences but with no special religious connotation.

6. Aurobindo respected but was uninfluenced by his grandfather, Rajnarain Bose, a prominent Brahmo leader.

7. Sri Aurobindo, 'The Religion of Vedanta', *Sri Aurobindo: Archives and Research* 8 (1984), p. 180.

8. Idem, letter to Mrinalini Ghose, 30 August 1905, translated from the Bengali.

9. This is not the place to go into the complex relationship between Aurobindo's spiritual interests and his political activities. I have examined this question in some detail in two articles: 'Religion and Revolt: Bengal under the Raj', *History Today* 43 (1993), pp. 29–35, and 'Bengali Religious Nationalism and Communalism', *International Journal of Hindu Studies* 1 (1997), pp. 117–39.

10. A.B. Purani, *Life of Sri Aurobindo*, Sri Aurobindo Ashram, Pondicherry, 1978, p. 60.

11. Sri Aurobindo, *Karmayogin*, Sri Aurobindo Ashram, Pondicherry, 1972, p. 4. The use of the name Vasudeva (Krishna) for the omnipresent Godhead echoes a verse of the *Bhagavad Gita* (7.19): *Vasudevah sarvam iti sa mahatm sudurlabhah*, 'Very rare is the great-souled one who knows that Krishna, the son of Vasudeva, is all.'

12. Ibid., pp. 4, 9.

13. Aurobindo would soon stop using this controversial term; he also removed it from earlier writings that he revised after the rise of Nazi Germany.

14. Sri Aurobindo, *Karmayogin*, p. 19.

15. Heinrich von Stietencron, 'Religious Configurations in Pre-Muslim India', in V. Dalmia and H. von Stietencron (eds), *Representing Hinduism: The Construction of Religious Traditions and National Identity*, Sage, New Delhi, 1995, p. 70.

16. Sri Aurobindo, *The Supramental Manifestation and Other Writings*, Sri Aurobindo Ashram, Pondicherry, 1971, p. 394.

17. Sri Aurobindo, *Social and Political Works*, Sri Aurobindo Ashram, Pondicherry, 1972, pp. 166–7, 169.

18. Sri Aurobindo, *On Himself*, p. 68.

19. In the Uttarpara speech, cited above. See note 11.

20. Some did so with the reverence typical of the traditional Indian approaching the holy man, others observing with some regret that a remarkable intellect had become somewhat deranged.

21. Government of India, Home Department, Political-A. January 1910, pp. 141–2, 4.

22. Letter, 7 November 1910, published in *Sri Aurobindo: Archives and Research* 9 (1984), p. 61.

23. Sri Aurobindo, *On Himself,* p. 68.

24. Diary of Anilbaran Roy, 19 November 1929, Sri Aurobindo Ashram Archives.

25. Sri Aurobindo, *On Himself,* p. 68.

26. Ibid., p. 424.

27. Letters of June (or July) 1912 and August 1912 (not 1913 as printed), both published in Sri Aurobindo, *Supplement* (to the Centenary Library), pp. 423–5, 433–4.

28. Sri Aurobindo, *On Himself,* p. 432.

29. Idem, *Record of Yoga,* 23 June 1914, in *Sri Aurobindo: Archives and Research* 13 (1989), p. 179.

30. Idem, *Social and Political Works,* Sri Arobindo Ashram, Pondicherry, 1971, p. 323.

31. Idem, *The Synthesis of Yoga,* Sri Aurobindo Ashram, Pondicherry, 1972, p. 19.

32. Idem, *Social and Political Works,* p. 248.

33. Ibid., p. 249.

34. Idem, *On Himself,* p. 375.

35. Idem, *Letters on Yoga,* vol. 1, Sri Aurobindo Ashram, Pondicherry, 1972, p. 139.

36. Ibid., p. 138.

37. The three paths of yoga (*jananyoga, karmayoga* and *bhaktiyoga*) are spoken of in the *Bhagavad Gita* and other Sanskrit sources and discussed by Aurobindo in *Essays on the Gita, The Synthesis of Yoga* and other works.

38. On three (later four) occasions in the year, Sri Aurobindo gave formal audiences to sadhaks and others. Following established practice, these audiences were given the name darshan. The same term is commonly used for viewing an image in a temple.

39. Sri Aurobindo, *The Human Cycle,* in *Social and Political Works,* pp. 3–10. *The Human Cycle* was first published under the title *The Psychology of Social Development* between 1916 and 1918.

40. Idem, *The Foundations of Indian Culture,* Sri Aurobindo Ashram, Pondicherry, 1972, p. 419.

41. Idem, *The Harmony of Virtue and Other Writings,* Sri Aurobindo Ashram, Pondicherry, 1972, p. 99.

42. Idem, *Essays Divine and Human,* Sri Aurobindo Ashram, Pondicherry, 1994.

43. Idem, *Supplement,* Sri Aurobindo Ashram, Pondicherry, p. 435.

44. Idem, *Social and Political Thought,* p. 250.

Index

Acculturative paradigm xii, xiv, xviii,
  xix, 4, 131
Acharya 10
Adam, William 9, 11
Adi Brahmo Samaj 10
Advaita Ashram 65
Advaitism 94, 95
Adyar 23, 159, 174, 187, 192, 193
Adyar Bulletin 181
Aestheticism xiv
Aesthetics, Indian 89
Agnosticism 5, 210
Agra 35, 47, 119
Agra Brahmo Samaj 35
Ahl-i Hadith movement 129, 130, 132
Ahmad, Mahmud xix, 134, 144, 145,
  150
Ahmad, Mirza Ghulam xix, 111, 128–
  31, 133, 135, 136, 138–41, 143,
  145, 149, 150
  writings of 134, 135
Ahmad, Nazir 41, 138
Ahmadiyya movement xii, xiv, xvi,
  xviii, xix, 111, 128–52
  numbers 129
  as missionaries 130
  W.C. Smith on 130, 134, 151
  social composition 134
Ahmadiyyat (M. Ahmad) 134
Ahmedabad 64
Ahrar 141, 149
Aiyer, Ramaswami 174
Aiyer, Srinivasa 174
Aiyer, Subramanian 162, 170, 173
Akhandananda, Swami xvii, 59–79
Akhbar-i-Anjuman-i Punjab 39

Akshardhan 66
Alambazar Math 62, 70, 71, 72, 73
Alasinga Perumal 71
Algeria 215
Alihadah nabi 145
Alipore jail 16, 24
Allah 128, 129
Allahabad 162
Almora 75, 87
America/USA 21, 67, 68, 69, 71, 72, 89
Amritsar 132, 133
Ancient Wisdom (Besant) 22
Anjuman-i Punjab 37, 41, 52n
Antahpura 48
Aqa 145
Arabic 109, 137, 146, 152
Aristotle 190
Arnold, T. 211
Arundale, Francesca 174
Arundale, George 174, 175
Arya Gazette 113, 114
Arya Pradesik Pratinidhi Sabha Punjab
  116
Arya Samaj xii, xiv, xvi, xviii, xix, xxi,
  3, 13, 16–18, 20, 33, 36, 39, 49,
  80n, 107–22, 129, 135, 163, 170,
  176, 220
Aryans xx, 166–68, 198, 213
*Aryopdesak*s 117
Asceticism xv, 15, 78, 161
Asram 94, 97, 215, 216
Atman 18
Aurangzeb 119
Aurobindo Ghose xi, xii, xv, xviii, xix,
  xxi, 3, 5, 10, 13, 16, 18, 24, 25,
  89, 162, 163, 164, 176, 209–21

western education 210
discovery of Vedanta 211
as revolutionary 212
cycle of religions 219–20
Auroville 219
Australia 185, 186, 188
Avatar 14, 26, 95, 108
Aveling, Edward 23
Ayurvedic medicine 65

Bagley, J.J., Mrs 85
Baird, Robert 3, 9
Bamabodhini Society 91
Bande Mataram 10
Banerjea, Surendranath 171, 172
Baptists 10
Baroda 24, 89
Basu, Chandramukhi 48
Basu, Kadambini 48
Beckerlegge, Gwilym xv, xvii
Bede Griffith xv
Bedouin Arabs 20
Belur xv, 86, 87, 90, 98, 100n
Benares 174
Bengal xviii, 13, 25, 34, 74, 92, 96, 100,
    163
partition of 212
Bengali 88, 210
Besant, Annie xx, 3, 4, 13, 19, 21, 23,
    83, 84, 159, 160, 164, 165, 166,
    167, 173, 174, 175, 180, 181–8,
    192, 193, 202n
her theory of evolution 193–4
Bethune College 48, 55n
Bhadralok 14, 55n
Bhagavadgita 24, 86, 212, 214
Bhairavi, Brahmani 13, 92
Bhajananda, Swami xv
Bhajans 108
Bhakti yoga xv, 95, 96, 218
Bhaktism 12, 15, 76, 220
Bharat Dharma Mahamandal 111
Bharatiya Hindu Suddhi Sabha 119,
    120
Bharatpur 119
Bhat, Jhandu 65, 66, 69, 76

Bhawani temple 25
Bhikku 100
Bhils 62
Bhuj 64
Bhupendranath 90
Bid'at 146
Bidyapati 211
Biradris xviii, 112, 113
Blavatsky, Helena xvi, xx, 3, 4, 13, 19–
    23, 83, 84, 159–63, 169, 172, 175,
    176, 187, 191, 193
Blavatsky, Nicephore 20
Bombay 17, 34, 68, 161, 169, 172, 173,
    174, 175
Bombay Presidency Association 171,
    172
Bose, Rajnarain 10, 222n
Bradlaugh, Charles 22
Brahma 18, 88, 92, 96, 97, 212
Brahmacarya 89, 98
Brahman Sabha 115
Brahmananda, Swami 24, 63, 67, 68,
    69, 74, 75, 89, 92, 95
Brahmanism xx, 108, 109, 161, 165, 175
Brahmins xviii, 88, 93, 112, 114, 117,
    166, 169, 170
Brahmo Gram 35, 36
Brahmo Sabha 9, 10, 11
Brahmo Samaj xvii, xxi, 3, 9–12, 16,
    17, 24, 48, 61, 69, 78, 90, 91,
    110, 170, 210, 211, 219, 220
as missionary movement 11
in Punjab 33, 34, 36, 37, 39, 41, 49
Braj, United Provinces 118
The Bride's Mirror (N. Ahmad) 138
British Indian Association, Bengal
    171
British Library 135
Brooklyn Ethical Society 86
Brunton, Paul 6
Buddha 14, 63, 64
Buddhi 42
Buddhism 66, 77, 84, 99, 112, 161, 165,
    218
in Ceylon 100, 184, 188, 201
Buddhists, Kalmuch 19

Bull, Sarah (Dhira Mata) 86
Burdett, S.H. 174
Burnier, Radha 99
Burrows, Herbert 22

Cairo 20
Calcutta 9, 17, 36, 39, 73, 74, 75, 84, 86, 87, 88, 93, 98, 100, 115, 172, 210
Calcutta Indian Reform Association 40
Calicut 174
Cambridge, Massachussetts 86
Cambridge University 210, 211, 212
Carlyle, T. 211
Caste xx, 11, 16, 18, 23, 25, 35, 41, 78, 94, 99, 108, 110, 113, 120, 163, 166, 168–9
and census 115
Census xviii, 115, 121, 129
Central Provinces 175
Ceylon/Sri Lanka 84, 100, 181, 183, 184, 186, 187, 188, 191, 193, 201
C.G. Jung Institute, Zurich 8
Chaitanya 12, 96, 220
Chakri 14
Chandernagore 215
Charisma 22, 25
Charlu, Ananda 171
Chaudhurani, Hemantkumari xvii, 33, 47–9
as author 48
as Gandhian 49, 75n
Chaudhuri, Bireshvar 35
Chaudhuri, Hemlata 35
Chaudhuri, Rajchandra 48
Chianod, near Baroda 24
Chicago 85
Child marriage xx, 108, 161, 162
Christ xiii, 10, 11, 12, 14, 145
Christians/Christianity xi, 9, 47, 61, 85, 87, 90, 91, 128, 145, 161, 162, 165, 167, 168, 170, 184–5, 210, 218
Church of the New Dispensation 10, 12
Colonialism xii, xx, 18, 183, 187, 188, 192, 201
Communalism xiv, xxi, 18, 107, 131

Community in India 166–9
Company Raj xiii, 11
Constantinople 20
Conversion xii, xviii, 112
Cooch Behar, Maharajah of 35
Counter-culture xx, 7, 187–91, 200–2
Cousins, James 181, 182
Cow-slaughter 111
Cults xxi, 3, 4, 6, 8, 12, 14, 15, 17, 18, 22, 23, 26
Dionysian 8
in Classical Europe 190
Cultural revivalism xiv

Dakshineswar temple 13, 93
Damascus marabouts 20
Darjeeling 75
Darsan 93
Darwinism xiii, xvi, xx, 3, 12, 23, 25, 163, 183, 191
Dasanami sannyasins 95
Daska 133, 150
Datta, Bhupendranath xii, 90
Dayanand Anglo-Vedic College 110
Dayanand Saraswati xii, xvi, xviii, 3, 13, 16–18, 23, 24, 26, 107–10, 121, 162, 170
Dehra Dun Hindu Sabha 117
Deism 11
Delhi 152, 174
Delhi durbar 18
Democracy 181
Deoband movement 129
Deobandi preachers 132
de Tassy, Garçin 37, 45
Detroit 85
Devaki Amma, Sannyasini 103n
Devalasmrti 117
Dharmapala, Anagarika 83, 84, 186, 187, 201
Dharma 24, 94, 108, 116, 164
Dharmasala 84
Divorce xix, 139, 140
Dostoevsky 20
Dreams/dream power 143, 144, 149
Druids of Mount Lebanon 20

Dupatta 143, 144
Durga 93, 97
Dutt, Akshoy Kumar 11
Dutt, R.C. 90
Dwarkadas, Jamnadas 173, 174, 175
Dwarkadas, Kanchi 174, 175

East India Company xiii, 11, 167
Eclecticism 14, 78
Education 16, 34, 35, 38, 69, 70, 78, 83, 84
  geography in education 45
  science in education 44
  mission schools 47
  English language 53n, 76
Education, female xviii, xix, 33, 39–49, 87, 88, 91, 94, 100n, 134, 138, 146, 151, 187
Egypt 161
Elitism 188
Emerson, Ralph Waldo 86
Enlightenment 191
Environment 189, 201
Europe xxi
  in 1960s xiv
European intellectuals xvi

Fabians 22
Famine 64, 73, 74, 75, 77, 78, 89, 168
Farquhar, J.N. 3, 10, 11, 18, 19, 23, 61
Fazl al-Rahman, Mufti xix, 135, 142, 143, 148
Feminism xiv, 13, 182, 186–9
Ferozpur 152
Fischer-Tiné, Harald 132
Foster, Mary Elizabeth 84
Fourier, Charles xx
France 215
French Revolution 4
Freud, Sigmund 6, 7, 8, 24
Friedmann, Yohanan 131, 132
Fundamentalism, religious xiv

Gambhirananda, Swami 63, 67, 68, 74, 75, 93, 96, 101n
Gandhi, M.K. 116, 164, 175, 188

Ganga 98
Gargi 99
Gatwood, Lynn 96
Gaya 84, 95, 118
Ghose, Baren 24
Ghulam 145
Gmeiner, Miss 174
Gokhale, G.K. 90
Golitsyn, Prince 19
Goodwin, J.J. 84
Gora (R. Tagore) 90
Greece 211
Greek, ancient 211
Greek philosophy 190
Greenacre Summer Camp, USA 86
Greenstidel, Christine 85
Gross, Otto 7
Gujarat xiii, xvii, 63, 64, 66, 67, 69, 76
Guntur 174
Gupta, Mahendranath 59
Gurdjieff 6
Gurubhai 62, 68, 70, 71, 74, 92
Gurus xvi, xxi, 3–9, 11, 14–16, 17, 18, 24, 25, 26, 42, 45, 75, 92, 95, 174, 212, 215
  Western 4, 5
  and creative illness 6
  and charisma 6
  and authoritarianism 6
  disciples 5, 7

Hadith 131, 137, 138
Haeckel, E.H. 7
Hafzah Qadiyani xix, 135, 136, 138, 140, 141, 142, 148, 150, 151
Hajj 147
Hale, Ellen 85, 100n
Hale, Mary 71, 72, 100n
Hardgrave, R.L. 117
Hawaii 84
Hayat-i-javadani 139, 140, 142
Health centres 83, 84
Heber, Bishop xiii
Heehs, P. 24
Hegelianism 4
Herzen, Alexander 16

Hierarchy, racial 180–2, 191–202
Higgings, Musaeus 187
Himalayas 161
Hindi xvii, 17, 33, 34, 36–9, 41, 46, 47, 48, 49, 69, 109
    Nagari script xvii, 36
Hindi Sahitya Sammelan 48
Hindu fundamentalism 9
Hindu reform 78, 79
Hindu renaissance 3, 4
Hodgson, Richard 19
Holy Mother Sri Sarada Devi (Gambhirananda) 93
Home Rule League, All-India xx, 23, 160, 171, 173–4, 176, 183
Homer 211
Homosexuals xx, 187
Honolulu 84
Hornes, Mabel 192
Hoshangabad 35
Hume, Alan Octavian xx, 162, 170, 171, 172, 175, 178n
Husain, Imdad 110
Husain Bibi xix, 136, 137, 141, 144, 148, 149, 150, 151
Huxley, T.H. 12

Idolatry 108
Imperialism xix, xx, xxi
Indian Association of Calcutta 171
Indian Daily Mirror 171
Indian National Congress xviii, xx, 16, 90, 115, 160, 171–6, 183, 212
    Madras Congress 1914 173
    Bombay Congress 1915 173
    Calcutta Congress 1917 175
Indian National Union 172
Indian Rebellion 1857 172
Indian Reform Association 39
Indramani, Munsi 110
Industrialization xiii
Infanticide 23
Inspired Thoughts (Vivekananda) 86
International Psychological Association 7
Ireland 180, 182

Irish nationalists xviii, xx, 187, 212
Isis Unveiled (Blavatsky) 22
Isvara 96

Jagaddhatri 93, 101n
Jalsa 137
Jamal ad-din al-Afghani 20
Jamiat-al-Tabligh al-Islam 119
Jamnagar 63, 64, 65, 77
Jandiala 133
Japa 95
Jati 119
Jayrambati 93, 101n
Jihad 130
Jnan 43
Jnana yoga xv, 14, 43, 218
Jnana Yoga (ed. Haridasi) 86
Jnanpradayini Patrika 39
John the Baptist xiii
Johnson, P. 20
Jones, Ernest 8
Jones, Jim 5
Jones, Kenneth xii, xiii, xiv, 3, 4, 131, 133, 141, 144
Jordens, J.T.F. 110
Judaism 161
Junagadh 64, 67
Jung, C.G. 5, 6, 7, 8, 13, 26

Kabir panth 220
Kafir 129
Kakar, Sudhir 14
Kala Pani 112
Kali (the Mother) xviii, 4, 14, 15, 25, 88, 92, 95, 97, 102n
Kali temple, Dakshineswar 92
Kalidasa 211
Kamarpukur 93
Kamensky, Anna 182
Kanya Kumari 71
Karma yoga xv, 15, 22, 218
Kashmir 92
Kathiawar xiii, 64
Kerala 103n
Khalifa xix, 130, 133, 134, 136, 137, 139, 144, 148, 150

Khandwa 67
Khetri 62, 64, 65, 67, 68, 69, 75, 77
Khetri, Maharajah of 62, 64, 68, 67, 71, 72, 73
Khilafat movement xix, 116
Kipling, Rudyard 89
Kopf, David 49
Koresh, David 5
Kossuth, L. 4
Krishna 212
Krishnamurthi (World Messiah) 23, 186, 202n
Krishnan, G. 118
Kropotkin, Peter 90
Ksatriya Upkarini Sabha 119
Kushnacht-Zurich 8

Lahore 35, 39, 40, 41, 47, 130, 132, 152
Lahore Brahmo Samaj 40
Lahore Christian Girls' School 47
Lahore Female Normal School 40
Lahore Medical College 36
Lahore Oriental College 35, 50n
Lahore Sat Sabha 38
Lahore School of Engineering 34, 50n
Lahore Shuddhi Sabha 113
Lajnat ul-Amaillahl 152
Lakshmi 44, 45
Laksmi-Sarasvati Samvad (N. Rai) 33, 41–7
Lal, Lala Bihari 38, 40
Lala Hamsraj 116, 118
Lamprecht, Karl 219
Lavan, Stephan 131, 132, 133, 135, 151
Leadbeater trial 23, 187, 199, 202n
The Leader 119
Leggett, Betty 87
Leitner, G.W. 35, 37, 51n
Lekhram, Pandit 111
Lele, Bhaskar 24
Lenin, V.I. 7
Lhasa 20
Ling, T. 60
Love 96
  M. Proust on 9
'Lucifer' 180

Lytton, Bulwer 20

MacDonald, Ramsay 90
Madras/Chennai 19, 71, 84, 171, 174, 175, 188
Madras Mahajana Sabha 171, 172
Mahabharata 65, 211
Mahabodhi 180
Mahabodhi Society xvi, 74, 75, 83, 84, 100
Mahamaya 95
Mahasabha 118, 120
Mahatma letters 21
Mahavidyas 96, 97
Mahdi 128
Mahila Samiti 48
Mahula 63, 74
Mahula famine 74
Majlises xix, 146, 151, 152
Malabar xix, 116, 117, 121
Malabar Thiyya community 118
Malabari, B.M. 162, 171, 172
Malcolm, Sir John xiii
Malkanas 119
Mamon, Paolos 20
Manazara 129
Manchester 210
Manoharlal, Munsi 109
Mappila rebellion 116
Mappilas 117
Marriage 139–43
Mary Magdalene 12
Masih Maw'ud 128
Masters, The (Mahatmas) 19, 20, 161, 172
The Master as I Saw Him (Nivedita) 88
Mathura 119
Maya 88, 96, 164
Mazzini, G. 4, 20
McLeod, Josephine xviii, 86
Mecca 147
Meditation xv, 70, 94, 95, 218
Meerut 34
Mehta, Pherozeshah 171
Melas 83
Mentana, battle of 20

Meritocracy 18
Metrovitcch, Agardi 20
Michelet, J. 4
Milap 119
Minault, Gail 136, 152
Mirat-al Arus 41
Missionaries, 9, 19, 76, 80n, 91, 108,
    110, 129, 131, 145, 181, 185, 188
Mitra Vilas Press 39, 41
Moksha 15, 17, 24
My Mother (Z. Khan) 148
Monotheism 18, 162
Moonje, B.S. 117
Mufassil 147
Mujaddid 128
Mukti 43
Müller, Henrietta 87
Müller, Max 24, 188
Multan, Sindh 118
Munshis 38
Murshidabad 74, 77
Musaeus Girls' College, Colombo 193
Muslim League xix, 115
Muslims/Islam xiv, xviii, xix, 10, 25,
    37, 94, 107–21, 128–52, 165, 170,
    181, 220
    Sunni 128, 129, 135, 145, 147, 150,
    152
Mysticism 84

Nabi 145
Namaz 146, 147
Naoroji, Dadabhai 171
Nariad/Nadiad xiii, 64
Nationalism xiv, xix, xxi, 4, 11, 23, 24,
    25, 38, 159, 168–9, 175, 176, 201
    Irish 87
Native Ladies' Normal School, Calcutta
    39
Nazism xx, 7
Neasden temple, London xiii
Negroes 182
Nehru, J. 175
Neo-Hinduism xix, 160, 162, 163, 169,
    170
Neo-Vaishnavism 10, 11, 12, 220

New Age movements 189, 201, 202
New India (ed. Besant) 173
New Light on Asia (Arnold) 91
New York 19, 84, 85
Newal Kishore Press 42
Nietzschean xiv, 7, 25
Nikhilananda, Swami 67, 68, 96
Niramayananda, Swami 69
Nirvana 24
Nivedita, Sister (Margaret Noble) xviii,
    16, 86, 87–90, 94, 100
Noll, Richard
    on Jung 7, 8
    on Blavatsky 19
North-Western provinces 33
Nur-ud-din xix, 135, 138, 140, 146, 148

Oberoi, Harjot 132
Occidentalism 25
Occultism xx, 19, 23, 26, 160, 161, 163,
    175, 189, 191
    Webb on 189–90
Olcott, Henry S. xvi, 23, 83, 159–61,
    169, 181, 184, 188, 193
On the Education of Hindu Females 91
Order of the Star of the East 183, 186,
    202n
Oriental Seminary, Calcutta 76
Oriental studies 191
Oudh 33

Pal, B.C. 90
Panchen Lama 20
Paris 215, 217
Parker, Theodore 69, 76
Parnell, C.S. 212
Parsees 170
Patna 10, 109
Pax Britannica xiii
Pax Swaminarayana xiii
Persian 37, 38, 46, 213
Philosophy of the Teachings of Islam
    (M.G. Ahmad) 134, 140
Plague 89, 144
Plato 191
Political reform 37

Polygamy xix, 135, 139, 140, 143
Polytheism 108
Pondicherry xi, xii, xxi, 3, 25, 215, 216
Poona Sarvajanik Sabha 172
Porbandar 68
Prabuddha Bharata 87
Prakrti 96, 97
Praman 45
Pranayama 24
Premananda, Swami 74
Prophecies 129, 130
Protestantism 5, 12, 18
Psychical Research, Society for 19
Psychoanalysis xiv, xvii, 6, 7, 24, 26
Psychoanalytic Endeavour, Society for 7
Psychological Club 7
Puja 44, 169
Punjab xiv, xviii, xix, 17, 33, 34, 36, 39, 40, 110, 112, 113, 128–52, 163, 175
Punjab Arya Samaj 113
Punjab Public Works Department 34
Punjab Textbook Committee 35, 41
Punjab University College 35, 36, 51n
Punjab University Intelligencer 39
Punjabi 38, 39, 48, 145
Puranas 114, 213
Purani, A.B. 24
Purdah 136, 137, 140, 141, 142, 149, 151, 152
Puri, Tota 14
Purusa 96, 97
Putta Parthi 9

Qadiyan xix, 128, 130, 133, 134, 137, 143, 144, 146, 150, 151
Qur'an 10, 109, 131, 137, 138, 139, 140, 146, 148, 149, 213

Race theory xx, 13, 180, 184, 191–202
Rai, Navincandra xvii, 33–49
Rai, Pandit Rammohan 34
Raj, British xx, 13, 94, 108, 112, 121, 130, 159, 164–9, 176, 212

Rajdharma 69, 77
Rajneesh 5, 6
Rajputana 70, 113, 119
Rama 66
Ramabhai Clubs, USA 89, 91
Ramakrishna xv, xvi, xviii, 3, 13, 26, 59, 60, 62, 84, 86, 89, 91, 92, 93, 95, 96, 97, 99, 220
'creative illness' 14
Ramakrishna movement xiv–xix, 3, 13–16, 59–79, 83–100, 101n, 196, 220
Ramakrishnananda, Swami 70, 71, 72, 75
Ramananda, Swami xiii
Ramayana 211
Ramier, Manjeri 174
Rantideva 65, 66
Rao, Krishna 173
Rao, Ranganath 162, 170, 171
Rashmani, Rani 92
Rastriya Svayamsevak Sangh (RSS) 120
Rasul, A. 174
Ratlam, Maharani of 48
Raychaudhuri, Tapan 15
Reconversion xviii, 118, 119
Reform movements xiv, 3, 9, 110, 132, 163
'transitional' and 'acculturative' 131
Reincarnation/karma xx, 10, 165
Revolutionary Society, Calcutta xviii, 89
Richard, Mirra ('the Mother') 215, 216, 217, 219, 221
Richard, Paul 216
Rig Veda 10, 17, 18
Ripon, Viceroy 172
Rishi xii, 17, 99
Rites 113, 117, 121
Roe, J. 187
Rolland, Romain xviii, 86
Rosicrucianism 20
Roszack, Theodore 23
Roti 147
Roy, Nobin Chandra 36

Roy, Ram Mohan 3, 9–13, 26
Rsiram, Pandit 116, 117
Russia 19, 20

Sabr ka ajar 139
Sacrifice 165
*Sadhak*s 218
Sadhana 13, 17, 19, 20, 21, 24, 25, 77
Sadharan Brahmo Samaj xvii, 10, 12,
    15, 16, 35, 220
*Sadhu*s 95, 99
Sahajanand, Swami xiii, 64, 66
Sai Baba 9
Sakta Sannyasini 92
Sakti xviii, 13, 25, 88, 95–7, 100, 102n
Samadi 14
Sampradaya 8, 99, 110
Sanatana dharma xxi 16, 24, 25, 120,
    213, 214
Sanatana Dharma Sabhas 111
Sanatanists 34, 115, 117, 118, 120, 121,
    122
Sanborn, Kate 85
Sankara 99
Sannyasin 64, 69, 71, 72, 73, 75, 76, 91,
    93, 98, 99, 100, 170, 212
Sanskrit 10, 17, 33, 34, 37, 46, 47, 88,
    92, 170, 211, 214
Santinavam ashram, Trichinopoly xv
*Sannyasa mantra*s 93
Sarada Devi (Holy Mother) xviii, 88,
    92–100, 101n
Sarada Mahila Ashram 97, 98
Sarada Math 97, 99, 103n
Saradananda, Swami 89
Sarala Devi 90, 98, 99
Sarasvati 44, 45, 46
Saratov 19
Sardhana 34
Sargachi orphanage 73,
Sarkar, Sumit 14, 15
Sarnath 84
*Sastra*s 44, 120, 184
*Sastrartha*s 108, 109
Sastri, Pandit Hathibhai 65

Sastri, Sivanath 11, 12, 34
Sati xx, 96, 161
Satsanga 64, 66
Satyagraha 101n
Satyartha Praksah (Dayanand) xii, 17,
    18, 109
Satyayuga 25
Science, western xvii, 42, 43, 45, 85,
    90, 91, 162, 165, 184, 191
Schwartz, A. 192, 204n
The Secret Doctrine (Blavatsky) 22, 191,
    193
Sects xii, 5, 11, 107, 110, 218
Sen, A. 78
Sen, Keshab Chandra xvii, 3, 9–13, 14,
    26, 35, 39, 93, 220
Sen, Narendranath 162, 170, 171, 172,
    173
*Sevaka*s 71
Sevashrama 94
Sevavrata, 59, 65–79
Sevier, Charlotte 87
Sevier, J.H. 84
Shaivite 17
Shakespeare 211
Shanars 114
Shari'at 134, 136, 137, 139, 141, 145,
    146
Sharma, Arvind 16, 17
Shaw, G.B. 185
Shivaprasad, Raja 33
Shivananda, Swami 101n
Shodashi 96
Sialkot xix 132, 133, 135, 144, 145, 150,
    152
Sikh revolt 23
Sikhs/Sikhism xiv, 113, 117, 128, 132,
    170, 220
Simhavahini 93
Singh, Bhagat Lakshman 36
Singh, Nazer 36
Singh Sabhas 113, 132, 135
Sinnett, A.P. 161, 170, 171
Siva 95, 96
Smith, Wilfred Cantwell, 130, 134, 151

Social reform xii, xiv, xviii, xix, 4, 10,
11, 35, 37, 38, 43, 47, 78, 83, 120
Social service (*seva*) xv, xvii, 15, 60, 61,
62, 64, 68, 69, 70, 73, 74, 75, 77,
78, 79, 80n, 94, 99, 102n, 162
Socialism xiv, 21, 22, 185, 188, 201
Solovyoff, V.V. 21
Spencer, Herbert 12
Spiritualism xiv, 21, 22, 160, 161, 162,
163
Spirituality xii, xv, xxi, 3, 14, 18, 91,
166, 189, 201, 209, 214, 219, 221
Sraddhanand, Swami xix, 119, 120
Sri Aurobindo Ashram 218, 219
Sri Narayana Guru 102n
Srimad Bhagavatam 65
Steiner, Rudolph 6, 189, 192, 202
Stories of Ahmadiyya Women 137
Storr, Anthony 5, 6, 14
Sturdy, E.T. 84
Suddhi movement xiv, xviii, 18, 108,
112–21, 125n, 218
Sudras 16
Sufism 20, 129, 131
Sugrhini 48
Swadeshi 15
Swaminarayan xiii, xvii, 5, 16, 64, 65, 66
Swaraj 25
Syed Ahmad Khan 18, 136
Sylhet Prarthana Samaj 48

Tagore, Devendranath 9, 11
Tagore, Rabindranath 90
Taki, Bengal 97
Tamil Nadu 220
Tanjore 174
Tantrism 13, 92, 95, 213, 214
Tapasyananda, Swami 65
Tariqa-i Muhammedi movement 130
Tashilumpo, Tibet 20
Tattvabodhini Society 9
Tblisi 19
Talang, Pandharinath 174
Telang, Kashinath 162, 171
Theosophical Society xx, xxi, 18, 19,

22, 83, 87, 99, 159–76, 183, 219
Simla Lodge 162
political influence 171–5
international 183
social composition 186
The Theosophist 21, 22, 159, 180–93
Theosophy xvi, xix, xx, xxi, 7, 13, 18,
19–23, 84, 91, 159–76, 180–202,
220
as counter-culture 187–91, 200–2
race theory 191–202
Tibet 19, 20
Tibetan Buddhism 10, 19, 20
Tinnevelly 113, 114, 116, 121
Tipu Sultan 118
Totalitarianism xxi
Tracts 129, 130, 134, 135, 137
Transcendentalism 86, 184
Transitional paradigm xii, 131
Truth-consciousness
('Supermind') 218, 220
Turiyanananda, Swami 67

Udaipur 70
Udbodhan 87, 98
Ulama 128
Unitarianism 9, 69
United Provinces 110, 113, 131, 152
Universalism 12, 13, 14, 18, 22, 26, 184
Untouchables/Dalits xviii, 108, 112, 113,
115, 117, 120, 121, 122, 125n
and census 115
Upanishads 10, 212, 214
Urdu 36–9, 46, 47, 109, 135, 145, 146,
152
Utopianism xx, xxi, 4, 16
Uttarpara 24

Vaikuntha 65, 66
Vaishnavasharan 14
Vaishnavism xvii, 14, 64, 66, 76,
77
Vancouver 85
Varanasi 10, 90, 94
Vasudeva 212–13

Vedanta xxi, 11, 13, 16, 24, 25, 85, 86, 90, 209, 211, 213, 216
Vedanta Centre, London 84
Vedanta Kesari 93
Vedanta societies, USA 86, 94
Vedas xx, 11, 39, 65, 77, 108, 112, 114, 120, 161, 170, 175, 176, 214, 219
Vegetarianism xiv, 113, 182, 185, 189, 201
Vermont, USA 160
Victoria Girls' School, Patiala 48
Vidya 42
Vidyasagar, Ishvar Chandra 11, 40, 55n, 65
Viharas 84
Virajananda 17
Viraraghavachariar, M. 171
Vishnu 66
Vishnupunya 96
Vivekananda xv, xvi, xvii, xviii, 3, 4, 5, 13–16, 18, 24, 59, 60, 62–78, 84–92, 97, 99, 100, 101n, 162, 163, 220
Vivisection 182, 185
Voice of the Silence (Blavatsky) 20
Vrat-kathas 42

Wadia, B.P. 174, 175
Wagnerism 7
Waldo, Sara Ellen (Haridasi) 86
War 109, 182
Washington, P. 20, 22, 23

Webb, James 189, 190, 200
Weber, Max 7, 8
The Web of Indian Life (Nivedita) 90
Weltanschauung 8, 110
Widows 11, 23, 40
Williams, George 15
William, Raymond xiii, 5, 8
Women, social position xvii, 11, 13, 16, 23, 33, 39–49, 78, 108, 155n, 182, 204n
Western influence 83, 100
in Ramakrishna Mission xvii, xviii, 83–100
in Ahmadiyya movement 128, 134–52
in marriage 136–46
as mothers 147–9
in Theosophical Society 186–7
World War I 115
World's Parliament of Religions, Chicago 67, 68, 84, 85, 88, 91, 92
Wright, Prof. 71, 72, 85

Yatras 93
Yoga, xv, xxi, 16, 24, 212, 215, 216
Yogananda, Swami 60
Young India 173

Zafrullah Khan, Muhammed xix, 135, 138, 142, 144, 148, 149
Zakat 146, 147
Zamindars 171